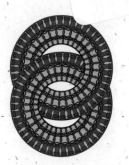

THE BREATH OF
PARTED LIPS

VOICES FROM THE
ROBERT FROST PLACE

VOLUME II

THE BREATH OF
PARTED LIPS

VOICES FROM THE
ROBERT FROST PLACE

VOLUME II

Edited by
Sydney Lea

Library of Congress Cataloging-in-Publication Data

The breath of parted lips : voices from the Robert Frost Place.
p. cm.
ISBN 0-9678856-2-0 (v. 1) — ISBN 0-9678856-8-X (v. 2)
I. American poetry--20th century. 2. American poetry--New
Hampshire--Franconia. I. Robert Frost Place (Franconia, N.H.)

PS615.B647 2001
811'.5408--dc21
00-047379

Cover photograph of Robert Frost by Ken Heyman, courtesy
Dartmouth College Library Special Collections
Interior photograph of Robert Frost, copyright: Lotte Jacobi,
courtesy of Jones Library of Dartmouth College. Reprinted here with
the permission of the estate of Robert Lee Frost
Interior photographs by Star Black
Cover and book design by Charles Casey Martin
Page compostion and production by Peter Cusack

Printed in the United States of America

CavanKerry Press Ltd.
Fort Lee, New Jersey
www.cavankerrypress.org

In loving memory of our friends and teachers

Amy Clampitt

Jane Kenyon

William Matthews

. . . and for Donald Sheehan

whose soul is the art of The Place

Contents

Democracy, the Spirit, and Poetic Passion

In a letter I received from him, the distinguished New Hampshire man of letters, Donald Hall writes: "Don Sheehan's disinterested passion for poetry, shaping the institution of the Frost Place, has made a monument exemplary in the purity of its attentions."

I sincerely hope that this second volume of *The Breath of Parted Lips: Voices from The Robert Frost Place* may likewise be a monument of poetic passion, something to which reader after reader may repair for the artistic and spiritual tonic that Donald Sheehan has made so abundantly available to the world of contemporary American letters. If it succeeds in that aim, then I shall be as happy with the project as I could ever imagine.

I've been involved with the world of American poetry for all my adult life. In those capacities, which have included visiting jobs at a wide variety of summer writers' conferences, I have seen almost as much to chagrin me as I have to encourage. As poetry becomes less and less a vocation than a profession, as poets become members of a guild rather than practitioners of a sacred art, politics and networking too often prevail over more humane concerns.

Not at the Frost Place. Not under Don Sheehan's careful and caring stewardship. I can think of few if any undertakings that are as thoroughly democratic as the annual Frost Place Poetry Festival—or any of the Frost Place–sponsored events and programs that have come into being in its twenty-five years. It is this democratic urge that Don Hall has in mind, I think, when he speaks of "disinterested passion." Something very similar moves Maine Poet Laureate Baron Wormser, another longtime associate and supporter of the Frost Place, to suggest that "What has made the Frost Place so special for so many people is Donald Sheehan's vision, a vision that puts our capacity to care for one another at the center of the activities of the Frost Place."

Disinterest is, of course, a word often misconstrued to mean indifference, though what it really means is impartiality. The passion that makes the annual poetry festival at Franconia all but throb is impartial in the sense that it takes no heed of anyone's reputation, status or influence. If a participant or even a faculty member should come to town with the hope that his or her career will be advanced by the forging of important connections, she or he will shortly be disabused. Important connections are made, to be sure, but they're made on the basis of the art itself and not of political or academic serviceability. They are, if I may use a tricky term, spiritual connections. Sheehan leads us all to understand that envy and competition are not only unwelcome at a Frost Place event but also, in the grander scheme, inimical to the very quality and survival of verse itself. Passion and care for one another as human beings not only can but also must coexist.

I am not Don Sheehan's spiritual peer. Few people are. Yet I have sought, however imperfectly, to assemble a book in his manner. I have tried to operate out of disinterested passion. I have looked to the work itself and not to the name of its contributor in making my selections.

Of course, I'm genuinely saddened to think of would-be contributors whose work does not appear in the following pages, but I am more than solaced to contemplate the work that does. I am further reassured to believe that even those whose efforts were rejected may rejoice in this book; it is the poetry, not the ego, which we must always prize, according to the Frost Place director.

I am above all pleased that persons whose poems have never been published appear here cheek by jowl with persons whose work has garnered the highest awards and distinctions available to American writers. The poems that follow are therefore arranged not with regard to whether an individual artist is luminary or tyro; I have chosen an alphabetical order of appearance not out of laziness but out of a desire to confute all imaginable hierarchical schemes.

But not everything here is equal after all—not in my heart. I'm delighted to have every entry in this volume, but I am particularly delighted by all the moving and deft poetry from writers whose names are at the moment unfamiliar to me and to most readers. Any decent editor will tell you that the surprise discovery is the truest reward he or she can savor. I have therefore been many, many times blessed by the scores of surprise discoveries I made in the process of editing this volume.

But once again the greater credit goes to Donald Sheehan. As an ardent advocate for the Frost Place, how reassured I am to see what fine writing the place attracts, and, more important, how that writing blooms and grows in power by virtue of the Place's attention and communitarian criticism.

No writers' gathering commands the fierce allegiance that the one in Franconia does. Participants and faculty members and resident poets alike testify to the Frost Place's benign impact on their craft. In letter after letter accompanying submissions to this book, the compound word *life-changing* appeared. I could desire nothing better than for the reader of *The Breath of Parted Lips, Volume II*, to feel his or her life likewise changed, however subtly, by its combinant poems. We often speak, though sometimes rather facilely, of poetry as "transformative"; if it reflects the spirit of Donald Sheehan and his programs, however, the poetry that follows will deserve that descriptive.

Sydney Lea
Newbury, VT
April 2004

THE BREATH OF
PARTED LIPS

VOICES FROM THE
ROBERT FROST PLACE

VOLUME II

Wild Onions

I want to touch the wildness in me Olya says
before she burns their dacha down. The night holds no moon
and the stars to her are cold—distant
though insects are singing in the summer heat

the river keeps flowing

  away

    away

My heart as well is flowing away she says
to herself igniting dried out August grass
with kitchen matches

flowing away   flowing away

The warmth from the burning walls of their dacha
her father had built with his own two hands
opens the wild onions in her heart
and there are no flowers there

flowers   flowers

red/red/red she says
flowing away on this

wild sea of petal and flame

this wildness fed by hungry fires—yes
her heart is spilling out from years
of letting the village mosquitoes suck her dry

from years of sitting at the wooden table
her *dyedushka* made from

fallen pine trees

from years of trying
at the village banya to steam out
the demons eating her heart
from years of watching Masha the goat

kicking

through fences, munching on grass
from years of staring at the wooden dacha walls

feeding matches to the old-style stove
boiling tea-water carrots eggs laid by chickens
her babushka had named

Yasha

      Dunyasha

            Sasha

In the morning
a breeze
of burnt wood
smoldering coal
fear
flesh
rotten peaches

blows over the river to the water's edge
where Olya sits her arms full of flowers.

She would like to feed them to Masha the goat
petal by petal by

petal …

Poems from the Fat Girl

1.

She lies in the twin bed
between line-dried sheets
watching night slide through
the open window. She worries

the seven bears lying beside her
are crowded, squishes herself
closer to the diamond wallpaper,
folds her hands across her chest.

The silent lift and unfurling
of the sheer white curtains
nudge her toward sleep.
From the other bed

her sister says, "Stop breathing,
You're making too much noise."

2.

Bathed and bed-redied
in cotton short-sleeved pajamas
patterned in rose buds

she follows her sister
into the late sunset
to chase fireflies

though she knows their despair
when they're caught
in tin-lidded clear glass jars.

On the porch, cigarettes arc

and rust-rumpled voices mark
the grown-ups drinking Jack Daniels

When the moon's sharpened with darkness
her mother calls them home.

3.
Zipped into the snow suit
she's poofed as a Twinkie
lying on her stomach
on the wooden sled with runners

her father hitches
with a thickly twined rope
to the salmon DeSoto
whose fins slice the air

and, oh, the slowness of the car,
the grace with which he takes
the curves of Glen Drive
leaning his head out the window,

watching the road as he calls to her,
"Okay back there?"

4.
She wants the shocking
pink with layers of crinoline

pushing the skirt
wide as a tutu.

Her mother says,
"You look ridiculous."

The velvet pants don't fit.

The striped shirt does.

Her mother says, "You can't
wear stripes if you're fat."

In the tailored dress
she feels like a funeral.

Her mother says, "Good.
You look thinner. We'll take it."

Where You Go When You Sleep

I

It is all conjecture: that dark place you drive to,
its vast ceiling flecked with the light of dreams
           your phototrophic senses turn to;
slaphappy with option, you hunger for the wildly improvised
           and open yourself
wide to sleep, to the trek towards the quickened, the
           ephemeral,
the damn-near-tangible understanding of the still sleeping.
You are the dreamer's dreamer, and until you are ransomed
           by wakefulness,
the candor of your passage keeps you solidly on your own.

II

There you go, off along the moonlit road where sleep
streams from you the way filaments of silver trail from the visible
           stars;
your myopic eyes drag it out along the darkness, a single bright
           track
you follow in, your heavy, somnolent feet deep in the teeming light.
You are artless and steady; you want only elbowroom for the
           profligate dream,
would trade decorum for the artifice of the unrealized, for
           sleep riddled with invention.
Overwhelmed and horizontal, again you would refresh your life.

III

This time the stars climb into your bed and carry you across a
           dark
field of sleep woven to the thickness of your dream, and far away
the light and the not light flicker like a familiar, patient eye.
           You travel
empty-handed; you bring nothing you know of with you, carried

off the way you are,
stolen, so to speak, giving yourself to the theft and grateful for it.
But this time you are sidetracked—your transient stars
      insist—and you are lost between dream
and not dreaming. You reach (you are lucid enough for reaching)
      but the dream
is slippery; unprepared for the stillness and the vastness, you
      slide back again
and find yourself blind in the depth and breadth of fathomless
      sleep, sleep like a cave, like a dark cave.

IV

And there are nights you travel backwards, blindfolded. You
      dream the mother god,
the father—it is different for us all, but the genius of this god is
      facelessness:
this is the worst, the anonymous relic, unnamed and unknowable.
These nights you would flee your dream; these nights fear
like a flame beneath your tongue incites in you the naming of all
      you would choose never
to name—the rocks, the pinnacles you would throw yourself from
if the dream were to take you in waking. You loosen the fabric
      that blinds you,
and yours becomes the desperate eye. And you, the ardent
      dreamer,
struggle for your own unencumbered vision, for your province, for
      a foothold in the culpable dream.

V

In one dream you rise with the archangel to the precious gates
but before you can squeeze past the keeper, a voice repels you
      the way you in your waking lifetime
repel the difficult and the dangerous, and you are jostled,
bit by bit, downward, and, from all around you, all the while you
      fall, the voices
in the gallery applaud your lack of grace in the falling. And this

hoary dream is nearer what you seek, the vehement climbing,
the strain in your groin, thin ribbons of muscle pulled taut in your
	thighs.
But familiar damnation is never enough. Even in your soporous
	need, you know:
better the kamikaze dream, or better the beseeching. Better
the dream in which you tangle with the dark thing in you that squats
	on its spindly haunches
and sees through your eyes. After all, it is only sleep, it is
	only the spidery figment of occasional lapse,
that marrow-like place between what you yearn for and what you
	might find.
Pursuit, then, becomes your obligation, and resolution hunkers
between the slabs of your need, between the finding
and the knowing, between night and the edge of the impious
	dream.

VI

And you lean into sleep as you would a lover, and the ribald
	trickster, fastidious rogue,
in turn takes you in. And love, like the notion of sleep, seems
	cogent and cocksure
and you are certain that your difficulty comes from the sorry fact
that no one told you sleep was concentric, no one explained you
	must go in
and come out, or that sleep is a bull's-eye, a wagon wheel, a tin
	can lid
and that it all means nothing if you do not at least consider the
	centermost path.
And you, the ragbag, dissolute lover, still bargain; needs would-be
	libertine, you barter—
bagatelle for the quixotic. Sidestepping the sublime, you pursue
	sleep layered with turmoil;
you, in your ignorance, court the bland space that surrounds the
	ecstatic center
and you pass through the shallow quadratura, the flat concoction

that passes for dream
at the edge of dream. You go up to and into the heart-stopping
        dark
but there you are stymied. You grope, you paw the black ground;
you are as anxious as a suckling mouth; you are horny with greed,
        and you know the roué
lousy bastard sleep, like love, is the birthplace of dreams.
You believe you would risk loneliness, every night, you would
        gamble all that you have cast out
or ever taken in, to reach the heedless landscape where everything
        dangerous meets the light.

VII

And, so how do you find it? What do you make of sleep, of
        your extravagant half-eyed muse,
feathered, dark, incandescent as dusk? You are the starry-eyed
        pilgrim; you mingle
with the shades of her kin. You are rapt with envy for the bursting
        of her bodiless light, for her dream
of the reckless, of the wastrel, and, solitary as the celibate moon,
you shake your fist at the bugbear that haunts you.
The vagaries that befall us all are behind you, and, reaching
        like the footloose beggar you are,
the lucid dream, once more, inevitably, evades you: you
        grasp nothing—
no one ever told you the prerequisite for peace is peace.
You are alone with your appetites; you sleep again.

Beautiful

At the pet store: no rabbits.
But plenty of mice, spinning
Inside what my son calls
Ferris wheels. He strokes the glass

Cages and feels fur,
The trembling of miniature hearts.
Next: fish. Here too he swipes
The smooth aquariums, sees

Goldfish back off. *Mommy*,
Sit right here, he orders,
Smacking the floor, then snags
Another pretzel from his bag.

An indoor outing today, the sky iffy,
Richardson Bay so gray
It looks smeared with dirt.
This morning, raking leaves, I hear

His voice, a few words warbling
What? I ask, shoving the leaves.
So beautiful, he says, pointing
At trees. *Beautiful*. The damn ordinary trees.

I Brake for Animals

for Baron Wormser

I spot it coming up on the courthouse
from behind, back from a park in Chinatown
where I've killed most of my lunch break
watching softball in a concrete field.
The bumper sticker penetrates
the thin state of my reverie, four words
affixing themselves to my brain—
as words will do—while I keep walking
past the side court doors (short man
in a maize suit talking to a woman
in a matching dress), and on
to the corner coffee cart where I stop
for a cool iced one, overhearing
"He was looking at 6 down to 3 . . . "
then safe through the metal detector;
these elements all pinned on
my brain's recent-past bulletin board.
Things stick with me like that.
Should anyone ask (and soon they will),
I could describe the couple in matching maize,
I could ID the coffee vendor, and *yes,*
your Honor, I brake for animals; it's the kind
of vigilance I believe we should keep up, and there's
that word *vigilance* setting off microalarms
in the lawyers' heads. I see them or I know
too much to be here, so I'm turned back
to the jury room, back to the pool, back
to a bolted-down chair, under a sluggish clock
waiting for heaven knows how long
in a room full of clock watchers.
I shouldn't have confessed to reading the *Times,*
shouldn't have said I like baseball, shouldn't have

for god's sake admitted being a writer, or was it
my shirt, my address, my way of looking
at the parties involved? I'm just here,
staring down at the impenetrable
bottom-left corner of the crossword—
I knew these words out there in my other life,
a few days ago, I could have filled them in—
now I'm waiting as we're all waiting,
waiting for the big hand to grab the 4,
for the little hand to sneak up on the 9.
I, too, will be released.

The Plenty

We two were streams
    conspiring the river.
We were ferns nodding under a tree
    with shade as our kingdom.

And when we were moss
    we elevated the lowlife,
invented 137 words for green
    we couldn't speak.

We were two sticks
    carried from opposite ends
      by the same bird.
Later as birds
    we lamented our hands.

And when we were rocks
    which of us was denser?

As hooves we were restless
      or swift.
As whiskers we fine-tuned
    the history of listening.

We gossiped as bells in the belfry.
    We were elusive as brooms.
As rails we tallied
    the lull
      between trains.

As flies we dropped together,
    as rain we dropped together,

as leaves we dropped together
or nearly, a second apart.

And as ash we were sorry.
As dust, demented.
As roots, good neighbors
who divvied the wealth.

When we were goats nibbling grass
night was our nanny—
Nyah nyah, goaded we
as the goatboy lost track of us.

Happiest (naturally) as shells
tumbled in the shallows
securing the calm of a clam . . .

Back to Zero

You sure told me
and I sat down to
feel your words.
You don't understand
neither do I,
you've had it
everything is a problem,
doors shut
windows come down
backs turn,
lights go out,
there is no sound,
you are gone,
no oxygen, it's finally dark.

MARVIN BELL

Short Version of Ecstasy

Up-welling of forces, serums and fevers,
tracking conduits of emotion,
following the longing of waist, elbows and knees
to crease to and fro, to be wind and wild
as any petal of in-growing rosebud in storm.
Until, and not until, each still quivering tendon
flops its last and pales;
until, and not until, something of a trance or sleep
blankets the bed; until, and not until, a dozen instances
lift and collapse in a headless consciousness
of release, and the gorged blood descends
by an intermittent elevator of stems,
will the lovers let go of themselves or each other.

Can they stand to get up now? So far have they slid
from the inflated lungs of love,
from the gasping expectation and the drag
of skin on skin as they sank after having held up
their coming, they who moved as one
raw from the separate rates of their falling,
such a distance have they gone, up and down then,
that each may recall the middle of the story
only by its fame. After the event,
the photo of the lover expels no scent, no invitation
sufficient to satisfy. It is truly over until,
and only until, some hidden residue of passion
sways into being, wanting to die.

Wednesday

Gray rainwater lay on the grass in the late afternoon.
The carp lay on the bottom, resting, while dusk took shape
in the form of the first stirrings of his hunger,
and the trees, shorter and heavier, breathed heavily upwards.
Into this sodden, nourishing afternoon I emerged,
partway toward a paycheck, halfway toward the weekend,
carrying the last mail and holding above still puddles
the books of noble ideas. Through the fervent branches,
carried by momentary breezes of local origin,
the palpable Sublime flickered as motes on broad leaves,
while the Higher Good and the Greater Good contended
as sap on the bark of the maples, and even I
was enabled to witness the truly Existential where it loitered
famously in the shadows as if waiting for the moon.
All this I saw in the late afternoon in the company of no one.

And of course I went back to work the next morning. Like you,
like anyone, like the rumored angels of high office,
like the demon foremen, the bedeviled janitors, like you,
I returned to my job—but now there was a match-head in my—
        thoughts.
In its light, the morning increasingly flamed through the window
and, lit by nothing but mind-light, I saw that the horizon
was an idea of the eye, gilded from within, and the sun
the fiery consolation of our nighttimes, coming far.
Within this expectant air, which had waited the night indoors,
carried by—who knows?—the rhythmic jarring of brain tissue
by footsteps, by colors visible to closed eyes, by a music
in my head, knowledge gathered that could not last the day,
love and error were shaken as if by the eye of a storm,
and it would not be until quitting that such a man
might drop his arms, that he had held up all day since the dew.

To Dorothy

You are not beautiful, exactly.
You are beautiful, inexactly.
You let a weed grow by the mulberry
and a mulberry grow by the house.
So close, in the personal quiet
of a windy night, it brushes the wall
and sweeps away the day till we sleep.

A child said it, and it seemed true:
"Things that are lost are all equal."
But it isn't true. If I lost you,
the air wouldn't move, nor the tree grow.
Someone would pull the weed, my flower.
The quiet wouldn't be yours. If I lost you,
I'd have to ask the grass to let me sleep.

Unless It Was Courage

Again today, balloons aloft in the hazy *here*,
three heated, airy, basket-toting balloons,
three triangular boasts ahead against the haze
of summer and the gravity of onrushing fall—
these win me from the wavery *chrr*-ing of locusts
that fills these days the air between the trees,
from the three trembly outspreading cocoons hanging
on an oak so old it might have been weighed down
by the very thought of hundreds of new butterflies,
and from all other things that come in threes
or seem to be arranged. These *are* arranged,
they are the perfection of mathematics as idea,
they have lifted off by making the air greater—
nothing else was needed unless it was courage—
and today they do not even drag a shadow.

It was only a week ago I ran beneath one.
All month overhead had passed the jetliners,
the decorated company planes, the prop jobs
and great crows of greed and damage (I saw one
dangle a white snake from its bill as it flew),
and all month I had looked up from everywhere
to see what must seem from other galaxies
the flies of heaven. Then quickly my chance came,
and I ran foolish on the grass with my neck bent
to see straight up into the great resonant cavity
of one grandly wafting, rising, bulbous, whole
balloon, just to see nothing for myself. That
was enough, it seemed, as it ran skyward and away.
There I was, unable to say what I'd seen.
But I was happy, and my happiness made others happy.

Paper Flowers

Hall of Revolutionary Martyrs
Tianjin, China, January 14, 1980

An official hands out paper flowers. We pin then
on our coats, my daughter and I, following
our Chinese cousins into the Hall of Martyrs.
Cold flows from stone: an ocean closes behind us.
Our footsteps speak the only language we know:
Stop. Stop. We shouldn't have come.

In the anteroom we sip black tea. We try
to warm our hands on the cups while guests
fill the table like a jury. I bow my head, feeling
my daughter accuse me of mourning a woman I hardly knew.
Dear girl: She was my father's only sister.
You don't know yet, how that is.

The bald man beckons. We file into a chamber where
hundreds of gray flowers clutter the walls. From a hood
of black crepe her photograph gazes. I close my eyes.
Last time I saw her, the wind flew her hat like a kite
over the seashells, over the blue umbrella, at my father's
old house. She laughed when he caught it,
my father her brother again.

Four times we bow to her ashes now boxed in a vault.
Men in gray suits collect all the flowers, stuff
them in cardboard for the next quick blooming. I'm dry
as the petals they crush, until someone touches my shoulder,
an old woman in black. She takes my daughter's hand,
reaches for mine. She says nothing, but her cheekbones
are wet, her eyes alive with the shock of love.

Burmese Girls
Sold into Prostitution in Thailand

In order that her parents not go deeper into debt
    she does not kill herself, she is
the bargain, the chip, she evens
    the odds even though she cannot speak
the language, Thai, it misaligns her tongue, sounds
    oily to her ears, the tongues of men, the forcing
of them, hundreds, thousands, how many
    places can they find on her, the body has only
so many openings and she loses value
    quickly once twice maybe three
times she can be passed off
    as a virgin even as she faints, even as she
counts the bricks in the windowless
    walls, corridors where she never sees
the sun unless—to settle the madam's score—she is
    arrested, hauled out from the underground
cells—then only the quiet ones are not
    redeemed, the ones who do not
know how to smile at men, but she is
    ransomed back to the metal
bed, the cement floor, the men again and
    again, especially the drunks
frighten her, so she feels nothing, nothing
    when the child moves inside her, nothing
when the poison she takes flattens
    her belly so that another girl will never
be born to turn eleven or twelve into nothing
    of value but the stories she makes even when
the fatigue claims her and she is coated with sores and sent
    back to her village where she is
whispered about, no friends, nothing
    but these mascaraed eyes, this fringed

cloth embroidered with the tales of luxury rides
    bringing the city to the village in a voice
hardened to the waste the man in her dreams
    who appears dressed in red brings—
until fevers overtake her and her
    mouth turns dry and she is
so thin the wind blows through her until she is
    parched, barely bones and so little flesh
left for the pyre, but they burn her body anyway, let
    flames arise around her, the heel the strongest
glowing coal, a searing eye staring back at
    them a long time as they burn all that is
hers, the city clothes, the plastic shoes, the drinking cup.

Sunday Drive

You can go with me he announces suddenly.
His teasing blue eyes smile at me from under the curved brim of his
        hat—
a tall white one like the cowboys wear—
You mean it? I jump up from my Uncle Wiggly picture puzzle
and grab him by his stiff pant leg,
Wait, I'll need my dolly.
The front seat of the Oldsmobile is wide as our neighbor's front
        porch
where wrinkled Mr. Mathis looks at his gold pocket watch as we pass
        by.
Restless behind the wheel Daddy unwraps a cigar,
clamps it in the corner of his mouth, chews hungrily.

I stand at attention near the open window,
Wind banks in my ears and balloons my dress.
My doll wears a soft cotton dress with a petticoat too.
Red ribbons on her braids tickle my arms.
I don't ask questions about Mama's headaches
or where Daddy throws his money away.
(He gives me silver dollars and tells me to save them.)
I try to hold still so he won't mind we're along
And watch as the cement sidewalks of town disappear into bumpy
        pastures,
wilted row crops and tired farmhouses where even the dogs are too
        hot to bark.

I think maybe the wind and speed will please Daddy on this sunny
        afternoon.
It is hard to know. Sometimes he smiles when I scold Dolly,
but then he's mad if I make too much commotion.
Pointing to a smudge in the distance,
he shouts that we're heading for the Blue Ridge.

Torn strips of tar paper hanging from chicken houses
are waving to us. A milk cow munching weeds near a wire fence
is a reddish blur. He laughs to see the road retreating in the rearview
          mirror,
lights his El Producto and lets out puffs like white blossoms.

Wind chases the smoke, tugs at my babydoll and makes me dizzy.
It seems as if we're flying and home is faraway,
still, he knows the way I tell Dolly, so we can't get lost.
I clutch her tightly to my chest edging closer to him,
I'm along for the ride wherever it takes me.

August

We are alone again,
     children and friends have come
          and gone, a hush of sage

wafts through the air,
     I sew a button to your shirt,
          it's August—placid, fair.

You're writing in your room,
     looking up now and then
          to stare at the nasturtium

and lavender I planted by the gate,
     for their gold and purple thrusts,
          their sedulous reaching,

and when I bring your old
     frayed shirt to my lips,
          cutting the thread with my teeth,

I hold it there simply
     because it is yours, and has
          our smell, familiar and common.

I press the denim against my face,
     tasting the air in it, the sun,
          and realize how light it is,

how easily it could slip
     out of my hands, out of this moment—
          how the smallest distraction,

the slightest inattention
      could leave me here alone,
            with nothing but my face in my hands.

The Worlds in This World

This is the world to love. There is no other.
—— Stephen Dobyns

Doors were left open in heaven again:
drafts wheeze, clouds wrap their ripped pages
around roofs and trees. Like wet flags, shutters
flap and fold. Even light is blown out of town,
its last angles caught in sopped
newspaper wings and billowing plastic——
all this in one American street.
        Elsewhere, somewhere, a tide
recedes, incense is lit, an infant
sucks from a nipple, a grenade
shrieks, a man buys his first cane.
        Think of it: the worlds in this world.

        Yesterday, while a Chinese woman took
hours to sew seven silk stitches into a tapestry
started generations ago, guards took only
seconds to mop up a cannibal's brain from the floor
of a Wisconsin jail, while the man who bashed
the killer's head found no place to hide,
and sat sobbing for his mother in a shower stall——
the worlds in this world.

        Or say, *one* year——say 1916:
while my grandfather, a prisoner of war
in Holland, sewed perfect, eighteen-buttoned
booties for his wife with the skin of a dead
dog found in a trench; shrapnel slit
Apollinaire's skull, Jesuits brandished
crucifixes in Ouagadoudou, and the Parthenon
was already in ruins.
        That year, thousands of thousands of Jews

from the Holocaust were already—*were*
still—busy living their lives;
while gnawed by self-doubt, Rilke couldn't
write a line for weeks in Vienna's Victorgasse,
and fishermen drowned off Finnish coasts,
and lovers kissed for the very first time,
while in Kashmir an old woman fell asleep,
her cheek on her good husband's belly.

     And all along that year the winds
kept blowing as they do today, above oceans
and steeples, and this one speck of dust
was lifted from somewhere to land exactly
here, on my desk, and will lift again—into
the worlds in this world.

     Say now, at this instant:
one thornless rose opens in a blue jar above
that speck, but you—reading this—know
nothing of how it came to flower here, and I
nothing of who bred it, or where, nothing
of my son and daughter's fate, of what grows
in our garden or behind the walls of your chest:
is it longing? Fear? Will it matter?

Listen to that wind, listen to it ranting
     The doors of heaven never close,
          that's the Curse, that's the Miracle.

A '49 Merc

Someone dumped it here one night, locked
the wheel and watched it tumble into goldenrod and tansy,
ragweed grown over one door flung outward
in disgust. They did a good job, too: fenders split, windshield
veined with an intricate pattern of cracks
and fretwork. They felt, perhaps, a rare satisfaction
as the chassis crunched against rock and the rear window
buckled with its small view of the past. But the tires
are gone, and a shattered tail light shields a swarm
of hornets making a home of the wreckage. How much
is enough? Years add up, placing one small burden on another
until the back yaws, shoulders slump. Whoever it was
just stood here as the hood plunged over and some branches snapped,
a smell of gasoline suffusing the air, reminding us
of the exact moment of capitulation when the life
we planned can no longer be pinpointed on any map
and the way we had of getting there knocks and rattles to a halt
above a dark ravine and we go off relieved—
no, happy to be rid of the weight of all that effort and desire.

The Good Devil

He was bad at torture. Flubbed his first flaying.
Dropped his pointed trident
into a lake of oil and had to scorch himself
diving in to retrieve it. Came out looking
like a channel swimmer
sheathed in pitch. Once he stepped
on his own tail during a papal dis-
embowelment, dropped
the stomach of His Holiness
on the flagmarl where it rolled into a nearby
flue. They had to fetch it out
with iron ropes and sticks.
And once, while the other demons drew
and quartered—neatly
splitting a false prophet like a chicken –
he was busy gazing off,
admiring the tapestry of fire
that flickered on the horizon.
He missed the special Days of Profanity,
the Blasphemers' Sabbath,
the millennial Parade of Pagans.
And when that poet showed up—
the Florentine with sallow skin—he was off
gathering teeth in the Betrayer's Oven
to polish and string for his mother.
The Gossips assembled, glad for work, tongues
humming like locusts
during the first Pharonic plague.
Rumor stretched its four necks and rose on leathery wings.
When the order came up
from below, winding its way through the bowels
of authority to ordinary drudges like him,
he was banished and had to hand in

his pitchfork, tines unbloodied,
shaft still immaculate of martyrs' grease.
He had to slouch in utter shame
through the Gates of Perdition into a new
and chastening light to make his living
by the sweat of his labor—
a poor farmer now,
condemned to delve in wet earth like a simple worm.
And everything he touched throve.
Everything he planted grew
in prolific, earth-nurturing rows
glistening with everlasting life.

The Day We Said So
for David

They lived there when their son killed himself,
a lot was wrong before, but got much worse.
She was unhappy with her husband,
so much so that even after fifty years
her sadness is still tangible in the old place.
The house, somehow unworthy of care,
has lost any bright hue, the windows have gone grey.
I won't marry in this pale house,
though the view would make our wedding album.

Her husband hardly worked this land at all,
only occasionally going to the barn for a tool.
He bought the place for the view of the notch in the mountain.
That was many years ago now, long enough to be history.
Her husband was a poet, so he did work the land after all,
with words like *woods, farmhouse near,*
bitter bark, good fences, touch and hand.

I will marry you in his barn with the doors of the house closed,
the curtains drawn over the colorless windows.
Before, you will chain smoke outside the open barn doors,
peering in at our bright decorations. So handsome
in your panama suit, white bucks and sweet pink face,
you will join me in the barn and we will marry.
Our eyes fixed on the clear blue sky and the notch,
rising over the house and the woods, and our hands touching.

Cafeteria

Some beauty will be born of this,
said my friend's blind mother,
across the hospital cafeteria table,
just hours after the doctor said
inoperable and closed her daughter up.
All morning we'd drifted in and out
of the flower-sweetened room,
watched the morphine drip; taking
Kate's hand, holding her gaze—useless.

I don't know about beauty, I said
and got up to order our lunch
from two women who'd been a comfort all week,
their small Scottish kindnesses a balm.
We ate our egg salads on whole-wheat
as though we'd never tasted real food;
the creamy sweetness of the filling, surprise
bite of green onion, and drank Diet Cokes
until we'd washed our mouths clean.

I loved everything about our lunch—
the newsprint placemats with their oily spots,
crumbs on the unbreakable plates,
and especially the metal napkin dispenser
recently replenished by someone's deft hand
with what the Scottish women would call
serviettes, *Help yourselves, dearie*, in that burr.
I loved the hospital employees on break,
smoking outside the window, jousting
and flirting with their serviceable bodies.

I loved Edgar Jones, the deaf man
interviewed on the radio last night—

a music archivist who says it doesn't
matter if he can't hear anymore: he still
feels the way he did when he first heard Sibelius,
It's in my heart, you understand?
I loved Kate's mother's lined, outdoor
face, the loose wisps of white hair
framing her fine bones, the lively, blue,
unseeing eye. I loved the shed paper
skin of the plastic straw, the way
the straws rose slowly in the Coke cans,
and we pushed them back down to drink.

I loved the terra-cotta walls around us,
freshly painted by people who'd done
their job adequately; loved the moment
someone else decided to place the poster
of a whitewashed Greek village *there*,
and not an inch higher or lower.
I wanted to eat all my meals in the hospital
cafeteria, each bite a tiny explosion.
I don't know about beauty, I said.

Sex Next Door

It's rare, slow as a creaking of oars,
and she is so frail and short of breach
on the street, the stairs—tiny, Lilliputian,
one wonders how they do it.
So, wakened by the shiftings of their bed nudging
our shared wall as a boat rubs its pilings,
I want it to continue, before her awful
hollow coughing fit begins. And when
they have to stop (always), until it passes, let
us praise that resumed rhythm, no more than a twitch
really, of our common floorboards. And how
he's waited for her before pushing off
in their rusted vessel, bailing when they have to,
but moving out anyway, across the black water.

Back, Sculpted in Relief by Matisse

Bronze twists and spends its power holding
to stone within the wall, barely defined,
full of bulky strength, remade from the spine,
bone growing out of notochord, into

the simplest living shape that's human
and can be desired. When I was nine
and in the children's ward of the Army
hospital at Orleans there was a girl

with leukemia. She had white, flecked skin
and thick hair in a braid shadow down
her back. She screamed each time they came
to draw her blood, bright and red and foaming,

into a syringe, arterial blood,
four times every day. It took two of us
and the nurse to hold her. Then she'd just lie there,
crying shaking her, curled away. This other,

this sculpted back, is only lines, but I'm
sure that if I drew her hair aside, exposed
her neck, I'd smell the bite of alcohol
and feel the stiff cotton hospital gown.

Picasso's Model

She warms in the sun
easing through the smudged windows of Bateau Lavoir,
sunlight dries the stinking mildewed walls,
erases the goosebumps on her thighs,
and reveals his thumbprints on the masks,
inscrutable and geometric, on the mantelpiece—
no Harlequins or Scapins ready to prance
for a market-day farce. She mustn't laugh.
Her thigh itches but she holds still as her eyes follow
the white twists of smoke escaping the chimneys.
Her breath raises and flattens the fold of silk across her breast.
She feels the history of posing in the ache of her neck.
A scent of turpentine rises from her skin
where he touched her the night before.
She considers this short Spaniard painting her
on the other side of the easel in his bare feet.
Her new lover at least makes the canvas creak passionately.

Slowly the rays stretch across the studio to unveil each
inch of splattered floorboard and cast her shadow
like a finger across the room. Downstairs a door opens
and some hung-over painter trudges up the staircase
trailing the scent of fresh baguettes.
She measures a handful of coins against due rent.
The carts clacking over cobblestones bring to mind
her unfortunate laugh last night when she saw herself
painted like a broken butter crock in his foolish art.
Her belly remembers the loops of brown
sausage in the window of Boulanger St. Claude,

will he remember she must eat?
She relives the small heat they made under cold blankets . . .
Sunlight falls on her best twill skirt splayed on his lumpy bed,
it has a newly torn seam to mend; indeed, just how is she paid to sit?
She shrugs.
He barks, "Be still!"

A Clothesline in Paterson
for Mary Carnevale (1914–1991)

I do not know why our five rooms upstairs
equal the evening stars
just coming out
over the cupola of Preakness Hill.

I looked up and it was so.

The equals sign says minus minus
and all comes around to where it was.

That must be how the reels of your clothesline
turn to the tires of Benny the Breadman
showing us each Paterson street

house by house
in his calm headlights.

Looking down the lower line,
you could count off the day in armlengths
beside a well-risen basket of clothes.

And now your armlengths equal the maple's.

And the maple's equal the sun's.

Through the big bedsheets
you cannot see it: the lines

keep going now
over the garage and easily

clear Preakness Hill.

There is no need to dry them all, dear.

I am sitting on the top stair
so we can talk about Ohio.

And, at the far end of your clothesline,
Venus is up, hanging out stars.

ROBERT CARNEVALE

Walking by the Cliffside Dyeworks

Even the dark end of Belmont Avenue
is floodlit today as though for postcards,
as though a tire, a rusted-out camshsaft,
rings that trashcans left in the snow
from now on belonged to history.

Shadows fall from the brick facets
to the windows of rundown houses,
but now they land on different faces,
not those *paesanos*
who manned the second and third shifts
through the fat Forties and lean Fifties
and, as you did, into the Sixties—
mostly spent now the bankrolls they shaved
against a death out of sight of their olive groves.

One was Frank Strangis
who came, like you, from Sambiase.
Nine years for stabbing a cardshark
made Frank a kind of celebrity.
Some of the women wouldn't visit,
some tried to keep their husbands away.
But you never singled him out,
even when you covered your glass
to keep him from pouring another.

I climbed the stairs of his three-family,
standing clear of the missing railings.
I could see the infield in Hinchcliffe Stadium
or halfway down the cleft of the falls,
could overhear through the screen
the women agree it was too much wine.

I could have stood there all day,
I could be standing there now
and still never have learned
if it was months or if it hit Frank
right then knife in hand
that the cardshark understood nothing
of Calabrese chivalry.

Once when I was out of work
one of the mechanics informed me
that I could show your union card
and get a job in a place like this.
Lie down, father.
Those bootprints in the old snow
leading to the Employee Entrance
are becoming shapeless as men.
And in one of the rusted-out rooms
a warping jig's burnished axle
rises from a welter of sumac
to tell them it's ten after two.

Still Life

I'm playing my videotape again of the beach scene:
Surf crashes, couple of girls walk by, palm trees
shake out their dreadlocks in the tropical breeze.
The lens zooms in on a man in his mid-seventies,
who looks like me in the future. I pause him. I
study the image to see what I'll become. Then
the man waves, hitches his trunks up, wades out
into the deepening water and dives right it.
Now we see only his head in a wave trough, after-
wards he's gone. I put the videocamera down and yell,
but there's no response. The lens sweeps the horizon
but it's just water and more water, sand and more sand.
The ocean is what anything looks like after a meal,
full and serene, a few seabirds over the empty waves.
This is the point where I push *rewind* and he reappears,
the top of his head first, then the whole body,
which swims for a moment in reverse—quite a trick
at that age—then backs just like a stunt man out
of a breaking wave. With a few more amazing strokes
he's in the shallows, he's regained his footing;
he walks straight backwards without missing a step.
He stands on the tide-line and he's safe. I do this
every evening after the six-thirty news, and if I
rewind further, he turns around, smiles and waves,
keeps walking backwards right to the chair beside me
and sits down. His face fills the whole screen, he
finds his glasses and puts them on, he waits for me
to speak. And all those questions I never quite got to
ask him, where are they? I can't find the words for them,
as I could never find words when he was here; so we sit
here together with the sound off, father and son,
looking out at Blue Hill across the river, or the sunset

he always loved. We get five minutes, which is as long as
the *pause* lasts, then he must go, as the instructions say,
or permanent damage may result. I push the *play* button
and he starts away again, hitches his trunks up, turns
around, waves once for the camera, and walks back in.

Hand Release

An old homeless guy saves his nickels and quarters
and heads for the Magic Touch Massage Parlor where
a nice call girl named "Cindy" who could be his niece
or granddaughter comes out and briefly dances around
a room that used to be some kind of office—there's
still the filing cabinets and a typewriter, and he
has a fantasy that it's his office and Cindy's his
secretary and every day after work she takes off
her top and shows him her nipples like a child
who has found two precious coins. She loves him so
much, his secretary Cindy, that she rubs him with
coconut oil, his old stringy legs with the hair gone
and his old belly full of stale bread and Thunderbird
and the stones of time that won't let the piss come
out; the nice girl who has typed for him all day is
saying "turn over" and rubbing his shoulder blades
that were as loose and useless as dinner plates but
now as Cindy caresses them with fingers made strong
from typing, they become massive and purposeful, like
wings. The old man would enfold her with these wings,
protect her from this terrible employment but the sign
says no touching the masseuses so he rests, and lets her
work oil into every feather, and beneath the feathers,
that meat of himself that has become dark and tender with
so much age, this old bum with lungs full of the spores
of death, his secretary Cindy brushes his bent back with
a breast; he can't see it but he knows, because he thinks
of his mother a hundred years ago in a half-open house-
coat and he can breathe, he breathes deeply and his lungs
open and he feels the blood pouring from the heart into
his old prick, that has lived the life of a street dog
but it is now ringing like a telephone and Cindy his
trusted secretary turns him over and picks it up and

whispers it's your wife, I will tell her you ain't here.
She's so clean, she wears rubber gloves over her red nails
and despite the sign over the massage table he is so special
that she lets him hold one hand while the other operates
a secret pump connected to his heart, which has been lost
and homeless but is now swollen with the two syllables
of a name he keeps saying to himself like a prayer so it
will last longer, so he will never have to leave this white
steel table and this angel secretary, Cindy, whose hand
is holding his whole body like a huge egg filled with blood
and semen which she cracks and it breaks open and he is free.

My Mother Prays for My Father

At night the muffled tick of rosary beads passes
through her fingers, pure mother-of-pearl. She prays
that he won't invade her side of the bed with the smell

of Lucky Strikes, of rye, that he'll fall in front of the 10:19.
For thirty days she prays to St. Andrew to protect her:
to keep the side of her face from the rose-colored

broadloom, soft as the cheeks of her China doll, the one with glass
blue eyes, there, in the music room, where her mother played Strauss,
her father read the *Herald Tribune*. She prays for protection

from the lightning of his fists, scarlet rain pouring from her mouth,
her ear onto chintz, starched organdy curtains. Did she make
a wrong turn in Poughkeepsie after summers at the lake

where she learned the breast stroke, the dead man's float,
or was it the beaded dresses, the Charleston, bathtub gin?
Every morning, she rises before him, wraps her hair in a French twist,

fries liverwurst and eggs. She wants to grow Japanese iris,
consider the secrets of scat, to leave this permanent evening
where even the larvae of caddis fly cast a stony sheath.

Window Blind

You keep the blind of our north window drawn.
Night after night we snuggle here and hold
each other in our reclusive unison
under our heavy blankets from Hudson's Bay
as if we were two clarinets beneath
the world's cellos and basses. We are devoid
of essence, two existences, thus neither
old nor young, male nor female, flesh nor stone,
which in existing and by existing are
only, onely, perfect—or nearly so.
Our song is a happy purring song. And yet
the blind is always drawn and at the back
of my mind I wonder why—why you at morning
dismiss the one clean pure light in the world
that comes to us from the north beyond the north,
from clarity there, unseen, unfaltering, and true.

The Woodcut on the Cover of Robert Frost's *Complete Poems*

A man plowing starts at the side of the field
Nearer his barn and works outward and away.
Why? Because plowing is always an adventure.
And then the slow walk home at end of day.

What to Do

Tell your mind and its
   agony
to the white bloom
   of the blue plum tree,

a responding beauty,
   irreducible,
of the one earth and ground,
   and real.

Once a year
   in April
in this region
   you may tell
      for a little while.

The First Signs of Spring

Because it was April
The tulip buds cracked then revealed
Satin sheened blood-red petals,
And the blossoming pear trees on Ninth Street
Filled the air with bridal stillness
The perfect setting for
The song of an unseen bird.
Then the woman in front of Balducci's screamed,
"Adam, give me your fucking hand,"
At the small boy with the dropped head
His fists clutching his jacket.
I knocked her down, picked up the boy
And fled up Sixth Avenue.
We stopped to get Toby, the ginger striped cat
Asleep in the lap of a drunk on Fourteenth
Who had scribbled on cardboard
"Toby and me are homeless PLEASE HELP."
I put ten bucks in his paper cup.
On the ferry across the Hudson
We tore the past off our skins
And threw the pieces into the river.
That night in my kitchen, windows wide open,
The fragrance of hyacinths filling the room,
Adam and I laughed, danced to a salsa beat,
While Toby stretched out on a blue velvet cushion
And scrupulously licked his fur clean.

Even When I Am Distracted,
I Am Thinking of You

The sky, grey around the edges, goes out for coffee.
"Hello," I say, wanting more hours than we have.
I insist on believing, music tearing my heart.
Morning lays a blank page. I soldier on,
ravished by art. What I miss is language,
stretching itself across emptiness. Grief, too,
has its necessary place. My sword wears rust,
my hair pillows your cheek, and the mummies
have moved to the second floor. Purple
as monkshood, they wonder what to do. Words
no longer fit. I grow old watching, begin to wear black,
practice aging. Your body next to mine, two commas
on a blank page. We could be mistaken for apostrophes,
those signs of possession. We fasten one more season
around us. I tried standing on my head, learned to like not seeing
what was coming. After darkness, it is not easy to see anything
but ambiguous shapes, the heart that wants to be a fence.

The Swim

Still, she has her silent say.

I swam nude in a creek with my mother once,
we kept a distance.
Then she said how nice I looked. Sun

on her dark hair, wet curls on her neck,
she painted cadmium red canvases. My flesh

cushions my bones, when will we get over
her drawnout death? That creek has filled

with thawed snow, her lilies are beginning
to bloom, the sky now is begging for notice.

Beach Rubble

"I love nature," Paul said, having walked the jetty
past the breakwater, tide fast filling in below us.
Thus began our long walk across the dunes to get back.
"Did you say *like* or *love*?" I asked.

He is saying, "that looks like bittersweet but it's not" and
". . . undulating grass . . ."

He shook rope from a bollixed net,
"good piece of rope," he said,
examined a flowerpot "good pot."
When he picked up a glove, I knew what he thought.

Traipsing toward the mainland through the dunes,
I thought of Jane and Flicka hiking in the sand
when the car hit, the driver asleep.
Later, my son found all that was left—
their sunscreen and walking stick.

In the dizzy light of this beach, I saw Paul
pick a plastic bottle out
from the sand. It looked like praying.

First Love

Forty times the wild geese have passed
across the face of a flower moon and

I still see my reflection in the heal of your eyes,
a boy locked in the blue shine, forever young.

I remember your hands, freckled and
almost as large as your laughter;

Hands that held mine and touched my face
behind the old mushroom barn by the dam.

You pressed against me in a '56 Chevy
as we rolled through town on our way to everything.

You leaned on my locker Monday mornings, waiting
for me in the west wing of the high school.

You could bring the whole school to a halt
with just your walk, the counterpoint

of your hips and shoulders flowing
in opposition to each other.

The first kiss that all others would be measured by,
behind your house by the grassy edge of the pond.

You gave me my innocence, forever.

PHILIP CIOFFARI

Racing the Uptown Express

When she left, I gave up girls for a year.
Saturday nights I gunned my father's '59 Fury up Tremont
to John's Paradise Inn, *Live Music Nightly*—
the bikes at curbside precise as headstones,
chrome trapping the bony light of streetlamps.
I drank Bud in large mugs, watched biker girls,
thin as kittens, slow-dance in place.
Sometimes I picked up Gerry and drove the Shore Road,
cars hunched along the rim of the bay, the frail breath
of love songs from dashboards in the dark.
I beamed the 6-volt out the window, slashed it
car to car, laughed
at what the light caused: a worried bob of heads, a clutter
of engines kicking in, the sudden red of taillights.
Once I drove alone under the El,
waited for the clacking of the Pelham Bay Express
on the uptown track.
I gave it a six-block head start, then chased
the dark clatter, the twitch of sparks.
I pushed the Fury past 60, 70,
the El's columns flickering by like mileposts.
I rode the shadow of that express head to head,
breathed its full-throttle scream
till the grey stone of the station wall came at me
and I hit the brakes—
some dreams you just have
to let go—
the tires holding,
fifteen feet to spare.

§

AMY CLAMPITT

1920–1994

I met Amy Clampitt on August 9, 1984, when she came as faculty to the writers' conference I direct at the Frost Place. We had lunch that day in the house, just the two of us, and during lunch I mentioned that I was studying Homer in Greek that summer, and she asked me to say some aloud. I had by heart the opening 50 lines of *The Iliad*, so I said them aloud. She listened with great alertness, her head tilted very slightly, her eyes bright, a tiny smile: as if her whole heart and very life depended on hearing Homer's Greek perfectly. She asked me to repeat several times the famous 34th line: "he went down to the shores of the loud-sounding sea" (*thina poluphloisboio thalasses*).

After her evening reading, she autographed my copy of *The Kingfisher*, writing: "for Don Sheehan, who knows the sound of Homer . . ." But she had heard Homer more deeply and truly than I had or could.

For Amy Clampitt's poems possess—all of them—a sonic exactness, in every line the syllables poised and alert, each sonic unit achieving a single and exact fit to its close neighbors. And in getting this fit right, the syllables themselves come to register the vibrancy of genuine aliveness.

But she uses this triumph to overcome—in every poem—what could have become the merely technical, instead seeking always a range of historic and dramatic richness. In lesser hands, the sonic alertness could well have yielded very fine and very tiny poems. In her hands it became the way to reach richness and width and depth and boldness.

In her 1990 book *Westward*, she published an extraordinary twenty-page poem called "The Prairie," one exploring the whole of American experience through the history of her family. Towards the end, she writes these lines about being on a boardwalk at Long Beach:

> What did it mean, that roaring?
> Existences, as they listen and then turn away,
>
> tremble: fate, memory, seaweed-clotted
> (*poluphloisboio thalasses*) pouring in immense,
> immersing all and every road not taken . . .

In the end of *Westward*, she adds this striking note:

The descriptive phrase transliterated here as *poluphloisboio tha-lasses* occurs for the first time near the beginning of *The Iliad*. It has been variously handled by translators—from "murmur-ing" to "loud-roaring" seas and back again. Tennyson perhaps had it in mind when he had his Ulysses say "the deep/ Moans round with many voices." Nothing in English, however, comes so close as the Greek to the hissing and tumultuous force of the breaking waves themselves.

With a wonderfully sly glance at Frost, she here beautifully knows the sound of Homer.

— Donald Sheehan

Iola, Kansas

Riding all night, the bus half empty, toward the interior,
among refineries, trellised and turreted illusory cities,
the crass, the indispensable wastefulness of oil rigs
offshore, of homunculi swigging at the gut of a continent:

the trailers, the semis, the vans, the bumper stickers,
slogans in Day-Glo invoking the name of Jesus, who knows
what it means: the air waves, the brand names, the backyard
Barbie-doll barbecue, graffiti in video, the burblings,

the dirges: *heart like a rock, I said Kathy I'm lost,*
the scheme is a mess, we've left Oklahoma, its cattle,
sere groves of pecan trees interspersing the horizonless
belch and glare, the alluvium of the auto junkyards,

we're in Kansas now, we've turned off the freeway,
we're meandering, as again night falls, among farmsteads,
the little towns with the name of a girl on the water tower,
the bandstand in the park at the center, the churches

alight from within, perpendicular banalities of glass
candy-streaked purple-green-yellow (who is this Jesus?),
the strangeness of all there is, whatever it is, growing
stranger, we've come to a rest stop, the name of the girl

on the water tower is Iola: no video, no vending machines,
but Wonder Bread sandwiches, a pie: "It's boysenberry,
I just baked it today," the woman behind the counter
believably says, the innards a purply glue, and I eat it

with something akin to reverence: free refills from
the Silex on the hot plate, then back to our seats,

the loud suction of air brakes like a thing alive, and
the voices, the sleeping assembly raised, as by an agency

out of the mystery of the interior, to a community—
and through some duct in the rock I feel my heart go out,
out here in the middle of nowhere (the scheme is a mess)
to the waste, to the not knowing who or why, and am happy.

Amaranth and Moly

The night we bailed out Jolene from Riker's Island
tumbleweeds in such multitudes were blowing through the dark
it might almost have been Wyoming. Built like a willow
or a John Held flapper, from the shoulders up
she was pure Nefertiti, and out of that divine
brown throat came honey and cockleburs.
She wore a headcloth like a tiara above a sack dress
improvised from a beach tower. She'd turned larceny
against the bureaucracy into an art form.
When they raised the subway fare and simultaneously
cut back on Human Resources, Jolene
began jumping turnstiles as a matter of principle.
The police caught up with her at approximately
the fifteenth infraction and the next thing
anybody knew, she'd been carted off
to the Women's House of D.
                                              Now that it's
been shifted to the other side of the East River,
bailing anybody out becomes an all-night expedition—
a backhanded kind of joyride, comparable
to crossing the Styx or the Little Big Horn
in a secondhand Volkswagen. You enter a region
of landfill, hamburger loess, a necropolis
of coffee grounds, of desiccated *Amaranthus albus*
(rudely known as pigweed) on the run.
No roots. When a tumbleweed takes off, barbed wire
won't stop it, much less a holstered guard
or signs reading No Authorized Vehicles
Beyond This Point. A shuttle bus arrives
after a while to cart you to the reception area,
where people paid to do it teach you how to wait,
with no message, while one shift goes off
and the next comes on, and every half hour or so

you feed another batch of change into a pay phone,
jiggling all the levers of influence you can think of
to no effect whatever.
                                    At a little after
three a.m., finally, Jolene came out—
the same beautiful outrageous gingersnap
with a whole new catalog of indictments.
On the shuttle bus, while a pimp was softly
lecturing his sullen girl on what to do next time,
Jolene described how at the precinct
they'd begun by giving her a
Psychiatric Assessment for which the City
then proceeded to bill her.
By the time the van arrived to take her
to the House of D., the officer
who'd brought her in in the first place
was saying, "Jolene, I love you." And she'd
told him, she told us, exactly what he could do.
All around us in the dark of Riker's Island
the tumbleweeds scurrying were no pigweed,
I was thinking, but the amaranth of antiquity.
And Jolene was not only amaranth and moly, she was poetry
leaping the turnstiles of another century.

Syrinx

Like the foghorn that's all lung,
the wind chime that's all percussion,
like the wind itself, that's merely air
in a terrible fret, without so much
as a finger to articulate
what ails it, the aeolian
syrinx, that reed
in the throat of a bird,
when it comes to the shaping of
what we call consonants, is
too imprecise for consensus
about what it even seems to
be saying: is it *o-ka-lee*
or *con-ka-ree*, is it really *jug jug*,
is it *cuckoo* for that matter?—
much less whether a bird's call
means anything in
particular, or at all.

Syntax comes last, there can be
no doubt of it: came last,
can be thought of (is
thought of by some) as a
higher form of expression:
is, in extremity, first to
be jettisoned: as the diva
onstage, all soaring
pectoral breath work,
takes off, pure vowel
breaking free of the dry,
the merely fricative
husk of the particular, rises
past saying anything, any

more than the wind in
the trees, waves breaking,
or Homer's gibbering
Thespesiae iaché:

those last-chance vestiges
above the threshold, the all-
but dispossessed of breath.

Beautiful Feet

They have beautiful feet
smooth toes adorned with rings
polished moon colors:
pearl, yellow fat of hunter moon,
thin slivers on tall black shoes.
Girls clang in and out of the house
flashing bits of colored silk
like cardinals darting through brush.
They sulk in the hammock
whispering of boys, of leaving.
I have been a good mother
spying at arms' length.
When they leave I will write
of my own youth,
aunts serving tea in china cups
their hair in smooth bouffants
discouraging breathing.
I will write of boys in cars
racing well past curfew
air streaming in
hiss of cardinal wings
red moon
damp, insistent grass
trailing my toes, legs
pale as a doe's.

Postcard from This Place

This bird on the branch can't feel the season. It flies from tree to
      tree, north-south, north-south.
This odd little car is stuck between two buses, which take it up the
      interstate at terrible speed.
This harbor frozen over is like no harbor I know. If I can't see the
      water it must not be there.
This strange little bar is tucked between two houses, which keep it
      from going anywhere.
This message arrived today: Leave now or be sorry later. I don't
      know which to choose.
This tiny traveling circus is setting up in my field. Will they ask me
      to perform?
So far down the ladder the pickings are slim, but I like slim and fit in
      fine.
This bag full of money means nothing to me, but no you can't have
      it.
This close to the border it's best to be a bird and fly over.

Postcard from Harmony Parking Lot

The teens have gathered, because they are teens.
They wear brown shirts faded to beige, black
boots, low-slung jeans. The way they stand
is called jaunty. Cigarettes burn through
their words, smoke blows through their hair,
and the way they stare at passersby blends
reptile with bird, spleen with wonder,
your past with their present to you.

Salt of Surrender

I am interested in the moment of change
the flying brush in Chinese paintings.

I am interested in the moment of breaking
levees, glass, the heart.

I am interested in the give-way-instant
dusk to dark, the spine of a book, loving.

I am interested in redemption
letting go, an apology, acceptance.

I am interested in catalysts
memory, desire, greed.

I am interested in the soul's emergence
truth, a lie, curiosity.

I am interested in consciousness
discovery, recognition, endurance.

I am interested in waking up
The Christ, The Buddha, The I Ching.

I am interested in drama
Shakespeare, Caravaggio, a wild night.

I am interested in the moment the poem
must be written
because there is nothing left to do.

Angler

We hadn't caught any fish
    afterwards we sat and ate our burgers
at the Union Grove DQ
marking time
I tried not to look

at my watch
tried not to say
    "well Dad I think it's time I got back"
we sat in the banana-colored booth
and ate our hamburgers

sun-stroked and grimy from having sat in a rowboat all that morning
    I'd driven from Chicago the night before
so we could get an early start
we're no fancy sport fishermen
we throw it out there and wait for the bobber to go under

Zebco rods
a few dozen night crawlers
perch bluegill the occasional small-mouth bass
something for dinner not the mantle
    it had been a perfect morning

by the time we'd rolled out of town
and into the country the sun was just coming up
we drove in and out of fog banks
settled to the bottoms of hills
    our footsteps and tackle boxes dropped to the planks

echoed through the harbor
    slipped the ropes drifted from the dock
clouds hung over the water around our oars

we dropped anchor
close to the shore

of a small island in the middle of the lake
    I didn't have the same impatience
I used to have
when I was a boy
in fact he set his bait and threw out

the first cast
I smoked took my time poured some coffee

knotted a new brass leader clipped an Eagle Claw
    sent my line far from the boat
he kept his in close

I used to believe I had a good feel for where they'd be
in the shade of a tree where the branches lean over the water
or near that outcropping of rock along the shore
    after a few hours we'd pulled a handful of bluegill
too small to keep we knew it wouldn't pick up

it was too late
in the summer
    I pushed my French fries aside and took a look
out the window
Dad asked was I going to finish them

oh
you can have 'em if you want
    across the highway
was the liquor store with the beer barrels
embedded in the walls

and down the road
the empty county fair grounds

a yellow light blinking from a wire above the four-way
same old Union Grove
    I told him

how lately
I'll catch myself thinking of everything as material
I told him it's like there's a glass wall around me
    he nodded
on guard

or not understanding
    I felt false for even having said it
it had gotten away
as soon as I opened my mouth
it was a lie

CHRISTOPHER CUNNINGHAM

Cows at the Salt Lick

When they lick, is it like thirst
or hunger, a parching thickness
of the throat, the slow tumble

of the belly? Or does the cow's salt urge come
from some other place,
some purely bovine emptiness,

like sleepwalkers' foragings for strange
fulfillment? Maybe it comes from the tongue,
thick and pink and black, hungry

muscle eroding saline blocks, white like ivory,
into the curves and dimples of bodies—
the alabaster absences of buttocks and breasts and knees

as if impressed in plaster. But the cows' need
is greater than any the human form can appease,
and days and weeks

and the slow work of want lick
these figures away, leaving only
dream forms, undulant concavities, the way

the wind weaves striae out of old
rock, marbling taut stone, or a cloud
is smoothed cirrus, as if by water

and time. But when the cows, their
salt thirst slaked, wander off, mulling
their cuds like questions, lulled

into motion by the siren-whisper of breeze
against grass, I wonder why I need these cows
and their tongues and these blocks to be

more than they are, why I need such beauty.

August 1
I couldn't get over my room at the Pinestead Farm. It reminded
me exactly of the attic room my mother grew up in at her aunt's
house. I felt like a real farm girl in it and adopted this persona as
my eyes and ears during the festival. I wanted everything to be
new to me while remembering everything that had come before.

New Hampshire Farm

Moira Mullen has come to the farm
and they have placed her
in the garret room
with nine pegs for her clothes.

Moira has tasks.

She has been dreaming about moose,
antlers like sea plants in a book,
flat and amber.

There is a barn with twelve windows
and a wide red door.
This is her solitude.

She speaks to the chickens
scratching under the firethorns.

She is remembering love, that old
country.

The Summer List

That summer we all took up yoga.
That summer we all got divorced.
That summer we all wrote our novel.
That summer we all found God.
That summer we all power walked.
That summer we all ate tofu.
And one of us got the Big C.

That summer we dabbled, some stood weeping
Fat tears, knee-deep in their pity weeds.

Yet Hammer Man Hal built his gazebo,
His goldfish paradise and backyard zoo.

And there's Alex with his biggest trout. There's
A snapshot of Kim perfecting her gams.

But Claudia, brilliant and brave, read Proust,
Grew kohlrabi. Queen of that summer list,

She waited for the grinning ax to fall.
She waved us farewell. Oh, goodbye we kissed,

And snuggled cold feet under plump comforts.
Oh, how could she leave for somewhere so strange?

Her eyes came to startle our sleep, her face
A charade of joy and translucent hope,

A brittle pale leaf. How could we plan?
—For indifferent white snow, down

Without sound on the stone near dark woods.

JESSICA G. DE KONINCK

Footprints of the Stars

Maria met Jesus wandering in L.A. in 1932.
The real deal, not some long-haired
messianic wannabe. He told her
he visited before. In 1849 he panned
the Sacramento Valley, but did not stop

to watch gold rise off the ocean
the way it does in Malibu at sunset.
He likes how California reminds him
of home, warm and dry,
full of decked out desperados

mining Hollywood Boulevard
for cash or a needleful. One time
he was born in East L.A.
Angelinos do not weather well
far from warmth. Jesus knows

the game of life in the wilderness,
the solitude of freeways,
how to avoid snow. Hiding
his face that blizzard winter
stuck outside the Donner Pass.

Now, for redemption, he waters
arid lots. Poinsettias with nugget hearts
bloom and bleed along the Boulevard.
Jesus watches the smog rise like amnesia
over the tar pits and cultivates

his fields, studded like rhinestones
among gold's rush and idols
of the silver screen. Few notice
his gardening, but in southern California
it never snows at Christmas.

The Doily

The end-of-the-worlders say anytime now.
They point to widespread catastrophic flooding,
three continents of deadly earthquakes,
children savaged, a general decline.
They match each new
atrocity, each horror, to Scripture.

But tomorrow we will rise again at five,
slip into the dark outside, look
to the silver stars, silk planets, and walk
as we have done for weeks.
Who knows? An owl might call *Who cooks for you?*
Be answered with the same.
In a patch of light from Stannard's driveway lantern,
shadows of our dog's quick legs
might move again like bickering sticks –
Me first! No me! No me me me! – then
vanish in the road's old dark.
Maybe close to home again
Scirpo's rooster will crow his brassy boast, and

all the while on the bird's eye maple
desk Big Unc gave us from the farm
a small fringed doily made
by someone long ago remains,
and on its tatted center square:
a tiny vase of eight gold mums whose
stems I beveled late
last night to keep them'til
I-don't-know-when.

Potter

Have you thrown a bowl on the wheel—loud slap
then the gentle application
of pressure—the mound slips round and round wetly
between your two cupped hands—feel it
bumping into your hands, bumping into your hollowed palms
more and more, pushing at them, pulling them, back and forth and
       back
till it seems that at the center where the clay should be there is
       something
inmovable something
not clay that has taken its place
repulsing it and your hands are closing in, hardening, trying
to contain it while the clay is forced inward and
upward and the oscillation becomes frenetic, head of an exotic
dancer spinning round and round
on her shoulders, faster and faster her hair
pulling towards the four corners, the four corners
screaming towards her till her soft throat is
ripped except the gash goes
all the way around
and you are left holding
a lump of clay
while the wheel spins emptily

From a Phone Booth

Friday night, supper over, the phone rings.
Fatigue honing her thin voice, my daughter
calling from a great distance from a phone booth
in a girls' dormitory thanks me.

Her thermal underwear, vitamins, my poem
arrived. Mornings the wind-chill index is forty
below. Insomnia, Plato. Words reaching out
in new concerns enter the blank pages

of her life. Snow falls. All roads are blocked.
It is 1978, and she, a freshman, seeks answers.
I utter directions for her safekeeping.
Silence comes back across the mountains

like a freight of steeples. Eyes and lips
have not changed. The loss of golden glow
and evening teas is a fledgling flying between us.
She is talking common sense; tension and stamina mix.

The world she describes is eighteen, snowy white,
    merciless.
She is in love. She, that white bloom I put out in
    December.

The Gospel Singer Testifies

When she spoke, I looked down
the way I would if she'd begun undressing
before everyone, not to entertain
but to show things about ourselves
we knew to cover. So aware that beside me
a Jewish friend listened—or didn't—
to her praise of Jesus.
I wanted to signal, "We're not all like that."
But my friend is, we are, all like that:
having something we'd get naked for
before a whole group of people.
That is, if we're lucky. So my body heard
before I did, with tears at the corners of my eyes,
as the words that had begun in song *Thank you, Jesus!*
dissolved back into song, or a finer
distillation, and the singer closed her eyes,
Thank you! bent like a bowstring,
shot forth her nakedness to save me.

The Nearness of You

The last time you wore clothes that hid your flesh
we drove down to the ocean and when I had to
convince you to enjoy March in the safety of the car

you wanted to wear lipstick, green eye shadow,
but were too tired. I was anxious to leave
the morphine, the hiss of the humidifier, the lushness

of flowering plants. You were restless,
trying to fit your bones to the seat. We listened
to Artie Shaw, Glenn Miller, your favorites:

It isn't your sweet conversation
That brings this sensation, oh no
It's just the nearness of you

Before your pain crashed through, Glenn held us
with his music. You patted my knee, rested your hand
there. We rode for a long time that way.

Eggs

We wanted to neck like they did, we'd heard, at parties,
on couches with people watching us work our jaws.
We wanted to slug from a bottle, eyes rolled back,
but we needed a party skill so we'd get asked.
The library book said, "a great trick for any party,"
so Evelyn and me, in her mother's kitchen, sucked eggs,
hard-boiled eggs, through the neck of a glass milk bottle.
A twist of newspaper, on fire, you put in first,
then set your clean, peeled egg on the bottle's neck
and the fire gets hungry for air and shivers it in
with a rubbery *BUP* of relief, and a puff of black breath.
We told Evelyn's mom we were practicing social graces,
but she charged us a nickel a pop, called it playing with food,
and as each gray egg, flecked with shell, smudged
with carbon thumbprints, grunted like a spelunker
and shot its guts, she got madder, shaking her head
like a cat with canker. When egg number eight
slipped its hips and blew its brains,
she hollered she knew why we never got asked to parties,
and clean up this mess, and the cat box too, goddamnit.
Evelyn wiped her hands on her yellow shorts,
smudging Davey Crockett's face with soot. We rolled up our mess
in the Friday Morning Call and cut out to wander Chadwick Street
at noon, swinging our butts, and all our eggs in two baskets,
shivering with our potential to fuck with fire.

Outboard

A drinking buddy gave our dad an outboard motor.
Dad kept it, up to its orange chin in bilge,
in an oil drum, up in the yard, and, after a few,
he'd go out and start it up, yelling, "Get back,
you kids!" but we were already back, and ready to bolt
if the green plastic men we'd thrown in up and busted the thing.
But no tiny-acid-stripped skeletons churned to the surface;
the army remained at rest with the worms and pear cores.
All that spring, when he felt good, he'd go watch his motor,
his nostrils straining to catch each oily fume,
a Chesterfield dropping ash down his nylon shirt front.
Once Shakey Louie, his pal, braved the terrible sunlight
to join him in motor-watching, and, chatty by nature,
told us Dad had said soon that our freezer'd be so full of trout
there wouldn't be room left for even one skinny Popsicle.
By August we'd scrawled "S.S. DAD" on the slimy oil drum,
but he never noticed, just stood in the din, smoking, staring.
He never did lug that motor out of the oil drum,
he let winter do in the only toy he had, though it spat
muddy rainbows and roared like a locomotive,
and gave off the piercing and molten stink of hope.

KAREN DOUGLASS

Crow's Daughter

Noisy, nosy, and familiar,
a murder of crows
blackens the tallest oak.
The city stands with its mouth open.
Who can hear their racket and not pause?

When I was four and angry,
I packed my wagon and ran away
down a long, sandy lane.
Not a soul around
save me and Crow.
She warned me about the world,
insisted, till I walked home again.

This week she feeds in the street,
scolds me from a low eave,
then—gone—my real mother.
I keep a civil tongue with her.

Crow does not die.
The same one drove me back
that saw Antietam, Gettysburg . . .
It's a long list.
I am still her child
pulling a red Radio Flyer
loaded with ghosts.
Her hundred sons
in the city oak
clack their beaks
as if the sky were talking.
The Sun sinks anyway.

The Marriage Bathroom

You're bent beneath the ceiling,
built by a smaller man,
and hunched up on the toilet seat
to get a better view.
Your knees just through the doorway.

Of course we decide to wallpaper.

Of course we choose the maddening rose.

I think I married you for your hands.
I watch your fingers spread into fans,
cajole and smooth each angled piece,
seductive music—paper, palm.

Our picnic table's tacky with glue,
the rolls scrolling back on themselves
as we work against dusk, the boom
of approaching thunder.

Four hours, elbow to cheek
trimming each edge with a razor blade.
Match and measure, lift and apply—
the sullen pulse of assembly line.

On your glistening forehead
a few stray hairs are twisting like eels.
We both avoid the mirror.

I wish I could say that we look
at each other and laugh, that we leave
the mess and climb upstairs
to our bed beneath the skylight.

Instead we wash in the other bathroom,
a couple of towels our luxury,
and sleep in the room with twin beds
because it's air-conditioned.

I think we say goodnight.

I pray that in the privacy of dark
half-rose will locate half-rose
and that when morning dawns on their embrace
the light will be clear . . . and generous.

The Old Boy

From the yard of his farmhouse
the view is pretty much the same
as from his cabin in Vermont:
mountains, those humpbacked things.
With the town off in the distance,
what he had, besides their beauty,
was a house with a porch on which,
in summer, he sat with feet
propped up and saved his days
with those other things called words.
I haven't spent much time looking,
or bent over a writing board
with my white hair showing plainly
like a trespass sign tacked to a tree;
but here on the screened-in porch
of my white clapboard cottage
at the North Country Motor Court
I have my own view of the mountains.
I have firewood stacked at my feet,
an old armchair and wooden desk
nearly as worn as his lap board,
a huge oak shading the porch,
flowering shrubs on both sides,
and neighbors, closer than his,
with whom I'm not disposed
to make small talk. Out back,
farther than I can see, bulldozers
rip out trees and savage earth
to make way for a house
the way the saw he wrote of did
the hand of a boy who lived close by.
I wonder what he'd make of these
machine-age beasts. A metaphor?

Or would he take them as he did
himself: storm troopers of the dark?
A path snakes uphill past birches,
through ferns and around a spring.
I don't know if it's the one less
travelled by, but of the end
that's in sight there is no doubt
if I should dare to walk away
into those lovely woods. *Gone,*
is all they'd say: my many friends.
The clouds turn purple as the sun sets,
streaking the trees against the face
of mountains like bloody fingertips.

Dismantling the House

Rent a flatbed with a winch.
With the right leverage
anything can be hoisted, driven off.

Or the man with a Bobcat comes in,
then the hauler with his enormous truck.
A leveler or a lawyer does the rest;

experts always are willing to help.
The structure was old, rotten in spots.
Hadn't it already begun to implode?

Believe you've just sped the process up.
Photographs, toys, the things that break
your heart—let's trust

they would have been removed,
perhaps are safe with the children
who soon will have children of their own.

It's over. It's time for loss to build
its tower in the yard where you
are merely a spectator now.

Admit you'd like to find something
discarded or damaged, even gone,
and lift it back into the world.

Monogamy

Start again, try to say it
with a little brio this time, a dash
of wasabi in the first sentence,
some paprika perhaps
for the sake of *p*'s, and turn loose
the drummer in you
(your best kept secret) who loves
the intermittent, yet heart-timed
clack of drumstick against metal.

After all, there's the suddenly desirable
mono in monogamy to celebrate,
the new freedom of wanting
only one person. Start again,
but admit you wouldn't advocate this
for anyone save yourself. Acknowledge
it's a state you've traveled far
to reach, motels and the overly careful
spelling of aliases behind you.
Acknowledge it takes long experience
in order to think of sameness
as an opportunity for imagination.

Call yourself a monk and call her
a nun, and remember the fun of words
lying down with other words.
Think syntax. Think combos
and ménages, it's all right, my friend,
to include the various in the one.
You're in love. It's springtime. Birds
are making a racket in the thousand thickets.

Turning to the Page

I remember that cavernous silence
after my first declaration of love,
then, feeling I must have been
misunderstood, saying it again,

and, years later, with someone else,
exclaiming, "That was so good!"
and the foreign language she—who was
speaking English—used in response.

I learned there's nothing more shaming
or as memorable as an intimacy
unreturned. And turned, therefore,
to the expected silence of a page,

where I might simultaneously assert
and hide, be my own disappointment,
which saved me for a while.
But soon the page whispered

I'd mistaken its vastness for a refuge,
its whiteness for a hospital
for the pathetic. Fill me up, it said,
give me sorrow because I must have joy,

all the travails of intimacy because
distances are where the safe reside.
Bring to me, I said, continual proof
you've been alive.

STEPHEN DUNN

Achilles in Love

There was no getting to his weakness.
In public, even in summer, he wore
big boots, specially made for him,
a band of steel reinforcing each heel.
At home, when he bathed or slept,
he kept a pistol within reach, loaded.
And because to be invulnerable
is to be alone, he was alone even when
he was with you. You could sense it
in the rigidity of his carriage, as if under
his fine-fitting suits were layers of armor.
Yet everyone loved to see him in action:
While his enemies were thinking small
advantages, he only thought endgame.

Then she came along, who seemed to be all
women fused into one, cheek bones and breasts
evidence that evolution doesn't care
about fairness, and a mind so good, well,
it was like his. She'd come to interview him
for a magazine, and Achilles had planned
to give her a bright package of nothing.
But it was love almost instantly.
You could see his body soften as he
realized that all of her questions suggested
the arc of what could be his best answers.

And days later, when finally they were naked,
she instinctively knew what to do—
as smart men do with a mastectomy's scar—
to kiss his heel before kissing
what he considered to be his power,
and with a tenderness that made him tremble.

And so Achilles began to live differently.
Both friends and enemies were astounded
by his willingness to listen, and hesitate
before responding. Even in victory he'd
walk away without angering a single god.
He wore sandals now because she liked him in sandals.
He never felt so exposed, or so open to the world.
You could see in his face something resembling terror,
but in fact it was love, for which he would die.

Taken

And that has made all the difference

It did, in a way, make a difference—
with one thing leading on to the next,
then on to the next, the way things do

—but not *all*, as I once thought; not
the essentials, the parts that come along
with me, the parts I've become, beyond

the mere quirks of the road I'm on,
those shades of use, or lack of use
that beggar comparison, like some

impromptu parlor game that lags on
well into the night with no real end
in sight, except foreseeable regret.

I forget the circumstances that loomed
so large, back then—a figurative woods
with inscrutable choices laid out before me.

I remember the dilemma the words made,
existential ploddings compounded by
a, too easily mistaken, deep forest scene.

But a person can sidestep, misdirect, mis-
appropriate and even completely mis-
understand the literal moment of choice.

He might miss it for what it is, with no
spotlight, nor theme song, just a lag, a
pause, a delay in his way. Then it's done.

The sun was too bright, so I went to the right.
The day had some heft, so I went to the . . .
If you must know, I needed somewhere to go.

Like God,

you hover above the page staring down
on a small town. Outside a window
some scenery loafs in a sleepy hammock
of pastoral prose and here is a mongrel
loping and here is a train approaching
the station in three long sentences and
here are the people in galoshes waiting.
But you know this story about the galoshes
is really About Your Life, so, like a diver
climbing over the side of a boat and down
into the ocean, you climb, sentence
by sentence, into this story on this page.

You have been expecting yourself
as a woman who purrs by in a dress
by Patou, and a porter manacled to
the luggage, and a man stalking across
the page like a black cloud in a bad mood.
These are your fellow travelers and
you are a face behind or inside these
faces, a heartbeat in the volley of these
heartbeats, as you choose, out of all
the journeys, the journey of a man
with a mustache scented faintly with

Prince Albert. "He must be a secret
sensualist," you think and your awareness
drifts to his trench coat, worn, softened,
and flabby, a coat with a lobotomy, just
as the train pulls into the station.

No, you would prefer another stop
in a later chapter where the climate is

affable and sleek. But the passengers
are disembarking, and you did not
choose to be in the story of the woman
in the white dress which is as cool and
evil as a glass of radioactive milk. You
did not choose to be in the story of the
matron whose bosom is like the prow
of a ship and who is launched toward
lunch at The Hotel Pierre, or even the
story of the dog-on-a-leash, even though
this is now your story: the story of the
man-who-had-to-take-the-train-and-walk
the-dark-road described hurriedly by
someone sitting at the tavern so you could
discover it, although you knew all along
the road would be there, you, who have
been hovering above this page, holding
the book in your hands, like God, reading.

Dressing the Parts

Here I comes.
— Anne Lauterbach

So, here we are,
I am a kind of diction

I can walk around in
clothed in the six-inch heels

of *arrogation* and *scurrility*.
And what are you

wearing? Is it those boxer
things again? I hope it is

those boxer things
and nothing else

except your eyes;
I like your eyes; do you

like the way my feet
are long, narrow,

with toenails like tiny television screens?
And hair is important.

A fog of hair floating
above the fields of the body.

Or the body as bald
as a truffle,

very French—
swine on leashes.

Like you, my pig.
I'm your truffle and

for you
reading is eating.

Is too.

When you were at the Brasserie
eating—

crêpes fourées, and,
légumes à la Grecque, and,

and, and—
you felt like you had read all of

Leaves of Grass at one sitting.
Wait, I see something

between your teeth:
it is a kiss as wet

and mobile as a gourami
in an aquarium.

Oh. God. Yes.
Describe the lips.

Describe what
the lips are wearing.

Is it that color called

Red-as-the-roofs-of-Brest?

That color that the lips
of the you is wearing?

That *you*, reader,
that you are wearing.

Elsewhere

This isn't Italy where even
the dust is sexual, and I am not
eighteen clothed in elaborate
nonchalance. Onions' *Etymologies*
says memory is related to mourning.
I'm always remembering myself
out of some plain place in the middle West,
some every-small-town-I-have-ever-hated-
and-grieved-my-way-out-of-in-poetry, chipping
the distance open with a train, awling
open with the train's hooting

a silence which is stolidly American, sturdy, woodsy.
Well, no, perhaps these woods are Dante's;
it's dark in here. I'm nearly fifty,
rummaging through the ruined beauty
of a girl at twenty who couldn't interrogate
her heart for more than five minutes.

—Just listen

even in Corsica where the repeated call of the
lighthouse throbbed like a piston, and the thin whine
of an engine garroted the quiet, and I stood good
as a flower in my pastel shirtwaist, poked and
nuzzled by my date, and listened to the mixing,
like a cocktail, of the water and earth, the cool
gargle, the slushy breathing of the surf, and
wished I were somewhere else

to her describing, even then, a longing
to escape. And, like me, she only does it on the page,

heaping up the elaborate scenery so
she can disappear into it.

On this flat EKG of horizon the silos are blips
repeating and repeating. There is a storm,
a thick, dark, hard knot of cloud, but it's stuck
in the chimney of my throat. Nearly fifty.

The fire is out, the cabin's dark,
and beyond, the woods are a platoon
of black trees. It's so quiet
I can hear my heart like the blows
of an ax, each blow blurred by an echo,

I can hear my heart inside my chest
trudging onward across the bleak tundra.
What was I thinking?

I look again at her poems flowing with
images, a restlessness, a terrible sense
of what's coming: She's writing me,
the woman she becomes, who could not
or would not save her.

The River Will Not Testify

— Connecticut River, Turners Falls, Massachusetts 1999

The river's belly swirls shards of bone gnawed by water.
The river is deaf after centuries of pummeling the rocks.
The river thrashes all night with the lightning of lunatic visions.
The river strangles on the dam, hissing at the stone eagles
that watch with stone eyes from the bridge.
Concrete stops the river's tongue at Turners Falls.

The river cannot testify to all the names:
Peskeomskut, gathering place at the falls;
Sokoki, Nipmuck, Pocumtuck, many nations, many hands
that speared the flapping salmon from the rocks,
stitched the strips of white birch into wigwams.
So Reverend Mr. Russell wrote to the Council of War:
They dwell at the Falls a considerable number, yet
most of them old men, women and children. The Lord calls us
to make some trial which may be done against them.

The river cannot testify of May 19, 1676.
The river's face was painted blue at daybreak.
Captain Turner's men, Puritans sniffing with beards
and flintlock muzzles, slipped between the wigwams
ghostly as the smoke from drying fish.
Their muskets lifted up the flaps of bark;
their furious God roared from every musket's mouth.
The sleepers drenched in rivers sun-red like the salmon,
and a wailing rose with the mist from the skin of the river.

The river cannot testify about canoes skidding
over the falls, their ribs in splinters, or swimmers
hammering their skulls against the rocks,
or bullets hammering the rocks and skulls,
or Captain Holyoke's sword lopping the branches

of grandfathers into the water, or Bardwell
counting the corpses vomited by the white cascade.
And Reverend Mr. Mather wrote:
The river swept them away, that ancient river, oh my soul.

The river cannot testify to who began the rumor:
a thousand Indians, someone yelled, a thousand Indians approaching;
so when a few dozen warriors read the smoke from gutted wigwams
and splashed across the river, the conquerors fled,
shrieking at the green demons that whipped their eyes
and snatched their ankles as they stumbled through the forest.

The river cannot testify to say what warrior's rifle
shot Captain Turner, the ball of lead thudding
between shoulder blades, flipped from his horse
and dragged off by the water to sink in a halo of blood.
His name christened the falls, the town, the granite monument
that says: destroyed 300 Indians at this place.
One day a fisherman would unearth shinbones
of Indians by the falls, seven skeletons
and each one seven feet tall, he declared.

Centuries gone, the fishing boats sucked over the dam,
the tendons of the bridge ripped out in the flood,
the children leaning too far and abducted by the current:
all as withered leaves to the river.
The lumber company fire that smothered the night watchman,
the cotton mill and the needles of brown lung,
the knife factory bricked shut during the Depression:
all mosquito-hum and glimmer of porch light to the river.
The Horse Thief Detecting Society that never caught a thief,
the German Military Band flourishing trombones,
the Order of Scalpers with fraternity war whoops,
the American Legion dinners beery against communism,
the Indians galloping undefeated onto the high school football field:
all like the glitter of fish to the river.

Centuries from now, at this place,
when chimneys are the shadows of monsters in the river,
when collapsed spires are haunted by crows,
when graves are plowed to harvest the bones
for aphrodisiacs and trinkets,
when the monuments of war have cracked
into hieroglyphics no one can read,
when the rain sizzles with a nameless poison,
when the current drunk on its own dark liquor
storms through the crumbling of the dam,
the river will not testify of Turners Falls,
for the river has swept them away, oh my soul.

The Shiny Aluminum of God
— *Carolina, Puerto Rico 1997*

After the pilgrimage
to the Office of Cemetery Records,
we pay fifty dollars in cash
for the free municipal burial plot,
the clerk hiding the bills in a manila folder.
El pastor Pentecostal forgets the name of the dead,
points at the ceiling and gazes up
whenever he loudly whispers the syllables
for eternal life, *la vida eterna*,
as if the stain on the tile were the map of heaven.
The mourners are palm trees in the hallelujah wind,
hands raised overhead. Once grandmother Tata's pen
looped the words of the spirits as they spoke to her;
now she grips a borrowed golden crucifix
in the coffin, lid propped open by mistake.
The coffin bumps into a hole of mud
next to the chain-link fence, and then
the family Vélez Espada gathers for dinner.

The pernil is frozen, pork shoulder congealed and raw
like a hunk of Siberian woolly mammoth.
But Angela tells us of the miracle pot
that will roast the meat in an hour
without a cup of water. She sells the pot
to her neighbors too, keeps a tower of boxes
with a picture of the pot resplendent on every box.
The words on her kerchief hail
the shiny aluminum of God: Dios te ama.

The scar carves her husband's forehead
where the doctors scooped the tumor out,
where cancer cells scramble like a fistful of ants.

In a year he will be the next funeral, when the saints
of oncology surrender their weapons. For now
Edwin lives by the finches he snares in the backyard,
wings blundering through the trap door of the cage,
sold for five dollars apiece to the neighbors.

He praises God for brain surgery and finches,
leans close and grins about the time
his brother somersaulted out a window
and two swooping angels caught him
by the elbows, inches from the ground.
Only one broken rib, Edwin says,
rubbing his stomach in the slow way
of a man satisfied with his meal.
Angela's brother passes out pamphlets:
God's ambulance found him and his needle
in a condemned building, no shoes
and no heartbeat. Then Edwin says:
God will not let me die.

An hour later,
the pernil is still frozen in the oven.
Angela stares at the sweating pork,
then the boxes of pots unsold in the corner.
A boy cousin taps his fork
and asks if we can eat the finches.
The trap clatters in the backyard,
an angel flapping in the cage.

At Omaha Beach

Lewis M. Ginsberg
d. June 7, 1944

The waves wash out, wash in.
The rain comes down. It comes down.
The sky runs into the sea
that turns in its troubled sleep,
dreaming its long gray dream.
White stars stand on the lawn.
We move on the edges of speech.

Sleep comes down. It comes down.
Dreams wash out, wash in.
Our fathers walk out of the sea.
The air is heavy with speech.
Our fathers are younger than we.
As the fog dissolves in the dawn,
our fathers lie down on the beach.

We're a dream drifting down on a beach
in the rain in the sleep of our lives.
White stars wash over a lawn.
We are troubled by sea and sky.
Our words dissolve in the waves.
On the edges of speech is the sound
of the rain coming down. It comes down.

A Starlit Night

All over America at this hour men are standing
by an open closet door, slacks slung over one arm,
staring at wire hangers, thinking of taxes
or a broken faucet or their first sex: the smell
of backseat Naugahyde, the hush of a maize field
like breathing, the stars rushing, rushing away.

And a woman lies in an unmade bed watching
the man she had known twenty-one, no,
could it be? twenty-two years, and she is listening
to the polonaise climbing up through radio static
from the kitchen where dishes are piled
and the linoleum floor is a great, gray sea.

It's the A-flat polonaise she practiced endlessly,
never quite getting it right, though her father,
calling from the darkened TV room, always said,
"Beautiful, kiddo!" and the moon would slide across
the lacquered piano top as if it were something
that lived underwater, something from far below.

They both came from houses with photographs,
the smell of camphor in closets, board games
with missing pieces, sunburst clocks in the kitchen
that made them, each morning, a little sad.
They didn't know what they wanted, every night,
every starlit night of their lives, and now they have it.

Rave On

> *. . . Wild to be wreckage forever.*
> — James Dickey, "Cherrylog Road"

Rumbling over caliche with a busted muffler,
radio blasting Buddy Holly over Baptist wheat fields,
Travis screaming out *Prepare ye the way of the Lord*
at jackrabbits skittering beneath our headlights,
the Messiah coming to Kansas in a flat-head Ford
with bad plates, the whole high plains holding its breath,
night is fast upon us, lo, in these the days of our youth,
and we were hell to pay, or thought we were. Boredom
grows thick as maize in Kansas, heavy as drill pipe
littering the racks of oil rigs where in summer boys
roustabout or work on combine crews north as far
as Canada. The ones left back in town begin
to die, dragging main street shitfaced on 3.2 beer
and banging on the whorehouse door in Garden City
where the ancient madame laughed and turned us down
since we were only boys and she knew our fathers.
We sat out front spitting Red Man and scanned a landscape
flat as Dresden: me, Mike Luckinbill, Billy Heinz,
and Travis Doyle, who sang, *I'm gonna live fast,*
love hard, and die young. We had eaten all the life
there was in Seward County but hungry still, hauled ass
to old Arkalon, the ghost town on the Cimarron
that lay in half-shadow and a scattering of starlight,
and its stillness was a kind of death, the last breath
of whatever in our lives was ending. We had drunk there
and tossed our bottles at the walls and pissed great arcs
into the Kansas earth where the dust groweth hard
and the clods cleave fast together, yea, where night yawns
above the river in its long, dark dream, above
haggard branches of mesquite, chicken hawks scudding
into the tree line, and moonglitter on caliche

like the silver plates of Coronado's treasure
buried all these years, but the absence of treasure,
absence of whatever would return the world
to the strangeness that as children we embraced
and recognized as *life*. *Rave on.*

                        Cars are cheap
at Roman's Salvage strewn along the fence out back
where cattle graze and chew rotting fabric from the seats.
Twenty bucks for spare parts and a night in the garage
could make them run as far as death and stupidity
required—on Johnson Road where two miles of low shoulders
and no fence line would take you up to sixty, say,
and when you flipped the wheel clockwise, you were there
rolling in the belly of the whale, belly of hell,
and your soul fainteth within you for we had seen it done
by big Ed Ravenscroft who said you would go in a boy
and come out a man, and so we headed back through town
where the marquee of the plaza flashed *Creature from
the Black Lagoon* in storefront windows and the Snack Shack
where we had spent our lives was shutting down and we
sang *rave on, it's a crazy feeling* out into the night
that loomed now like a darkened church, and sang loud
and louder still for we were sore afraid.

                      Coming up
out of the long tunnel of cottonwoods that opens onto
Johnson Road, Travis with his foot stuck deep into the *soul*
of that old Ford, *come on Bubba, come on* beating
the dash with his fist, hair flaming back in the wind
and eyes lit up by some fire in his head that I
had never seen, and Mike, iron Mike, sitting tall
in back with Billy, who would pick a fight with anything
that moved but now hunched over mumbling something
like a prayer, as the Ford lurched on spitting
and coughing but then smoothing out suddenly fast
and the fence line quitting so it was open field, then,
then, I think, we were butt-deep in regret and a rush

of remembering whatever we would leave behind—
Samantha Dobbins smelling like fresh laundry,
light from the movie spilling down her long blonde hair,
trout leaping all silver and pink from Black Bear Creek,
the hand of my mother, I confess, passing gentle
across my face at night when I was a child—oh, yes,
it was all good now and too late, too late, trees blurring
past and Travis wild, popping the wheel, oh too late
too late

and the waters pass over us the air thick
as mud slams against our chests though turning now
the car in its slow turning seems almost graceful
the frame in agony like some huge animal groaning
and when the wheels leave the ground the engine cuts loose
with a wail thin and ragged as a bandsaw cutting tin
and we are drowning breathless heads jammed against
our knees and it's a thick swirling purple nightmare
we cannot wake up from for the world is turning too
and I hear Billy screaming and then the whomp
sick crunch of glass and metal whomp again back window
popping loose and glass exploding someone crying out
tink tink of iron on iron overhead and then at last
it's over and the quiet comes

Oh so quiet. Somewhere
the creak and grind of a pumping unit. Crickets.
The tall grass sifting the wind in a mass of whispers
that I know I'll be hearing when I die. And so
we crawled trembling from doors and windows borne out
of rage and boredom into weed-choked fields barren
as Golgotha. Blood raked the side of Travis's face
grinning rapt, ecstatic, Mike's arm was hanging down
like a broken curtain rod, Billy kneeled, stunned,
listening as we all did to the rustling silence
and the spinning wheels in their sad, maniac song
as the Ford's high beams hurled their crossed poles of light
forever out into the deep and future darkness. *Rave on.*

I survived. We all did. And then came the long surrender,
the long, slow drifting down like young hawks riding on
the purest, thinnest air, the very palm of God
holding them aloft so close to something hidden there,
and then the letting go, the fluttering descent, claws
spread wide against the world, and we become, at last,
our fathers. And do not know ourselves and therefore
no longer know each other. Mike Luckinbill ran a Texaco
in town for years. Billy Heinz survived a cruel divorce,
remarried, then took to drink. But finally last week
I found this house in Arizona where the brothers
take new names and keep a vow of silence and make
a quiet place for any weary, or lost, passenger
of earth whose unquiet life has brought him there,
and so, after vespers, I sat across the table
from men who had not surrendered to the world,
and one of them looked at me and looked into me,
and I am telling you there was *a fire in his head*
and his eyes were coming fast down a caliche road,
and I knew this man, and his name was Travis Doyle.

Anniversaries

for Donald Sheehan

This is the day of Hiroshima,
the flashpoint day of bodies, bright
as the briefest star. And you remind me
that this day is also a high holy day,
the transfiguration, when Christ went up
on the mountain and in the company of three
disciples, became light just as those
Japanese bodies became light.

I am sitting on a gray folding chair
thinking about connections . . . August 6th,
my God—the day my father died. Not moving,
not taking my eyes from the compassion
in your face, I stumble back to my tenth summer,
the phone call that blasted something away forever.
Suicide leaves survivors wanting something
to explain it, the way even now I want
some cloaked guide to step from the shadow
of a casket saying: *This, child, is how it was.*

Noontime, on the gentle slope of lawn,
a woman tells me on this day
last year, she set flowers and candles
adrift on a long river for the world.
And I wonder how, against the immensity
of Christ or of arms, incandescent in a cruel
cloud, one small death can matter,
can share the same syllables in the throat,
the same vowels floating across the vaporous air.
My father. My father.

Later, from one small bedroom window,
I watch the soft arching of Mt. Kinsman,
a blue sky and a cloud rising,
a lightning rod atop a cupola.
The day gathers itself: this festival,
Hiroshima, these hills, your voice,
and yes, Christ, in whom I may not even believe,
and the suicide of my father, all lifting
into this pine-laden air, all rising
and igniting like candles,
like a procession of flowers and candles
over these wavering White Mountains.

PATRICIA FARGNOLI

Watching Light in the Field

It may be part water, part animal—
the light—the long flowing whole
of it, river-like, almost feline,
shedding night, moving silent
and inscrutable into the early morning,
drifting into the low fields,
gathering fullness, attaching itself
to thistle and sweetgrass,
the towering border trees,
inheriting their green wealth—
blooming as if this
were the only rightful occupation,
rising beyond itself, stretching out
to inhabit the whole landscape.
I think of illuminations, erasures,
how light informs us, is enough
to guide us. How too much
can cause blindness. I think of memory—
what is lost to us, what we desire.
By noon, nothing is exact,
everything diffused in the glare.
What cannot be seen intensifies:
rivulet of sweat across the cheekbone,
earthworm odor of soil and growing.
The field sways with confusion
of bird call, mewlings,
soft indecipherable mumblings.
But in the late afternoon, each stalk
and blade stands out so sharp and clear
I begin to know my place among them.
By sunset as it leaves—

gold-dusting the meadow-rue and hoary alyssum,
hauling its bronze cloak across the fences,
vaulting the triple-circumference
of hills—I am no longer lonely.

BARBARA A. FLAHERTY

Company

Sad comes to visit
often lately wearing a
large Victorian hat, the
brim tilted town shading
the stories in the eyes.

Sad, thy garb is pale,
demure, yet cool with
loneliness.

You sit in the wide wicker
chair, poised for tea,
waiting for conversations to
continue from the past.
Then, talk about the weather.

How long will you linger this time,
gauging how to be
polite, listening to the
counting of the mantle clock?
A muffled pass of whispers,
the tea cup shatters on
the empty shadow.

Word Hunger

Doctor's orders: we had to swaddle him.
Colic. Tough to watch: he'd flail the air
and kick so hard it would have sprung a diver
into air, a newborn from the womb.
Words were of no use: so I tied him
into a fetal tuck, his chin so tight
against his chest he couldn't cry—
and still he'd wriggle free and yell.
"Born hungry," said the nurse.
When I couldn't understand his baby talk,
he hated me. I loved him for it.
It's a family trait, this appetite
for words, for eating them like bread.
I didn't get my mother's rich soprano,
but I'm loud—I can hyperventilate.
I spend a lot of time talking to myself.

The Page

See the page as a snowy field
you must cross. It is evening,
your tracks fill with blue.
Stay close to the snow fence,
its slats leaning into the drifts.
Keep your eyes on the farmhouse,
the lit yellow squares.
Imagine holding
the mug with both hands,
bending your face
through the steam.
When you finally arrive,
there is no mother.
Upstairs, a baby cries
and cries. Your brothers huddle
under the bed, away from the father's
broom handle. Swearing, he prods and jabs,
then slams out to the barn, yelling at you
to follow. He leans his head
into the flank of the cow,
his breath making
beads in her fur.
She sighs and settles
to his touch. When you try,
she kicks over stool and pail
and the warm milk spills
across the page.

After Dark

She is thinking of the delta
shimmering with tidal and freshwater urgings

as his hand opens on the flat
of her breastbone. So much sediment

there, the Mississippi argues its way
through the bayous, pausing for the ibis,

the tall-legged cypress, the heron
that cannot decide, walking backwards,

it seems, while moving ahead.
A million years of water

in which sturgeon, carp and crustacean
sink and rise with the leaves

of the ancient willow,
half-dissolved root, pungent bone.

In this ambiguous world, both fluid
and firm, she drifts between the blurry borders

of the current, and beyond,
through cottonwood nebulas, pollen, and siftings

of alluvial plain, admitting
love can exceed our intentions,

those levees built against flooding.
But mainly she is struck

by its patent, persistent nature.
The constant nibbling of the river

like a fiddler crab
whose tiny legs (tickling like his beard)

weaken a soft bank until, thunder from afar,
it collapses into water.

Sea Change

After the flood, fresh water
green as the fields had been
in early spring

traveled a thousand five hundred miles
from the sunken farms,
and, like the snakes that invaded homes

as the floodwaters rose,
flowed into the salty Atlantic:
the Mississippi come to the Keys.

With it came the secrets
of where it had been.
So the men

who discovered the green river
ten miles wide in the blue
current of the Gulf Stream

could almost see the Midwest
as if it had been their land,
their homes erased

as the moon in eclipse
absents itself in stages:
first a crescent in shadow,

quarter moon, half, threshold,
lintel, windows and eaves darkening
until the whole house goes under.

Later, it seemed to them
as far away as the moon.
Florida to the blood, fresh water

to that other world of the sea.
But as the cells of the body
gossip to one another like neighbors

spreading this and that,
as one failure begets another,
as the pain of a woman whose breast,

also like that moon in shadow,
belongs to us all, your hunger,
his death—it keeps coming back to them

like the truth that, out,
casts everything we thought we ever knew
in doubt.

DANA GIOIA

The Room Upstairs

Come over to the window for a moment—
I want to show you something. Do you see
The one hill without trees? The dust-brown one
Above the highway? That's how it all looked
When I first came—no watered lawns or trees,
Just open desert, pale green in the winter,
Then brown and empty till the end of fall.
I never look in mirrors anymore,
Or if I do, I just stare at the tie
I'm knotting, and it's easy to pretend
I haven't changed. But how can I ignore
The way these hills were cut up into houses?
I always thought the desert would outlive me.

How did I get started on this subject?
I'm really not as morbid as I sound.
We hardly know each other, but I think
You'll like it here—the college isn't far,
And this old house, like me, still has its charms.
I chose the site myself and drew the plans—
A modern house, all open glass and stone,
The rooms squared off and cleared of memory.
No wonder Mother hated the idea.
I had to wait until she died to build.
It was her money after all.

                              No,
I never married, never had the time
Or inclination to. Still, getting older,
One wonders . . . not so much about a wife—
No mystery there—but about a son.
I always looked for one among my students
And found too many. Never look for what

You truly want. It comes too easily,
And then you never value it enough—
Until it's gone—gone like these empty hills
And all the years I spent ignoring them.

There was a boy who lived here years ago—
Named David—a clever, handsome boy
Who thought he was a poet. That was back
When I still dreamed of writing. We were both
So full of dreams. He was a student here—
In those rare moments when he chose to study—
But climbing was the only thing he cared for.
It's strange how clearly I remember him.
He lived here off and on almost two years—
In the same room that you are moving into.
You'll like the room. David always did.

Once during a vacation he went off
With friends to climb El Capitan. They took
A girl with them. But it's no easy thing
To climb three thousand feet of granite,
And halfway up, she froze, balanced on a ledge.
They nearly killed themselves to get her down.
At one point David had to wedge himself
Into a crevice, tie down to a rock,
And lower her by rope to another ledge.
When it was over, they were furious.
They drove her back, and he
Surprised me, coming here instead of home.

His clothes were torn, his hands and face cut up.
I went upstairs for bandages, but he
Wanted to shower first. When he called me in,
I watched him standing in the steamy bathroom—
His naked body shining from the water—
Carefully drying himself with a towel.

Then suddenly he threw it down and showed me
Where the ropes had cut into his skin.
It looked as if he had been branded,
Wounds deep enough to hide your fingers in.
I felt like holding him but couldn't bear it.
I helped him into bed and spent the night
Sitting in this room, too upset to sleep.
And on the morning after he drove home.

He graduated just a few months later,
And then went off to Europe where he wrote me
Mainly about beer halls and mountain trips.
I wrote that they would be the death of him.
That spring his mother phoned me when he fell.
I wonder if you know how strange it feels
When someone so much younger than you dies?
And, if I tell you something, will you not
Repeat it? It is something I don't understand.

The night he died I had a dream. I dreamt
That suddenly the room was filled with light,
Not blinding but the soft whiteness that you see
When heavy snow is falling in the morning,
And I awoke to see him standing here,
Waiting in the doorway, his arms outstretched.
"I've come back to you," he said. "Look at me.
Let me show you want I've done for you."

And only then I saw his skin was bruised,
Torn in places, crossed with deep red welts,
But this time everywhere—as if his veins
Had pushed up to the surface and spilled out.
And there was nothing in his body now,
Nothing but the voice that spoke to me,
And this cold white light pouring through the room.

I stared at him. His skin was bright and pale.
"Why are you doing this to me?" I asked.
"Please, go away."
                    "But I've come back to you.
I'm cold. Just hold me. I'm so very cold."

What else could I have done but hold him there?
I took him in my arms—he was so light—
And held him in the doorway listening.
Nothing else was said or lost it seemed.
We waited there while it grew dark again,
And he grew lighter, slipping silently away
Like snow between my fingers, and was gone.

That's all there is to say. I can't explain it,
And now I'm sorry to have bored you so.
It's getting late. You know the way upstairs.
But no, of course not. Let me show you to your room.

Words

The world does not need words. It articulates itself
in sunlight, leaves, and shadows. The stones on the path
are no less real for lying uncatalogued and uncounted.
The fluent leaves speak only the dialect of pure being.
The kiss is still fully itself though no words were spoken.

And one word transforms it into something less or other—
illicit, chaste, perfunctory, conjugal, covert.
Even calling it a *kiss* betrays the fluster of hands
glancing the skin or gripping a shoulder, the slow
arching of neck or knee, the silent touching of tongues.

Yet the stones remain less real to those who cannot
name them, or read the mute syllables graven in silica.
To see a red stone is less than seeing it as jasper
metamorphic quartz, cousin to the flint the Kiowa
carved as arrowheads. To name is to know and remember.

The sunlight needs no praise piercing the rain clouds,
painting the rocks and leaves with light, then dissolving
each lucent droplet back into the clouds that engendered it.
The daylight needs no praise, and so we praise it always—
greater than ourselves and all the airy words we summon.

Unsaid

So much of what we live goes on inside
The diaries of grief, the tongue-tied aches
Of unacknowledged love are no less real
For having passed unsaid. What we conceal
Is always more than what we dare confide.
Think of the letters that we write our dead.

DOUGLAS GOETSCH

Smell and Envy

You nature poets think you've got it, hostaged
somewhere in Vermont or Oregon,
so it blooms and withers only for you,
so all you have to do is name it: primrose
—and now you're writing poetry, and now
you ship it off to us, to smell and envy.

But we are made of newspaper and smoke
and we dunk your roses in vats of blue.
Birds don't call, our pigeons play it close
to the vest. When the moon is full
we hear it in the sirens. The Pleiades
you could probably buy downtown. Gravity
is the receiver on the hook. Mortality
we smell on certain people as they pass.

The Key

I have memorized the coastline
of your key, fingering it
in my pocket all morning.
One chink reminds me of the gap
in your teeth. Another, the space
between your first two toes.
This whole jagged ridge could be
your heartbeat on an EKG.

Lunch hour, I drive over,
slip it in your door,
sit in your closet, smell
your clothes, run your silk
between my fingers,
lie on sheets we melted on
the night before, when you reached down
and whispered, *This belongs to me*.

Our Lady

Our Lady of Perpetual Surprise is how
she looked after she had her eyelids

lifted. Who is this stranger I must
be kind to? Where is the dark one

who couldn't feed me? She went under
the knife and dyed her hair blonde.

After a splendid day at the beach
he dropped dead in the hall, she

in the kitchen wrapping coldcuts.
The next year she spent looped

on pep-up pills, playing duplicate bridge,
traversing the distance between them

that way. I crept down to rec rooms
foraging for crumbs from pimply-faced

boys, their clumsy tongues. Surfacing
for breath, I too smelled of Old Spice.

I was a stitch in her side, a splinter,
a thorny reminder. I was her darling,

her *liebchen*, her sweetie pie. Oh Mother,
what big eyes you have, and wide.

A Sabbath

Shortly after the death of my grandmother,
my husband brought home a tzaddik
for Shabbos. I was so angry I pretended
I'd forgotten to buy candles. But the tzaddik
just smiled. "Even darkness," he said,
"is a form of healing." He mocks me, I thought.
I am a Jew riddled by doubt, and he mocks me.
But, because of my dead grandmother and
the mother of my dead grandmother, I offered,
in his tradition, to take him around the neighborhood.

The world was bright on 106th Street and Broadway.
The tzaddik philosophized about neon, conversed
with the gentlemen in the bodega and
filled out a lottery ticket at the newsstand.
I introduced him to the local blind girl
who once again had found her spot
in the center of the sidewalk. Cross-legged,
she refused to beg or accept offers of help,
her face turned to the sky, indifferent as a pan.
"Listen," the tzaddik said.
"Helplessness, too, is a form of seeing."

Brazen, I took him into the new Tex-Mex
restaurant, where the loud diners pretended
they were in California, even on the Sabbath.
I plied him with blue drinks while
the waitress playfully showed him
her brown belly and asked to see his license:
"No i.d., no surfin'," she said, tickling herself
with the end of his long, white beard.
The Lord's name was not invoked. Instead,
the tzaddik shrugged, grinned, and

pointed to the fish painted on the window:
"What is the mind without the body?"

And so I took him to my grandmother's grave.
Between the stones in her cemetery grew tree ears
and boletus, and lilies sprouted
in the clay along the path. When we reached her
plain pine box, I asked to see his papers.
The tzaddik emptied his pockets and stacked my palms
with certificates and emblems and one
slightly ridiculous snapshot of himself
leaning into the Western Wall. One eye prayed
while the other faced the camera. This, he
insisted, was his finest credential.

But when I asked him to sing Kaddish
so we could bend down and lower her,
the tzaddik clapped his hands over my mouth. "No,"
he said, "No. We haven't got a minyan."
I blazed, I railed, I stamped my tiny foot
against God. But the tzaddik laid his palm
across his chest, where the text was stored
and would not draw it out. We stood, facing
each other over my grandmother's freshly dug grave.
To pass the time, for I was sure I could
sway him, I told stories about her talent
for flirting in six languages, for juggling,
and how she was a refugee three times
if you counted her death. Sabbath darkened

across our drama. We tossed fruit
back and forth, scrawled city names on her stone,
and yes, we made a few eyes at each other.
Morning came. And day. We opened our coats.
The tzaddik invited me to join the mourners
at the head of the hill. For reasons

I can't explain even now, I followed.
Here is the end of the story:

A crowd had gathered, grieving so vigorously
I thought they must be actors. The tzaddik wept
louder than anyone, tore his hair, rent his clothes,
played with himself and stumbled to the ground.
Day passed. The Sabbath ended.
We drew our coats closer. We slept, we dreamed.

Toward morning, the tzaddik woke me from
our hammock where we lay, barefoot and spent.
He motioned to the ridge below. A wave
passed over, or maybe it was a cloud—
who knows?—we were nearly sightless
from the exertion of so much sorrow.
Nevertheless, as we mouthed a lullaby, the stones
began to rise. The tzaddik admitted
this was not his miracle, and I
do not mean to suggest the dead ripped loose,
then flew upward as a constellation
in the sky above us. But they rose.
Our common field rose and hovered.

NOTES

Sabbath or Shabbos is the Jewish day of rest, called the "queen of the week" or "the Bride" and regarded in religious homes as a miraculous time. In *The Joys of Yiddish*, Leo Rosten notes that the Friday night lighting of the candles, one of the few religious tasks reserved for Jewish women, makes them momentary priestesses.

A *tzaddik* is regarded as an extremely pious and honorable man, often possessing mystical powers. However, the word can be used ironically for a wicked, cynical man. Or even a fool.

Kaddish, one of the most solemn and ancient of Jewish prayers, is recited at funerals even though it contains no references to death or resurrection.

The ten male Jews required for religious services are called a *minyan*.

SARAH GORHAM

Half Empty/Half Full

Reasons to grieve: diminishing flesh,
weeks that scroll by unnoticed.
Chic coarseness of image and voice.
Rain of ash on Montserrat,
milkweed that loosens in a sudden gale.
The mirrored hall of adolescence,
rootlessness of politicians.
Books that end up in the air, seas
that pare away the shore. The black horse,
black horse that throws its rider.
The sinking of foundations, or moral standards.
Blur of small print, medicine that comes too late.
The reduction of great literary characters
to one or two dismissive sentences.
Pale skin, cold coffee,
wandering attention. Unpainted bats.

Reasons to rejoice: skin closing
after an abrasion. First attenuated hours
of vacation. Swell of rivers
and waves and the White Mountains.
Simple accounts: *I'm relieved. I'm first in line.*
The red hot blaze before the ash, milkweed
feathering down. The transformation of sisters
into late-life companions.
Fresh sheets, a bar of glycerine soap.
Open-ended novels. Tram tickets, teatime,
little red spiders, the other minutiae
behind great open-ended novels.
Aspirin that prevents, caresses that sway,
primer to hold the bright coat of paint.

Aphorisms, epigrams, succinct parables:
Two horses fighting, one black, one white.
Which horse will win?

The one you feed the most.
Again: the one you feed the most.

Happiness

I think it aims for all of us,
a range of hellos running up
and down the scale. Once in a while
someone like me risks silliness
and actually listens. Once I could tell you
the sound it makes:
Tumble of lost pennies in the dryer,
swish of a cotton skirt against panty hose—
How easy to hear the happiness of others.

I do think it's hungry for my attention
and grows in spite of me, discarding the past
like children's shoes. How else to explain
the sudden tinniness of cicadas
when I return from the mountains
where an entire *jubilate*
thundered through the trees?
How else to account for the letdown
of home.

I have a notion where it lives.
Something I'd read, how happiness
is for the body, suffering for the mind.
Wish I could be one of the physical types
who leave the dinner talk
to chase it across a dewy field,
daisies wilting in their overheated fists.
Their fingers open slowly like a damaged child's;

but shame, shame on me
who thinks happiness is for simple folk,
just because it's easier for them to find,
and they'd rather live than describe it.

You Have Entered the Twilight

A zone the two of you have never explored
an unchartered wilderness on a nonexistent map
a place once bordered by three humanoid sons
The borders gone now
Nothing defines this land mass
The two of you don't know what to name this place
You don't know
if this is a city or a state
a country or a new planet
You venture into the geography
explore barren hollow caves
craters void of noise   activity
You shuffle about this stark lunar landscape
approach the outer limits
of this mysterious netherworld
Perhaps you'll establish a new government
the two of you, a two-party system
one democratic, the other
        democratic

SHAUN T. GRIFFIN

Late Letter to Walter Sisulu
for Cath

Absent the heavy wings of trees, Soweto
steams a carnival of Combis at the taxi stand.
In the distance lie the fields of tailings,

hard rock mines scooped from memory—
even the tour guide is lost in her answers.
We have no name for the child of stone

who woke these streets, his face a memorial
that fronts the bus loads of slumber.
History is a church of weary covenants,

the bullet holes through which a country screams.
The sun buries its treasures, its insect voices
over Jo'berg. You have left us Walter and revenge

has broken its teeth on your grave. Albertina
weeps to shake the dust from your hands,
oh South Africa, when you lay down for freedom.

At the Piano

In the March morning, an old wind eats
from the goldfinch sock beyond the piano.
He is dressed for mountain baseball—
long johns, knee-high socks and hat.
His fingers are slow to release the notes
of another in the stillness of the room.

Today, this gruff wind will carry a boy
from the dugout to squat behind the plate.
Beethoven flecks the nerves in his gloved hand.
He kneels, as if at the piano, a pinch of dust
punctuates the sign for a slider. No one hears
Für Elise but father, high in the bleachers.

The ball burrows in the oversized lips of his mitt.
For the moment there is no catcher to receive
the quick white shadow. He thinks of the months
at the window when there is only snow,
a trace of baseball under the shed roof
and the pianist, almost deaf against the drifts.

ANDREY GRITSMAN

This Is a Test

"This is only a test,"
I hear on the radio on the way to work,
driving by the mall,
shallow river with ducks,
a vacant lot, family restaurant,
"Timberland" billboard.

"This is only a test,"
I hear, passing the scattered woods,
smashed little animals on the highway.

"This is a test,"
I think, is transmitted
from the clouded dentate island
of the city, rising on the horizon.

"This is only a test,"
I hear the voice whispering
as I pass roadside shops, the school building,
her, standing at the entrance,
by the statue of a boy with a horn at his mouth.
(She still has my book!)
She looks the same
as when I left her.

"This is only a test," I hear
and see my grandmother,
standing in the phone booth,
her eyes alert, nodding, calling me.

It's dinner time and it's getting dark.
And I still hear my own voice:
"This is a test. This is only a test."

Catbird Rhapsody

The catbird's song
begins with a question
but just like me, he doesn't wait for an answer.
The actual cat needs scolding
and the heady scent of honeysuckle
commands his praise.
Have we noticed the kouzas
decked out in white stars?
And just where is that stranger going,
the one driving by in this dusty red car?
Look! The ferns have unfurled
under the spruces.
Those few wispy clouds are soft in the sky.
Have we noticed
the limbs of the cherry are a map of rivers,
a loosened love knot, a maze
to keep your gaze entangled for hours
as you lie in the light net hammock. Listen!
Look! It's a fair June evening
on a day after rain.
All the dust has washed off
the spicy geranium leaves.
The snake plant's spears are shining
and darkness still two hours away.
Listen, Listen, the catbird cries.
Choose a question
to govern the rest of your life.
Name which god deserves
your continual praise.

Japanese Student of English

Iron-bird fly god-bird of death,
And death fall in great flower.
Iron-bird paint people shadow on earth,
And rejoice death devour.

Tea garden here remember place of death.
Water flow by teacup flower and pagoda.
Bells and night flow in water
To remember place of death forever.

Here lantern remember in tea garden.
Lantern of no light remember death.
No light char sun, eat convict child.
No light make child lifefire in heaven go out.

River Tracks

Who but Jesus walks on water?
And I'm not sure about him. Footprints
must end where the river begins and swallows them.
But I see them anyway—huge pockets
tracking from one shore to the other
before the water fills in.

Near the bank, a dream-laden train
always leaps, clacking through a childhood
home to reclaim a death the parents—
in their own notion of protecting—had hidden.

And the avalanche repeats—Hitler's face
on the Palisades breaking apart with a terrible
rumbling. The grown-ups like frightened children,
racing the trolley nonstop, believing
the war had finally brought home bombs.

I need to walk on sand and sink,
but water extends. I remember those before
me, all claimed by the trains and the river
into a living sleep. Their tracks
form, dissolve, form again.

ELIZABETH HAHN

The Ghost

It's Mother again,
healthy, breezing in,

and not a moment too soon
what with the soup
getting warm on the table.

Shall we use
the large, old spoons
or the round ones
meant for consommé?

It all makes a difference,
although exactly how
is hard to say:

take care with the way
Mother is seated
(the Sheraton chair,
tricky under
the drop-leaf table),
now the napkins
in our laps,
the blessing, thought
or spoken,
the pause before
she lifts her fork,
the decorum
of proper chewing.

Even though she's
been dead four years,

the meal
is going very well.

Neither of us
says a word,
but Mother's eyes
brighten at the sight
of the sorbet
flanked by delicate
lemon wafers.

Dear specter,
even though
one Concord grape
has just rolled past
your polished shoe,
I believe
we have finally
pulled it off.

Mount Kearsarge

Great blue mountain! Ghost.
I look at you
from the porch of the farmhouse
where I watched you all summer
as a boy. Steep sides, narrow flat
patch on top—
you are clear to me
like the memory of one day.
Blue! Blue!
The top of the mountain floats
in haze.
I will not rock on this porch
when I am old. I turn my back on you,
Kearsarge, I close
my eyes, and you rise inside me,
blue ghost.

DONALD HALL

The Man in the Dead Machine

High on a slope in New Guinea
the Grumman Hellcat
lodges among bright vines
as thick as arms. In nineteen-forty-three,
the clenched hand of a pilot
glided it here
where no one has ever been.

In the cockpit the helmeted
skeleton sits
upright, held
by dry sinews at neck
and shoulder, and by webbing
that straps the pelvic cross
to the cracked
leather of the seat, and the breastbone
to the canvas cover
of the parachute.

Or say that the shrapnel
missed me, I flew
back to the carrier, and every morning
take the train, my pale
hands on a black case, and sit
upright, held
by the firm webbing.

Smile

She was twenty-five when they settled in our town.
When they moved from the city into their colonial,
they unpacked wedding china and silver from boxes
labeled Tiffany, Bergdorf Goodman, and Kresge's.
Both men and women leaned like hollyhocks
toward the luster and power of her unlimited
determining smile. They brought with them a small son
and she bore two daughters in the next five years.
She dressed her children in primary colors
so that they resembled child models in a catalog,
yet they played with such charm they made childhood
seem happy. Her handsome husband adored her.
Many remembered the photograph in the *Courier*
when they first came to town: She sits upright,
baby on her lap and husband smiling behind her.
Even the baby smiles, but it is her mouth
that brightened outward from the gray of newsprint.
When her photographs appeared, over the years
of dances and fund drives, they repeated
the same smile shining from an aging face.
She confessed to a lover how she summoned
her generous smile for the camera: As she gazed
into the lens she thought prick asshole cunt.

We loved her and nothing diminished our love.
When they arrived they joined the Purple Hills Club
which provided them a set. Many husbands
from the Club followed her the way kindergartners
follow their teachers, but even the plainest wives
never disliked her for long. When a friend
turned cold, she telephoned and suggested lunch
at the Club. After an engaging conversation,

with many smiles, the friend was convinced
of warmth, fidelity, good faith, and disinterest.

She played an energetic game of tennis,
mostly doubles on Tuesday and Thursday afternoons
with her seven closest friends. She was elected
president of the Purple Hills Garden Club.
Mornings before his day school she drove her son
to hockey practice, afternoons her daughters
to ballet. For their birthdays she hired a team
of puppeteers or a magician. With contract bridge
partners from the Club, she and her husband
went to numerous cocktail and dinner parties
on Friday and Saturday evenings, so many
that they found it difficult to reciprocate.
In spring and autumn, they mounted cocktail
parties employing a jazz trio they imported
from the city. Six times a year, she prepared
dinner for twelve. She cooked for two days
and hired students to help with the serving.

In their first decade here, Purple Hills Club
people danced together at their weekend parties.
If there was a husband for whom she smiled
least, we speculated that he was the moment's
favorite. Sundays she and her husband played
mixed doubles with three other couples, then
concluded the busy weekend by meeting for potluck
at somebody's house. It was her crab bisque
that we praised the most. When we complimented
her cooking—or her tennis or her bridge—
we received the smile we looked for. Monday
mornings her husband fixed her French toast
and coffee in bed and delivered the children
to their schools. Tuesdays from 10:30
until lunchtime she read aloud to a blind widow

from Joan Ruskin's Fors Clavigera. Her hair
appointment was for three p.m. on Fridays.

As they advanced further into their forties,
Purple Hills couples went to fewer cocktail
parties and played less tennis. Some died.
Some stopped drinking. Her smile remained
all the more bright for the lines on her face.
One child gave them problems; it seemed unfair
for trouble to visit her house. Her husband's
sideburns went gray; her own hair turned auburn
and no one was unkind. For five yeas running
she was first runner-up in Senior Singles; she
might have won, we thought, if she had tried.

After her children were grown, she returned
to the State University to pick up an M.A.
in the History of Art, writing on a graphic
designer from the belle époque. When a young man
whom she met in the Department—teaching fellow
and Ph.D. candidate—boarded with them, taking
a child's room, we understood that the lines on her face
wrote desperation. It was after the young man died,
as the malicious rumors neglected to mention,
that someone broke into the house in their absence,
ripping upholstery and the Picasso print, carving
prick asshole cunt into the bedroom wallpaper.
For two weeks she remained housebound, then
returned smiling, despite the gossip. Some years
later, in her illness, she was a beautiful invalid.
If anything her smile remained set in its place
for a moment longer. When she lost flesh
her cheekbones stood out. The whole town spoke
of her courage and cheer; everyone offered to help.
The child who had become a problem returned
to her bedside at the end, which made her smile.

All this happened long ago. She lies under
ground in a box perfect with darkness, her flesh
fallen away except for corrupted shreds of her skull
where the mortician fashioned a replica of her smile.
Each of her aging grandchildren displays
her photograph on a staircase wall of family
photographs. Visitors take notice of her smile.

Gravy

                        Forced to listen to the body's sentence
            as   it   hesitates   &faults,   you learn to
      trust   its limitations

            Even love isn't enough.

      Now   even our coming together
    in the first place   gets questioned.

            It's like that at Fifty.

                              I'm thinking again
                        about B i g things —
            Happiness & Peace
        — no longer vague,
      they take on
    a muscularity,
      a defined
        shape
      like a   chest or   a back
        that starts with   a feeling
                that   t h i c k e n s
                in the belly   then   Pushesup
                        into the biceps   finally
                                    collecting
                                at the bend
                          in the throat.

            Life crystallizes
                        & we're not looking
      so much for higher purpose   but nuts & bolts:

            I have it or I don't.

That's where we are now.

Our love I take for granted.   Strange as it seems, it's gravy.

Psychotherapist
with Black Leather Binder
Sits in White Oak Chair
That Came Through a Fire

I do God's work here.

People bring their marriages,   saints & demons, mothers & fathers,
   the cloaks of their shame.

Catholic

remnant I live here   performing Works of Mercy: feed the
hungry, clothe the naked,
visit the sick, bury the dead — & free will:

the bottom line that will throw out every commandment.

Frankly,
I'm grateful.   It's the saving grace of the Church.

Brought up on Thou Shalt Not &
Mortal Sin,

I float safely

now   through all nuns habits, knowing the last judgement
was always infineprint: the asterisk
at the bottom of every doctrine:

let your conscience be your guide.

Let's face it, every religion has its Advantages: huManity, FLAIR,
   Abraham   negotiating
with God   as an equal.

But conscience is the final God:
   if you believe you are right, then you're right;
   if you believe you are wrong, you are wrong.   So

this time
I rewrite history
              placing the baby before Him, emptying the Church of
                        all Pharisees:
                              nuns, priests & self-proclaimed
                                   prophets
                        of doom.
              No dogma here,
lust & pride are no longer deadly. Saints & angels loosen their halos.
              I once expected vaulted ceilings,
                   a long
                        climb
                        up the
                        steps
                        to the
              Massive Bronze Door.

                              Once holy only on dark afternoons
now Church is all   small
         goodnesses   like one's home,
                   or a father's favorite chair,
                   a book of Joyce's stories
                        or a violin safe in a velvet lined box.

              And anyone who wishes can be Jesus:
         Perhaps
Chekhov is
         Jesus   & Brahms & da Vinci,   the midwife & yogi, the
                                   altar boy, soldier &   cantor.
              Godparents all,
                        I place the baby among them
         pour the water,   anoint &   free her
                        of all past promises.
She is clean;
she is warm.

So the scaffolding is gone:
I don't go to Church,

                    can't even say I believe.   Saints & Lucifer
                        seem preposterous to me now,
          though the residue at the bottom of
          the wine glass remains.

         My hands have gotten old:
      freckled with spots
like a nun's or a priest's.

               Skin is I a x, loses flexibility,
                    finally

          falls into its

    inevitable map

              with thousands

      of thresholds
   to be balanced on,

                wavered at,

                    then

flug
  into   or
    from,   r a v a ging still   another   piece of my soul.

SANDRA HANDLOSER

Christmas in Florida
for my father (1901–1979)

Family trips south, my father driving:
oleander bloomed
and birds of paradise.
Seminoles wrestled crocodiles,
their unscathed bodies glistening.
Down Dayton Highway now
armadillos on saw grass shoulders
grow still as coconuts . . .

I slip the car between
his bag of irons and the wall of tools.
With his spade I dig a trough
around the wax-myrtle tree
to bury the hard evidence,
too heavy, I think, for ashes.
So I carry him now, as a
deep-sea diver might carry coral.

In Morrison's Cafeteria I sit
beside mother in dark glasses
idling over a vegetable plate—
his perfect physique, (how could he
go . . . anyway)—
I watch steam from her coffee
die, how she shies off
from men who eat alone.

The gorgeous weather invites
but cannot rescue me,
neither the ocean

nor the sand
from seeing only white
downhill on a sled
my father holding me
my father holding me under him.

Arrival

After Christopher Smart

I will consider my son William,
who came into the world two weeks early, as if he couldn't wait;
who was carried on a river that gushed from his mother;
who was purple with matted black hair;
who announced his arrival not by crying but by peeing,
      with the umbilical cord still attached;
who looked all around with wide slate-blue eyes and smacked
      his lips as if to taste the world;
who took to his mother's breast right away;
who sucks my little finger with such vigor that it feels as if
      he's going to pull my fingernail right off;
who sometimes refuses my finger, screwing up his face in
      disgust as if I have stuck a pickled radish into his mouth;
whose face is beautiful and not like a shriveled prune;
whose hair, though black, is soft as milkweed;
who was born with long eyelashes that girls will someday envy;
whose fingernails are minuscule, thin, and pliable;
whose toes are like caterpillars;
whose penis is a little acorn;
whose excrement is like the finest mustard;
who can squeak like a mouse and bleat like a lamb;
who hiccups and his whole body convulses;
who screams and turns red and kicks sometimes when we
      change his diaper;
who when he stops screaming is probably peeing;
whose deep sobs from the back of his throat bring tears to
      my own eyes;
who likes to be carried in a pouched sling;
who thinks he is a marsupial;
who has soft fur on his shoulders, back, and legs;
who is nocturnal and whose eyes are widest at night;
who will sleep sometimes if I lay him across my chest;

whose eyes flutter, whose nostrils dilate, and whose mouth
       twitches into strange grimaces and smiles as he dreams;
who is full of the living spirit which causes his body to
       wiggle and squirm;
who stretches his arms and arches his back and you can feel
       his great strength;
who lies with the soles of his feet together, as if praying
       with his feet;
who is a blessing upon our household and upon the world;

who doesn't know where the world ends and he begins;
who is himself the world;
who has a sweet smell.

Family Dog

A succession of Newfoundlands
of diminishing nobility
and with names like English maids—
Flossie, Rosie, Nelly—
gave way, long after I'd left,
to this hyperactive black lab
who (like me?) never grew up,
always the exuberant puppy
to almost everyone's annoyance,
and whose name—Jess—is so much
like my own that when I'm home
and hear my father call the dog
or say his name in irritation
when he's gotten in the garbage
or chewed up someone's shoe,
I'm forced to relive an unpleasant
split second I lived many times
as a teenager, when my father
and I were chronic enemies—
a quick shock through my heart
and the thought, *Oh God, what
have I done now?* Followed now
by the realization, *It's only the dog*,
a sigh of relief, a quiet laugh . . .
I'm almost always fooled,
as if the pitch of my father's voice
triggered some switch
in my nervous system, my body
still wired for sound
decades later, bringing back,
before I have time to think,
the fear, the rancor,

things I would rather forget,
the way a dog forgets
and always comes back, comes home
when his name is called,
knowing his master loves him.

Ploughing in Fall

Outdated crops
Sometimes only by weeks
Find themselves now
Exposed
On furrows' crests:
Ploughing in fall.

I remember deep old smells
Of upside-down earth
The Obscenity of it,
The trueness of it,
Like skilled, humble butchering.

Brown-black and wet and straight
The furrows were,
And shiny was the soil
Underneath its worn-out
Coat of stubble.

I don't remember any talking
During this task.
Already too much lay unearthed:
Weed-roots now for safely freezing,
Last-minute scavenging
for geese and mice

Before frost freeze-framed it
All in silver.

It's my turn to be plowed
To lie exposed and fallow.
I find it restful;

SIEGFRIED HAUG

Glad to see those dark-
Lush trenches.
Good earth
Where secretly
I'd dreaded rock.

That Afternoon in Harvest

Look: A snapshot of my parents. Like a picture
of folks I know I ought to know but don't.
1938:   They're in a cornfield. Smiling.
More than forty years before she died.

I remember most that she was weary.
"If I could just write letters in the barn,"
she said. "What I want to say is clearer
when I feed calves." The pails

of water, cans of milk, the winter
snow—they pulled her down. And at the end,
when she lay quiet in the hospital, Dad saw
her shoulders. Broad. "So many bales of hay."

His voice
          cracked. Was he thinking
of that day when someone caught
her sitting on the end of a lumber wagon,
in a dress of solid color, patent leather pumps

laced up. She wears a hat. Her face spells
mischief. He kneels on the ground,
he's husking corn. He wears the English
racing cap a boy might wear. His face

clean shaven. Left eye-brow raised. Glasses
give the look of the scholar he'd prefer to be.
Pipe stem poking out from the pocket
of his shirt. No doubt the shirt is blue,

a cotton chambray, like one he'll wear
every working day of his life. In his lap, three cobs

of just-shucked corn. I think they've been married
eighteen months. I know they have a child.

I wonder: Were they scared? What were
their hopes? their dreams? One afternoon
in harvest they were smiling. And they loved
each other. They did what they knew to do.

Pietà in Camera

Dark-haired still, leanly handsome Peter
Sits in 251, that long corner
Room, telling you about his summer with
Your new-look girl of the past academic year.

Is he smoking? That you cannot see.
But yes, now you find you can, for when
He pauses, smoke curls from under his straight nose.
We all smoked then except of course for Tom.

But his innocence is another tale.
In this one now you see Peter's slender
Fingers tapping a cigarette against a lighter
As you stand naked before him after your shower—

Or nude, rather,— and you're enjoying his
Discomfort, your moral superiority,
But you're enjoying at least as much the fitness,
The hardness of your body after its summer

At Great Pond muscling the pushmower and trimming
Edges, swinging sure the sharpened sickle,
Making sparks shoot from its back edge.
You toweling yourself are feeling stronger

Than he and quite as handsome and not upset
At all by his confession there in September
In that college room. In that room
With a different number if the scene is set

After a summer's labor, which is when
It feels like. But it also feels like the far
End of the long room, and if it's there,

It cannot also be then, then being

When you lived in another hall, on a different floor,
In a room with a different number. And if you are there,
Then it is winter, it must be winter, take
My word for it. But it does not feel like winter,

My flesh has no goose bumps, there's no cold
To make me shiver. Peter may be shiv-
Ering, not that he is afraid I may
Turn violent, but he, rather, may be

Feeling the pressure of playing The Boy Who Loves
The Girls. Petey Weety, who may have been doing
Simply what seemed to him the manly thing
To do, as surely it was. Elegant Peter,

Good at bridge and dressing (Walt remembers
Still a stylish overcoat in gray),
Who may be looking for something more from me
Than forgiveness and understanding. Well, those

at least he has from me now at last. Peter
Playing Smoking Mary there to my
Unpierced Jesus. My erstwhile neighbor Peter,
Acquainted with douches and other feminine things,8

Unacquainted as yet with grief. Gay Peter,
Who, according to the report we heard, put
The barrel of a gun in his mouth and fired sometime
Before the Age of AIDS. I take it back:

It is not for me, unpierced me, to forgive
You, Peter. And what is it I understand? The mystery
Of the gift of the body is what your passion
Brings me closer to in these rooms we haunt.

Darkfall

Outside the side a deeper green overshadows bark
Close by a too gray sky on the ground

Today is a brown picture
She is too tired to say "I"

Turning to her lap she sees another spot of dried food
What else didn't make it to and from

Her mouth isn't a surprise
To herself and mainly to herself

"The reds of fall and the yellows"
No

That's not why this part of her life is
Even this paper knows it

This view is different
The dress she's wearing was clean this morning

DEMING P. HOLLERAN

Trash Day

Pajama-clad, his slippers
parting pebbles into
an unkempt double wake,
our elderly neighbor
must have gauged the distance
to the curb within his strength,
not reckoning the return.

His wife, now keeper, slept.
Can a man not be of use?
To lug a weekly plastic bag
from house to street links
a man with neighbors, makes
a kind of brotherhood.

Proud of deed, he turned to will
his heavy feet toward home,
and fell, and lay, and waited.

Must it come to this,
that his rescuer, a man himself
past sixty, unknown, should
heave him up and together stagger
to the door? For what did that
younger neighbor see? The eyes
of an animal, trapped
inside a body, seeking what?
Forgiveness. For the shame
of growing old.

Conversations with My Son

Houdiniesque and 8,
snaking out of his seatbelt
on our way to Peabody Elementary,
he rests his little mug just behind my ear.
There he puts a metaphysical question,
a prestidigitation of the mind:
"Where is Cleveland, Ohio?"
And before I can answer, another:
"Would you rather be buried or
crucified?"
I ask if he means "cremated."
He asks what's the difference.
I tell him and he says, "I just don't think
you should take up too much space
when you're dead, Dad."
For Pete's sake, I mutter.
And he's right there with another: "Who's Pete?
and what's Pete's ache?"
Together we watch the road to school
unfold like a familiar story.
I tell him the story of Pete.
The guy who said he loved Jesus so much
he would die for him.
That was his ache, I say.
But when the time came,
when the soldiers came with their swords
blazing like the sun,
Pete got scared. He ran away.
And he didn't do what he said he would do.
And that was Pete's ache, too.
"I think I'd rather be crucified," he says
as I pull in behind a school bus.
And I'm not quite sure if he means

he'd choose the pain of the nails
over the pain of the betrayal,
or the fire over the pine box.
Before I can ask him he's out,
he's unbuckled the belt, unlocked the door
and reappeared outside, running up the hill,
his little backpack full of tools
bouncing on his shoulders,
a head on his shoulders full of questions,
questions escaping all over.

April Saturday, 1960

I mean, Berkley Osborne and I had
small interest in each other, and

it was happenstance the afternoon
we found ourselves in the ballroom

of Wytheville Country Club, nobody
else around except Judy and Bobby,

her cousin and my pal, so serious
a couple they lost interest in us

immediately, put on a slow record
and stepped out on the dance floor

to do something that could hardly
be called a dance. An undulating

embrace was what it was. Berkley
and I—joking—started a mannerly

box step. We'd spoken hardly ten
sentences before—maybe I grinned

at her one day in the hall or she
at me in band practice or history

but we'd never touched fingertips
let alone tried to dance. So it's

no wonder we began in awkwardness
and humor, poking fun at the kiss

Bobby and Judy showed no signs of
breaking off. It's strange enough

two couples dancing in a ballroom
with all the invisible chaperones

tsk-tsking, the other dancers not
yet having arrived, full daylight

reflecting over the parquet floor,
a line of chairs for wallflowers

along three walls, tables whitely
waiting for punch bowls perfectly

centered among cups, small plates
for cookies, party napkins placed

exactly so. Music stands awaited
sax man, trumpeter and trombonist;

the discreet piano widely grinned,
and the drums and cymbals yearned

to be punished. Meanwhile Berkley
and I box-stepped our laps nicely

around the ballroom. "Oh my God!"
whispered Berkley; she gave a nod

toward Bobby and Judy, only their
pelvises moving, his hands on her

butt and hers on his. They stood
in place, clothes on, a very good

boy and girl except for movements
of their tongues, hips, and hands.

The record that kept on repeating
was the soulful "Unchained Melody"

which cast a spell over the whole
room—it was like a space capsule

floating endlessly toward unknown
galaxies of eternal midafternoon

light with Berkley and me in orbit
around a red-hot Bobby-Judy planet.

Well, the boxstep grows tiresome
after you step out box number one

thousand and four. Berkley and I
shifted position, she gave a sign

then snuggled in close. I noticed
her warmth and her nice fragrance,

also her astoundingly small waist,
and the way her chest fit against

my chest. I think that's actually
what caused the glandular anomaly

that followed—we sort of scooted
our chests around as if we needed

to get comfortable, the sensation
being about as erotic as anything

I've ever felt. So Berkley and I
were acquaintances transmogrified

suddenly into your basic two-part
hormonally effervescent lust-unit.

One minute we were innocently box-
stepping away our lives, the next

we were groins and nipples, pubic
hair, teeth and tongues, a public

display of live pornography—well,
I shouldn't exaggerate. We still

had our clothes on, and we didn't
collapse to the floor. The event

was so mental and over so quickly
that the annals of sexual history

don't even mention it. All right,
maybe it was no more than a tight

embrace with a remarkably intense
kiss and maybe the body movements

of accomplished lovers like Bobby
and Judy. Maybe a favorite hobby

of theirs was leading mere casual
friends into situations of carnal

possibility—Berkley and I locked
into each other, parts of a clock

fitting perfectly, moving in time.
We were just kids really, sixteen

and seventeen, we hadn't had much
experience, certainly not of such

intensity or strangeness. I think
Eros looked at Cupid, gave a wink,

and suddenly Berkley sighed, "O,"
which took me over the edge. "O,"

I said, too. We just stood there
breathing and shuddering together.

Embarrassment set in very quickly,
but it was of the bonding variety,

and of course we couldn't go back
to the box step. We tried to chat

and stand where we were, our arms
still around each other, our aims

a bit vague and sentimental. How
kind words were to come to us now

that we had learned such a lesson
of recapitulating ontology, human

folly, and the utter indifference
of stars drifting through silence.

"I have to go to tuck my shirt in"
or "I should splash cold water on

my face" or "Shouldn't we get out
of here?"—our exact words aren't

the point. At a certain emotional
pitch, the tone of a voice is all

that matters, *somebody just croon
to me please, and I'll be ok soon.*

Ten thousand days have flown away
since that small piece of a sunny

afternoon. Berkley's had her life,
I've had mine, and who can say if

what happened made any difference
to either of us? Her remembrance

may bring her a twitch of a smile
but that's all. Sometimes I feel

I'm a sliver of dust in the great
pattern of creation, I think fate

is a vast intelligence. But then
I recall blips of cosmic nonsense

like that afternoon with Berkley:
Galactic energy started crackling

along the stratospheric periphery
with Darwin and Freud spastically

heaving in their graves and a boy
and a girl in a Virginia town, by

the whimsy of chaos, the theology
of random chance, were flung body

against body. Bless their hearts,
they played their ludicrous parts,

saying "O," and standing in place,
with astonishing kindness & grace.

Red Radishes

Brilliant buds rising two feet from the stand,
Perched in a precarious bouquet.
Rubies hung strand upon sun-shot strand
homage to beauty and bounty and order.
There, on 16th Street, next to waxy turnips,
round and smooth and polished to opalescence
And parsley, curly and kelly and upright
enough to crackle with crispness.

The November air blows my hair halfway
round my head, across my eyes.
"Don't Walk" furiously blinks red, red, red.
Bike messengers pass in a quick rush.
Sirens squeal and a flag-draped fire truck
bears down on cabs jockeying for position.
But, those radishes
how still and constant they remain.

On Thanksgiving, always the relish plate
with celery, olives green and black and radishes.
He despised olives, thought celery a waste.
But, those radishes
he always ate them all.

SOPHIE HUGHES

Nothing Stands Still

Nothing stands still.
Landscapes self-destruct.
If you look away,
when you look back
you cannot find
Suzy's begonias,
Nanna's rocking chair,
goats in Oscar's shed.
Something obliterates.
Something succeeds.
Rank growth invades the site
of garden, porch, and pen.
Whole farms are forest now
whirring in the wind,
"Where have you been?"
"Where have you been?"

Lumbar Puncture

Sacrifice to the deities of the dead was made with averted
face; no looking, only the voice, was allowed in the realm
of the departed. This could work miracles.
— Karl Kerenyi, *The Heroes of the Greeks*

Lying on my side,
my knees drawn up to my chest,
I offer them my back,
stretching forward to open
the muscles along the spine,
to relax the tight squeeze
of little bones. Turned away
from the room, curled into
myself, I do not see
the face of the nurse holding
the bottle of alcohol, the hands
of the doctor with her long needle.
This is their work, to speak
with averted eyes, to draw the fluid
up from around the living nerves,
into the narrow tube, to measure
and weigh the drops as rare as tears.

The needle pricks my skin,
pushes in deeper. I turn my face
down, coil tight. Grade school drills:
we learned to hide under our desks,
our arms crossed over our heads,
shielding our eyes from white light,
glass flying from the great blast
shaking tiles from the ceiling.
If that inferno had come
the metal legs of our bolted desks
would have heated to a thousand

degrees and melted over us.
Our hands over our eyes
would be a film of water.
To turn away availing nothing.

The nurse and doctor are speaking
to one another in quiet tones. I
cannot see them. The nurse
tells me to lie still: was I trembling?
What I protect, curling inward,
exposes this frail column of nerve-
strung bone that prods the flesh
under skin stretched tight. Lie still.
For the long needle to enter safely,
along the spine, with its bundles
of nerves and bone, the meninges
and vertebrae, to search deep
and probe into the smallest spaces
where a colorless fluid hides secrets.
It can be weighed.

I am waiting beneath my desk
for the fireball, my eyes covered,
obedient, as if one alone
might be saved. I am huddled inside
my house, under the volcano
my arm over my child's small back,
as if the ash and fire might pass
over us. Or perhaps only to taste
another breath before we are dead.
I am dead. I am traveling back
through my mother. I am in the earth,
curled on my side, clutching stone.
I lie still; the voices I cannot see
are all around me; the needle
hesitates, turns and probes, is held

and withdrawn. Perhaps a drop
glistens on the point. I close up, rock shut,
fall into the dark. Then someone touches
my shoulder, tells me to turn over
on my back, not to raise my head.

CYNTHIA HUNTINGTON

The Strange Insect

The lights have gone out in the hallway.
The boy who polishes the stairs has found
a strange insect—he wants me to see.
It clings to his rag and won't shake off.
It is black and long, like a widow, or a
sacred priest, has a yellow necklace and
yellow beads upon articulated leg joints,
has a tail eight inches long, three plumes
of a tail, black like ripped lace; is thin,
thin like a straw, like a wasp, thin as a
quill, is hanging on a piece of what was
once a shirt, appears to have no wings
and not to know night or day, to neither
look up nor to acknowledge our regard:
ancient, hieratical, the most mutant
butterfly, the wickedest jeweled queen.
The boy shakes the rag again, beats it
against the wall, and it drops, deigning,
into the dry fountain; grazes the brick,
drops further, lowering its banded legs
on to the blunted grass, drumming small
horny feet in a cadence, beginning to speak
with its hands moving in air, a message
beat against the floor of patriarchy, ceiling
of the world's brain, speaking reason to
desire, order to confusion, state against
state, telling another version of the world.

You Knew Her

for Linda Silva

Was it even dark yet it was getting dark
September the street filling with voices
just before dinner hours people going
home late. Six-thirty maybe getting on to
seven. She fell and she lay with her head
in a puddle of rain of motor oil salt wet
of blood from her temple she was breathing
she had stopped breathing it was reflex
motion in the nerves the muscles she was
warm she seemed to be breathing she was
getting cold when she moaned it was the air
let out from her last breath when they
turned her release of that last gasp a gasp
or a sigh or a sound of someone running.

Small town even so a crowd the police
put up barricades and questioned a green
pickup somebody saw a man in a yellow
slicker a truck heading out of town he
wrote these words on a pad four hours
they wait for the medical examiner and
she is lying in the rain in a puddle of water
of grease oil salt water blood cold coming
up rain trickling the tight skin of her face
her bare ankles her legs splayed out so
oddly. If you knew her would you leave her
there no you would put a blanket over her
cushion her head you'd comfort her like a
daughter a sister like any of the helpless dead.

Retro

I should have liked to live in Paris
in the fifties.
It would have suited me to wear
my flared voile dress with polka dots,
matching pumps, and wide brimmed hat.
So dressed, I would descend the stairs
from my compact apartment to check the mail,
delivered twice daily in the fifties,
and look for the vellum envelope
postmarked Marseilles with his initials
inked across the back.
Then I would walk my dog—
no not a poodle, even in the fifties
I retained my sense of individuality—
A Terrier, let's say.
I would sit in an outdoor bistro drinking
coffee, faintly trying not to meet the eyes
of a gentleman facing me under the canopy
of smoke that swirled around cafés.
I would pretend not to notice how he lowered
his *Le Monde* to admire my well-turned ankles—
I had well-turned ankles in the fifties—
Then off to market to buy a fresh baguette,
Gruyère and brie. Yes, I should have liked
to live in Paris in the fifties.
That would have suited me I think.

From the Porch of The Frost Place
August 2002

It is milkweed smells so sweet, Peter and Joan tell me,
      and the last daylily's bloomed
in the bed that rims the porch. A single shrunken
      bloom, yesterday's, clings to a bare
forked stem among a forest of stems already withering.
      I notice melancholy's begun to veil
my thought because I can no longer shake a sight
      I caused last night returning
along Ridge Road—slammed my brakes but hit
      a chipmunk, not straight on,
but partially, and felt compelled to watch its grisly
      dance of flops until it stilled.
These small deaths, and the news of human ones
      constantly barraging us. And
now rumors of a second, coming war with Iraq.
      As always, the antimonies line up:
good, evil, but whose side is which? Last night Jessica
      read a poem about her friend,
in flames, choosing to throw herself from one
      of the towers. Throughout the festival,
the trauma of last September's attack kept asserting
      itself, signaling how deeply scarred
we are. Lincoln's charge is on my mind, *to bind up*
      the nation's wounds, then Don
reminds us that yesterday was the anniversary
      of Hiroshima: that vast incineration—
was it 135,000 died in one great radiating ball
      of conflagration? We've heard
the justifying arguments all our lives, but they
      haven't redeemed an instant
of human suffering. The interest compounds *ad infinitum*:
      no moral nation can pay the debt.

Add it to our slavery debt, our genocide of native peoples
        debt, our bilking of The Third World debt.
Now a glider from Franconia's gliderport comes into view,
        circles around and across Lafayette
with its spill of rocks that each spring keeps a cross
        of not yet melted snow.
Time to plant corn the locals say when the cross shows
        above the fields. How I wish
the Christian Cross had enough potency, after all these
        years, to have leached warmongering
out of us. When our President signs the order to attack,
        he'll do it with God's blessing,
so he believes. I'd rather stake my faith in this creation
        before me, trusting that if there's
redemption and ease from suffering and grief, it comes
        in beholding this great blue dome
of sky, the varied mottling shadows and shapes of clouds,
        these blue-green mountains
and deep green hills, the pines and tamaracks, poplars,
        birches, the chipmunk who,
moment's ago, dared the porch, spotted me, scampered
        off in a scurry of cheeps. I want
to think he showed himself to forgive me for the maiming
        death of his kin, but that's
a fanciful wish that tells me I long for forgiveness this
        bright, clear, scintillate morning,
and I do, shameful, sorry creature that I am, who knows—
        but does not always abide by what
she knows—only the song is worthy of us and it is praise.

After Midnight

Moon, stars, clouds over the roof, and inside,
quiet rooms, sleepers, one insomniac. Rain
An hour ago, now the smell of metal screens
And, from the garden, iris. Peace opens the spirit
And art bears no dissembling. The damp earth,
Cool air, an open window. One moment, the next,
And nothing stops, *ad infinitum*, the repetition
Of primal scenes: birth, death, accident, joy,
Each glance of love, war, terror. One listens
And writes while something stands outside
And above, abounding in voice and character,
Ready to mock and tease, or simply bestow.

Like a Pear

With a rotten core, or a jack-o-lantern that slowly blackens
with mold and caves in on itself, caring for him
has exhausted her, so that even now,

after the vexing wounds of last decisions,

after his funeral and burial, weariness consumes her.

For three years, when he messed himself, she wiped
and washed him, and when he didn't wake to ask for a bedpan,

she woke to the smell of urine
which carried out the night and carried in

the bleached blank abandonment of day.

Diaper pail in the bathroom for a grown man. The odor of disinfectant
like a craven beast rubbing its brindled muzzle against her.

Cancer eating his spine, yet she, too, was devoured,
as if minnows worked thousands of small cold mouths against her
        flesh.

His mind was no more than globules of occasional light,

yet how to account for a sweet nature, his to the end?
Or how is silence before his world's stern reductions,

his humor even in pain, grabbed at her with a force she could not
        explain,
love swelling the way a drought-shrunken root

swells in warn August rain.

Still, how brown and dank and illimitable her exhaustion is.

Does she have shoulders, breasts, a face? Anything to touch
below her waist?

Is she the one dead?

Everything smells of rot, his sheets, pillow, even his false teeth.

She places his clothing and shoes in plastic bags and heaves them
into charity's white Dumpster.

Its hole opens before her, a passageway,
and for an instant she thinks to climb in. She is picked clean.

What manna can feed such a hollowness?

What meadow can she wake in with her bones restored?
With her flesh?

Derelict vagabond, her mind long gone.

Will it find its way back home?

The Ex

In the placable air of long dissolved discord, we wait
with our daughter, days overdue, our single shared
goodness. She carries our first grandchild.

In thirty years, not a word has tiptoed across
the continent between us. We've led vastly different
lives. He's not unkind, only holds a dizzying number

of opinions. Like bombarding mosquitoes they fly in
and out of range. Across my face I draw a tight mask
of passive acquiescence. The skeleton underneath

threatens to grin, but he's the one who's dying—
of AIDS and its complications—the effeminate,
virginal boy I married when I was twenty-two.

Can anything be said to those we betrayed and
abandoned? Neither of us knew ourselves; each
feared we'd be destroyed by the other's needs.

That fear seems exorbitant from here, and pointless,
yet I remember staggering about for weeks feeling
as though a beast were daily ripping the sternum

out of my chest. We shred our nerves against the grate
of one another's youthful insecurities. Weak, slight,
vulnerable, only his voice is unchanged—

I must have loved its sound once! Maybe, strangely,
in the unreckonable realm of human life—our daughter's
and her child's—whoever we marry is ours forever.

And in some sense he is mine, and I almost want him,
but only out of pity, or forgotten guilt. All the dross
that had to go was long since skimmed off. Here

we are, his once-wife, my once-husband, the child
we made who is with child, this summer evening's
sterling light and the mystery of how each moment

goes on and on and holds us present until the last.

The Purple Metallic

Was the last loaner on the lot
On a top down day in May.
With the family sedan safely
In the mechanic's hands, I peeled
Away from the dealership.
Convertibles automatically subtract
Ten years off your driver's license.
Midlife mother became "Lolita" in sunglasses
With blond hair flying in a car I'd never pick.
Drivers honked, as my briefcase
Bounced to the Beach Boys:
". . . fun, fun, fun, 'til her Daddy
takes her T-Bird away…"
sometimes a day just takes you.

Sometimes a day just takes you, like
A hundred-dollar bill in the envelope day,
Or a sudden call from a long lost lover day,
That takes you to a secret room in yourself,
And you

Burst right through its closed door in a
Purple metallic convertible
With the Beach Boys blarin'
And you do something you have never
Done before, like blow off a workday,
Or spend the money all on yourself,
Or go out to lunch with the married man.

And even if it rained all day on the beach,
Or the money only purchased useless lottery tickets,
Or the long lost lover was nothing more than an oil slick,
That night in the convertible

With your hair hung over the head rest,
While you are gazing at the moonlit night
You feel satisfied that you sampled
The cookies when they were passed;
That you searched around in that room
You never explored.

Sometimes we just need to shift to another gear.

The Tears of Horses

When Achilles' horses wept
to mourn his comrade's death,
the churning world grew quiet—

you could hear the sound of
teardrops raining slowly down
across the war worn globe

could feel the pain of soldiers
wounded in the field, could touch
the hopes of fathers and of wives,

in waiting for the footsteps
that would never sound again,
could taste the sweetness drying

on children's hopeful lips,
could see the sobbing breath
of mothers making evening meals

their sons would never eat,
could gather up in weeping horses' tears,
whole oceans full of misery and loss.

Creed

after Jack Wiler

I believe the chicken before the egg
though I believe in the egg. I believe
eating is a form of touch carried
to the bitter end: I believe chocolate
is good for you: I believe I'm a lefty
in a right-handed world, which does not
make me gauche, or abnormal, or sinister.
I believe "normal" is just a cycle on
the washing machine; I believe the touch
of hands has the power to heal, though
nothing will ever fill this immeasurable
hole in the center of my chest. I believe
in kissing; I believe in mail; I believe
in salt over the shoulder, a watched
pot never boils, and if I sit by my
mailbox waiting for the letter I want
it will never arrive—not because of
superstition, but because that's not
how life works. I believe in work:
phone calls, typing, multiplying,
black coffee, write write write, dig
dig dig, sweep sweep. I believe in
a slow, torturous sweep of tongue
down the lover's belly; I believe I've
been swept off my feet more than once
and it's a good idea not to name names.
Digging for names is part of my work,
but that's a different poem. I believe
there's a difference between men and
women and I thank God for it. I believe
in God, and if you hold the door

and carry my books, I'll be sure to ask
for your name. What *is* your name? Do
you believe in ghosts? I believe
the morning my father died I heard him
whistling "Danny Boy" in the bathroom,
and a week later saw him standing in
the living room with a suitcase in his
hand. *We never got to say goodbye*, he
said, and I said I don't believe in
goodbyes. I believe that's why I have
this hole in my chest; sometimes it's
rabid; sometimes it's incoherent I
believe I'll survive. I believe that
"early to bed and early to rise" is
a boring way to live. I believe good
poets borrow, great poets steal, and
if only we'd stop trying to be happy
we could have a pretty good time. I
believe time doesn't heal all wounds;
I believe in getting flowers for no
reason; I believe "Give a Hoot, Don't
Pollute," Reading is Fundamental,
Yankee Stadium belongs in the Bronx,
and the best bagels in New York are
baked on the corner of First
and Twenty-first. I believe in Santa
Claus, Jimmy Stewart, Zuzu's petals,
Arbor Day, and that ugly baby I keep
dreaming about—she lives inside me,
opening and closing her wide mouth—
I believe she will never taste her
mother's milk; she will never be
beautiful; she will always wonder what
it's like to be born; and if you hold
your hand right here—touch me right

here, as if this is all that matters,
this is all you ever wanted, I believe
something might move inside me,
and it would be more than I could stand.

Longing

Terror is a mirror in which your eyes belong
to a woman wearing sunglasses. There she is
now, pulling out of the parking lot across

the street in a new convertible, bottle
of Cabernet brooding like a teenager
on the front seat. Longing is that bottle

of wine you may never open. But there is
the woman again, lighting a cigarette
on the corner of Sixth and Twelfth.

St. Vincent wraps a shadow around her
shoulders as she flicks the cigarette
onto the ground and ducks into the dark

of Fat Tuesday's You have spent years
following this woman across the city,
gathering her cigarette butts

and stuffing them into your mouth.
Longing is a form of terror. It is
the same woman hovering over postcards

in the small, White Mountain town. First
you are surprised she has anyone
to write home to. Then you realize maybe

she's been following you. But that's
impossible. Because this is your
mother. She abandoned you long ago.

Letter to Howard Levy

How often I've missed you
and had nothing to fill that void with.
This was last weekend, I was helping
at a local art opening, (good food, nasty wine)
when I noticed a girl quietly reading
off to one side, oblivious to the people milling around.
Nothing so remarkable about the girl, pretty,
in a blue dress, still young enough
you couldn't tell what she'd look like as an adult.

I moved close enough
to see the book, an older one
judging from what I caught of the typeface
and yellowing paper, and it was titled Mozart.
She looked up from what it said only
at the flash from a photographer
who'd spotted her the same time I had,
and went on reading. That girl, alone,
her summer dress and her concentration, reminded me
that someone said you healed yourself once
of some heartbreak I never heard the details of,

that you did it, listening to Mozart
over and over. I think that his music
finally must have filled you so completely
there was no room anymore for your particular pain.

I always hope that people I love
will be made beautiful by that love, or happy.
That I will be happy. That it will help.
And I admire that sense you have
of what might lead us to take up our rightful lives
like a crutch thrown down in despair,

not so much healed as able to get around
in our bodies again.

Mostly the rest of us go on playing and re-playing
the same small songs we thought would help, but there's
hardly any real music in hours of the stuff.

No wonder we're never restored in any way
that might last more than the three or four minutes
a song takes. Half the time I don't even know
what made e want to hear something,
even my own ragged heart.

Perhaps that young woman will grow into
the quiet beauty of someone truly listening.
Mozart would like that. I would. So would you.

Sharing the Secrets

This barn belonged once to Robert Frost.
People come to visit, bringing their children,
for some association with the place
and the mountains hidden in cloud this evening.
He had children too, Frost,
although you wouldn't think so. One boy,
the eldest I imagine, killed himself
over some issue, sex, or a love he couldn't obtain.

If I had a daughter the most difficult thing
would be to explain what I am.
She would want to know, of course, but I worry
what she would think, hearing the stories
I make, the children in them
growing more distant from her each year.
The man speaking in the front is a friend.
His wife is pretty, and their little girl.
I wonder how she will turn out,
what illnesses and angers have kept
her parents awake nights and afternoons
they damn well wanted to disclaim all children
and drive off to make love or to sit, not speaking.

I see how secret, how sexual I am:
how I imagine my child a daughter,
holding her breath to keep from growing up,
and how much I am afraid:
the ecstasies of women, their bodies

and what they know. I have thought
of a daughter so often I'm surprised she's not real.
My friend reading tonight, he too must carry
things he'd like to weep over and forget.

The child here sits on her mother's lap.
The light runs its soft strands
down the wife's blouse
and the child's hair like a silk scarf,
as if this one child were all desires
spoken, in safety.

I wonder what Frost's children asked him,
and if he bothered to answer.
My friend here has written a poem
for his daughter, too, he says, and begins. The child
smiles quickly at her mother, at all this
just for her. Their look
seems to exchange knowledge of this man
they live with and share, something the child
knows about longing and its inventions
her mother has yet to fathom.

§

JANE KENYON

1947–1995

Jane Kenyon's three poems come from the latter part of her life, when she was at the height of her powers. I remember seeing each for the first time, and my continuing astonishment over the work of the woman I loved.

Once I told Jane the title I chose for a new book, *The Happy Man*. She looked skeptical. "Sounds too depressed," she said. She wrote her late, bountiful "Happiness" with a depressive's ecstasy, in the surging reverse of melancholia. Only a depressive could write such a poem. I love her strange, exactly right particulars, like the uncle landing his single-engined plane, like the wineglass weary of holding wine.

"Woman, Why Are You Weeping?" is her best religious poem, and like so many great Christian poems it was written out of a crisis in her faith. She loved India so much—the rigorous sweetness and complexity of Hinduism—that she felt her own beliefs challenged.

"Having It Out with Melancholy" was more difficult to write than any other of her poems, not for technical or intellectual reasons, but because it took courage to express and expose her illness. We did not show each other our poems in progress but sometimes we would speak of an ongoing poem, and thus I knew of her effort, struggle, and pain in drafting "Melancholy." And I remember the first time she read it aloud. It was at The Frost Place, which by its generous nature, encourages intimacy. It was emotionally difficult for her to speak the poem; I remember a long pause during which she collected herself. She was making her disease public, a disease which has been looked down on and made light of, and which governed so many wretched passages in her life. She stood in front of The Frost Place audience saying that "A piece of burnt meat wears my clothes." The triumph of reading it aloud was small compared to the triumph of writing it, but it was a triumph.

When she finished, the response of The Frost Place audience was immediate and overwhelming. Many listeners had experienced depression and everyone had known or loved someone with this affliction. Jane wrote the poem to embody the lineaments of her condition, to put feelings into images and metaphors that would leap from poet to reader and listener. She wrote the poem so that the miseries of depression might be heard and taken in. When she had finished saying it, many people crowded around, to thank her for the poem, for what she had done for them and for people close to them.

— Donald Hall

Happiness

There's just no accounting for happiness,
or the way it turns up like a prodigal
who comes back to the dust at your feet
having squandered a fortune far away.

And how can you not forgive?
You make a feast in honor of what
was lost, and take from its place the finest
garment, which you saved for an occasion
you could not imagine, and you weep night and day
to know that you were not abandoned,
that happiness saved its most extreme form
for you alone.

No, happiness is the uncle you never
knew about, who flies a single-engine plane
onto the grassy landing strip, hitchhikes
into town, and inquires at every door
until he finds you asleep midafternoon
as you so often are during the unmerciful
hours of your despair.

It comes to the monk in his cell.
It comes to the woman sweeping the street
with a birch broom, to the child
whose mother has passed out from drink.
It comes to the lover, to the dog chewing
a sock, to the pusher, to the basketmaker,
and to the clerk stacking cans of carrots
in the night.

It even comes to the boulder
in the perpetual shade of pine barrens,
to rain falling on the open sea,
to the wineglass, weary of holding wine.

Woman, Why Are You Weeping?

The morning after the crucifixion,
Mary Magdalene came to see the body
of Christ. She found the stone
rolled away from an empty tomb. Two
figures dressed in white asked her,
"Woman, why are you weeping?"

"Because," she replied, "they have
taken away my Lord, and I don't know
where they have laid him."

Returned from long travel, I sit
in the familiar, sun-streaked pew, waiting
for the bread and wine of Holy Communion.
The old comfort does not rise in me, only
apathy and bafflement.
      India, with her ceaseless
bells and fire; her crows calling stridently
all night; India with her sandalwood
smoke, and graceful gods, many-headed and many-
armed, has taken away the one who blessed
and kept me.
      The thing is done, as surely
as if my luggage had been stolen from the train.
Men and women with faces as calm as lakes at dusk
have taken away my Lord, and I don't know
where to find him.

§

What is Brahman? I don't know Brahman.
I don't know *saccidandana*, the bliss

of the absolute and unknowable.
I only know that I have lost the Lord
in whose image I was made.

Whom shall I thank for this pear,
sweet and white? Food *is* God, *Prasadam*,
God's mercy. But who is this God?
The one who is *not this, not that*?

The absurdity of all religious forms
breaks over me, as the absurdity of language
made me feel faint the day I heard friends
giving commands to their neighbor's dog
in Spanish . . . . At first I laughed,
but then I became frightened.

§

They have taken away my Lord, a person
whose life I held inside me. I saw him
heal, and teach, and eat among sinners.
I saw him break the Sabbath to make a higher
Sabbath. I saw him lose his temper.

I knew his anguish when he called, "I thirst!"
and received vinegar to drink. The Bible
does not say it, but I am sure he turned
his head away. Not long after he cried, "My God,
my God, why have you forsaken me?"
I watched him reveal himself risen
to Magdalene with a single word: "Mary!"

It was my habit to speak to him. His goodness
perfumed my life. I loved the Lord, he heard
my cry, and he loved me as his own.

§

A man sleeps on the pavement, on a raffia mat—
the only thing that has not been stolen from him.
This stranger who loves what cannot be understood
has put out my light with his calm face.

Shall the fire answer my fears and vapors?
The fire cares nothing for my illness,
nor does Brahma, the creator, nor Shiva who sees
evil with his terrible third eye; Vishnu,
the protector, does not protect me.

I've brought home the smell of the streets
in the folds of soft, bright cotton garments.
When I iron them the steam brings back
the complex odors that rise from the gutters,
of tuberroses, urine, dust, joss, and death.

§

On a curb in Allahabad the family gathers
under a dusty tree, a few quilts hung
between lightposts and a wattle fence
for privacy. Eleven sit or lie around the fire
while a woman of sixty stirs a huge pot.
Rice cooks in a narrow-necked crock
on the embers. A small dog, with patches of bald,
red skin on his back, lies on the corner
of the piece of canvas that serves as flooring.

Looking at them I lose my place.
I don't know why I was born, or why
I live in a house in New England, or why I am
a visitor with heavy luggage giving lectures
for the State Department. Why am I not
tap-tapping with my fingernail

on the rolled-up window of a white Government car,
a baby in my arms, drugged to look feverish?

§

Rajiv did not weep. He did not cover
his face with his hands when we rowed past
the dead body of a newborn nudging the grassy
banks at Benares—close by a snake
rearing up, and a cast-off garland of flowers.

He explained. When a family are too poor
to cremate their dead, they bring the body
here, and slip it into the waters of the Ganges
and Yamuna rivers.
                    Perhaps the child was dead
at birth; perhaps it had the misfortune
to be born a girl. The mother may have walked
two days with her baby's body to this place
where Gandhi's ashes once struck the waves
with the sound like gravel being scuffed
over the edge of a bridge.

"What shall we do about this?" I asked
my God, who even then was leaving me. The reply
was scorching wind, lapping of water, pull
of the black oarsmen on the oars . . . .

Having it Out with Melancholy

If many remedies are prescribed for an illness,
you may be certain that the illness has no cure.
— A. P. Chekhov, *The Cherry Orchard*

1 FROM THE NURSERY

When I was born, you waited
behind a pile of linen in the nursery,
and when we were alone, you lay down
on top of me, pressing
the bile of desolation into every pore.

And from that day on
everything under the sun and moon
made me sad—even the yellow
wooden beads that slid and spun
along a spindle on my crib.

You taught me to exist without gratitude.
You ruined my manners toward God:
"We're here simply to wait for death;
the pleasures of earth are overrated."

I only appeared to belong to my mother,
to live among blocks and cotton undershirts
with snaps; among red tin lunch boxes
and report cards in ugly brown slipcases.
I was already yours—the anti-urge,
the mutilator of souls.

2 BOTTLES

Elavil, Ludiomil, Doxepin,
Norpramin, Prozac, Lithium, Xanax,

Wellbutrin, Parnate, Nardil, Zoloft.
The coated ones smell sweet or have
no smell; the powdery ones smell
like the chemistry lab at school
that made me hold my breath.

3 SUGGESTION FROM A FRIEND

You wouldn't be so depressed
if you really believed in God.

4 OFTEN

Often I go to bed as soon after dinner
as seems adult
(I mean I try to wait for dark)
in order to push away
from the massive pain in sleep's
frail wicker coracle.

5 ONCE THERE WAS LIGHT

Once, in my early thirties, I saw
that I was a speck of light in the great
river of light that undulates through time.

I was floating with the whole
human family. We were all colors—those
who are living now, those who have died,
those who are not yet born. For a few

moments I floated, completely calm,
and I no longer hated having to exist.

Like a crow who smells hot blood
you came flying to pull me out

of the glowing stream.
"I'll hold you up. I never let my dear
ones drown!" After that, I wept for days.

6 IN AND OUT

The dog searches until he finds me
upstairs, lies down with a clatter
of elbows, puts his head on my foot.

Sometimes the sound of his breathing
saves my life—in and out, in
and out; a pause, a long sigh. . . .

7 PARDON

A piece of burned meat
wears my clothes, speaks
in my voice, dispatches obligations
haltingly, or not at all.
It is tired of trying
to be stouthearted, tired
beyond measure.

We move on to the monoamine
oxidase inhibitors. Day and night
I feel as if I had drunk six cups
of coffee, but the pain stops
abruptly. With the wonder
and bitterness of someone pardoned
for a crime she did not commit
I come back to marriage and friends,
to pink fringed hollyhocks; come back
to my desk, books, and chair.

8 CREDO

Pharmaceutical wonders are at work
but I believe only in this moment
of well-being. Unholy ghost,
you are certain to come again.

Coarse, mean, you'll put your feet
on the coffee table, lean back,
and turn me into someone who can't
take the trouble to speak; someone
who can't sleep, or who does nothing
but sleep; can't read, or call
for an appointment for help.

There is nothing I can do
against your coming.
When I awake, I am still with thee.

9 WOOD THRUSH

High on Nardil and June light
I wake at four,
waiting greedily for the first
note of the wood thrush. Easeful air
presses through the screen
with the wild, complex song
of the bird, and I am overcome

by ordinary contentment.
What hurt me so terribly
all my life until this moment?
How I love the small, swiftly
beating heart of the bird
singing in the great maples;
its bright, unequivocal eye.

GALWAY KINNELL

How Could She Not

for Jane Kenyon (1947-1995)

It is a day after many days of storms.
Having been washed and washed, the air glitters;
small heaped cumuli are carried across the sky;
a brief shower, its parallel diagonals visible
against the firs, douses the crocuses.
We knew it would happen soon.
Hearing that she died but hours ago, I go
to the open door and I look eastward toward her,
inNew Hampshire. There, too, the sun is bright
and a few clouds make their shadowy ways
along the horizon. How could it not have been today?
In another room, Kiri Te Kanawa is singing on a CD
the Laudate Dominum of Mozart, faintly,
from deep in the past, barely hearable
over the whisperings of a line of scythes
and soon the rattling of horse-drawn mowing machines
drawing their cutter bar's little intricate
reciprocating triangles through the timothy
being made to lie down in the sunshine.
In the dark of early this morning, did she wake
almost used up by a full year of pain and despair
remitted briefly now and then by a hope
that had the undertaste of death?
At first light did she glimpse
the world as she had loved it and see
that now it would not be wrong for her to die,
for she could leave him in a day like paradise?
Near sunrise did her hold loosen a little?
Having these last days spoken her whole heart
to him, who spoke his whole heart to her,
might she not have felt that now, in the silence,
he would not feel that any word was missing?

When full daylight filled the room, how could she not
have slipped into a spell, with him next to her,
his arms around her, as they had been,
it may then have seemed, all her life?
How could her cheek not press itself a moment to his cheek,
which presses itself to hers from now on?
How could she not rise and go, with all that sunlight
at the window, familiar arms around her, and the sound,
somewhere, fading, deepening, hard to say, of a single-engine
plane in the distance no one else hears?

Feathering

Many heads before mine have waked
in the dark on that ancient pillow
and lain there on its prisoners' ticking,
wondering at the strangeness within themselves
they had been part of moments ago.
Yesterday she ripped out its stitches
at one end, and today, standing on the stone bench
and gripping the stained shapeless thing like a sack,
she delves with her hand and extracts
a small puffy fistful of duck down.
Bits of it drift toward the ground
and suddenly tree swallows appear.
She raises the arm topped by the down
straight up in the air
and stands there like a mom
at a school crossing or a god
of seedtime about to release
a stream of bits of plenitude
or herself, long ago, at a pond, chumming
for sunfish with bread crumbs.
At accelerations of the breeze her fist
loosens and parcels out upward
tumbles of these fluffs near zero
on the scale of materiality.
With a flap, a swallow, one of the dozen
now looping and whirling about her,
streaks at a feather, misses, twists
on itself and streaks back and now
snaps its beak shut on it and soars
out over the field to mislead or to gloat,
then circles back to where its nest box is.
After many tosses and catches, she ties off
the pillow, ending for today

the game they make of it when she's there,
the imperative to feather one's nest
come down from the Pliocene.
At the window, where I've been watching
all this through bird glasses, I see
her traipsing back to the house,
her face lighted, a sidewise lurch
in her walk, as if she's a bit tipsy
from still being where she has been.

White Mountains

Sky is seen piecemeal—between clouds, or reflected in the smooth stretch of water beside the bridge. Clouds bleed their shadows over the hills, patches of dark and light that, in turn, create contour. And the hills ripple outward, row after row, in fading tones of blue until the last ones are swallowed in sky, just a hint on the horizon. Distance is vicarious, measured in sound—occasional birdcall, dogs barking up from the valley, or a truck shifting gears.

So the summer eye pulls inward, finds focus on something close. Cattails by the roadside. Lupine, lifting its purple fingers. Or the individual leaves of the lilac bush outside the door, chattering in the wind before the storm. The spider who weaves his web above the woodpile is carefully out of sight while the sun, caught for an instant in the filaments, turns what was invisible visible. What else has gone unnoticed? Sunlight is blue. Is brilliant on the mountains. Is sliced wafer thin and stacked ready for whatever season will follow. The gardener's shears chip steadily away at the afternoon—*shrnk, shrnk, shrnk*—and it is only in the imagination that the hedge behind the house takes on the shape it constantly defies. Tonight when I emerge, blinking, it will catch me by surprise with its neatness, the way it fits itself into the wide sweep of yard as though it had never resisted.

Everything for the Seeds

In May, we sowed four rows of corn.
I furrowed a perfect V that you noticed
was not the way your father hoed.
You dropped each kernel eight inches apart,
yet stalks grew in rows raccoons
could pass between, or in clumps
like clustered cosmos bouquet.

Early in July, I put in giant marigolds.
In August you tore the blossoms
to show the way your mother gathered seeds.
Black and white like wild rice
little needles spread to dry into autumn.

After the stroke,
caring for you all September,
I ignored my garden.
Pumpkin vines strangled the peppers.
Cobs hung like thirsty tongues.

Now I shred the shriveled corn for geese,
and it's time to burn the stalks.
Marigolds, butter orange and yellow
lean against their hollowness.
Thirteen swollen pumpkins
you laughed at this summer,
hold their ground and wait,
while I pull at blossoming radishes,
open pods like hands in prayer,
remove the pebbles green within.

Here in my October garden,
my fingers redolent
with radish, marigold, onion and earth
I bind with lavender,
a sachet to plant beside your pillow.
Can you smell this?
Mother, if you can, nod "yes."

Joseph

What about Joseph? Not the guy bent over your metal *auto's*
urchin's complaining engine /
but the Joseph we don't say prayers to /
whose face is not the one discovered
on the veils that never bear the imprint
of his face but of his Son's,
you know the one.

What about Joseph, not the one who knicked
your Formica countertop and left you to
discover it but the simple guy
who never knew of plugged-in tools,
but did it all by hand, trained his
circumcised Son to read Torah, to join a minyan,
to build cabinets. You know the one.

What about Joseph, not the Father,
not the biological father, but the father
no different from us, expected to find a resting place,
expected to instill, by example, a respect for whipless
authority for an absolute and unquestioned love
of family as his son stands on his shoulders,
even his not-his-son child but
his Son. You know the one.

What about Joseph?
If I were able, I would offer him
latkes at my house, some of Grandma's
sweet thick grape wine, a chance to lave in a tub
porcelain and fit for a Pharaoh.
Give me the lead rope, relax for a while,
I'd say to the saintly man, we'll talk later.

What about Joseph?
his caring hands, his grief
when they nailed his son to a cedar cross, not you.
You can tell me it still hurts.
He is not the one you pray to, dear Joseph,
but, like any good father, the one you
pray for/even as he left you sonless
with less than a postscripted note.
We know the feeling.
You know the one.

CHRISTINE KORFHAGE

My Father's Voice

That rare night together ended
with mom asleep in the front seat,
me forgotten in back,
and dad, a little intoxicated, I think,
driving home from the Officers' Club.
I remember the wet sheen of that black
volcanic rock, the rough slide of pebbles
washed by the sea, those few scattered stars,
and the glow of his cigar that seemed lit
by them. And, oh, I remember the slight
lean of his head as he began to sing
with a longing so deep I held my breath
and followed him to his mother's land
in a distant sea. And though I could only
make out the wave of blond hair
along the back of his godlike head,
I pierced the curve of his neck
till through his clear tenor voice I saw
the rounded white collar and big red bow
around the throat of a 10-year-old
choir boy standing next to his mother
beside a cold-water flat. And, oh, now
I remember, slowing down, that turn
in the road, our darkened bungalow,
my own silent voice crying, *Oh, no, not yet!*
as he glanced at my mother
and I shut my eyes, till like mercy
that car drove on for one last spin,
another round of *When Irish Eyes Are Smilin'*,
and I filled myself up with the blessing
of that sound, the thick cigar smoke
knowing tomorrow he'd leave us again.

My Mother on an Evening at the Cottage

When the sun sets
and a few spray-stung cedars
glisten with a light
slanted and salty,
my mother, with her hair in tight curls,
stands near the clothesline
and watches the sun's russet glaze
wash over the Japanese garden.

Soon the cottage, with its windows still open, will send
songs of bells and flutes
into the dusk and the Japanese garden
will begin its unblooming
and the stones, tide smoothed spheres
will seem to hide
the secrets of earth.
And my mother, under summer's spell,
will think how we yield each day
to tides of forgetting
and she will not know
why she stands here
or what she is bound to.

My mother will go indoors and the roses, the stones
will wait for dawn.
Only the fireflies will flash,
small flecks
in the bee-eaten fruit of the pear tree,
in the dewed lawn, in the dark air,
in the garden that keeps silent.
The tree is not yet leafless;
the stones, not yet words.

Friar Laurence: Nightmare

I was in the garden harvesting tomatoes
and you were supposed to be writing.

I had written your assignment on the blackboard,
in the softest, sea-green chalk,
and was turning up the leaves
to find the truly ripened fruit
and you were supposed to be writing.

I had even taken the trouble and time
to erase, powder out and rewrite the word
or two that I thought weren't clear
before I left. I thought the writing
would be enough to grip your mind
and guide and even stay your hand.

Didn't you get it? Didn't you grasp
that the channel and force
of the cursive circle and line and curve
can be the spiraling path of peace?
At the place where the ways
of inscription meet, thought
crowds out killing. My God,
it's the difference of ink
and blood! What didn't you see?

When I found you, you'd lost
your disposable pen and the souvenir
lighter I'd brought you. Instead,
there were shells scattered round
and a juicy, teeming red blotch
in place of your eye. The crows
gathered round but said they knew

nothing. Your other eye grazed
the mountain trail to my cell.

What could I have done?
You knew I had taken a vow of silence,
and you were supposed to be writing.

ELISABETH KUHN

Mother's Advent Ritual

We watched, squirming around
the wreath as Mother lit the second
candle. On the wall table
sat her homemade nativity scene:
hand carved shed, animals, shepherds.
Mary, Joseph, and Jesus
would not arrive until Christmas.

We huddled closer, chewing
our lips, eyed the crib
and the two small tins behind it
(one filled with threads, one with needles)
as we sang for our savior:
Oh come, oh come, Emanuel!
Mother conducted.

My sister had been good.
She was allowed
to pick a woolen thread
for Jesus' crib so he would be
warm and comfortable.
I had done something to anger Mother.
I had to pick a needle.
Jesus would have to suffer
for my sins.

Before I could drop the needle
into his crib, I had to give it to Mother.
She held my trembling wrist
and stabbed the needle
into the tip of my index finger.
I screamed, clutching my bleeding hand.

Screaming was not allowed,
so Mother grabbed
the wooden spoon and started hitting
my legs, my hips, yelling
that she would not stop
until I stopped crying.

Then she turned to my brother.

MAXINE KUMIN

A Mortal Day of No Surprises

This morning a frog in the bathtub
and not unhappy with his lot
hunkering over the downspout
out there in the pasture.
Strawberries, morever,
but not the bearing kind, scrub
growth, many-footed pretenders,
running amok in the squash hills and valleys.

Out of here! I say
ripping the lime-green tendrils from
their pinchhold in my zucchini blossoms
and out! with a thrust of the grain scoop
to the teal-blue frog who must have fallen
from the sky in a sneakstorm that slipped
in between 2 and 3 A.M. when
even God allows for a nap.

Last night at that sneakstorm time
(God sleeping, me working out
among the rerun dreams)
two white-throated sparrows
woke me to make their departmental claims—
Old Sam Peabody peabody pea—
wrangling like clerks in adjoining bureaus
only to recommence at dawn
saying their names and territories.

Now for good measure
the dog brings home one-half a rank
woodchuck no angel spoke up for
but won't say where he's banked
the rest of the treasure

and one of this year's piglets
gets loose again by rooting under,
emerging from mud like a crawfish
to stumble across the geese's path
and have an eye pecked bloody by the gander.

All this in a summer day
to be gone like cloth at the knees
when the dark comes down
ancient and absolute as thistles.
A day predictable as white-throat whistle.
A day that's indistinguishable
from thirty others, except the mare's
in heat and miserable,
flagging, rubbing her tail bare.

When I'm scooped out of here
all things animal
and unsurprised will carry on.
Frogs still will fall into those
stained old tubs we fill
with trickles from the garden hose.
Another blue-green prince will sit
like a friend of the family
guarding the doomspout.
Him asquat at the drainhole,
me gone to crumbs in the ground
and someone else's mare to call
to the distant stallion.

Strut

Every morning to guard against glut I chop
zucchini zealots for the lambs
who are not particularly grateful.
They prefer mashed apples and fresh grain.
Every morning I rethink how common green
—pond scum, a thousand sumac sprouts
orchard and rye grass, birdsfoot trefoil
milkweed, poke, dock, dill, sorrel

bush and shrub, soft- and hard-woods, all
leafy-headed—must go down again in
frost and come again. Is this a deep
head-tilting meditative thought, or

vernal instinctual, nothing more?
Here come the marbleized rat-wet new foals
blowing blue bubbles like divers into air
on their feet in minutes finding

the mares' teats by trial-and-error blind
butting stagger-dance. And here comes
cakewalk-cocky with the whole mess
of birth and rebirth the strut of the season.

Almost bliss.

In the Upper Pasture

In the evergreen grove that abuts the pasture we are
limbing low branches, carting away deadwood,
cutting close to the trunk so the sap does not bleed,
to make a shelter, a run-in for foals and their mares.
We will not shorten the lives of these hemlocks and pines
in the afternoon of our own lives, yet I am sad
to think that the dell will outlast us and our bloodlines.

Is this a pastoral? Be not deceived
by the bellows of leathery teats giving suck,
by the fringe of delicate beard that pricks
its braille notes on the muzzle of the newborn.
When instinct whinnies between dam and foal
at night in the rain, do not be lulled.
Each of us whimpers his way through the forest alone.

With galvanized nails and scrap lumber we fence off
a triad of trees that have grown so close to each other
a young horse darting through might be taken prisoner.
Let the babies be safe here, let them lie down on pine duff
away from the merciless blackflies, out of the weather.
Under the latticework of old trees, let me stand
pitchstreaked and pleasured by this small thing we have done.

Tonight the peepers are as loud as all
the grandmother of the world's canaries, those
Petey- and Dicky-birds trilling vibrators
from their baggage-handle perches, perpetual
singing machines stoned on seeds of hemp.

Tonight the peepers are a summer camp-
ful of ten-year-olds still shrilling after taps.
Winter will have us back with cold so harsh
our nose hair freeze. Martens will spring the traps.
But peepers tonight—spring peepers hallow the marsh.

Five Small Deaths in May

Somehow a mole has swum too far
downstream from the tunnel and drowned
in the pond. On his nose the star
he wears for a wise fifth hand
is losing its pink. His eyepits blacken.
Now the sun can sink
into those two particulars
and eat away the last wires.

A milk snake has come to this cup
of straw at the cleft of a rock.
It has drunk the good yolk up.
When the meadowlark flicks back
she turns and turns like a dog
making a place to lie down.
The shell specks fly out between her legs.
They are flecked lavender and brown.

A heron is fishing for minnows.
In the shadow of the bird
they crowd together
lying straight out to leeward
a see-through army in the shallows
as still as grains in a rice bowl.
Scooped up they go down whole
exchanging one wet place for another.

The owl, old monkey face
will have his nightly mouse
culled from the tribe
disgorging here and there
down in his pine-lined bog
and on the pathway to the house

a chip of rib, a flake of leg
a tuft of hair.

I will not sing the death of Dog
who lived a fool to please his King.
I will put him under the milkweed bloom
where in July the monarchs come
as spotted as he, as rampant, as enduring.

Utshimassit (Davis Inlet), Labrador

The ship will go no farther. Already the ice presses down from
      Upernavik,
and the light turns to stone where it falls. A soft night fog covers
      bear-claw
scars of glaciers that scoured the land, retreated, and drowned the
      shore.
Only these islands are breathing.

An old trapper's hut leans into the sea like a wolf drinking.

A clumsy bell tower without a bell.

Cliff's covered with graffiti: RCMP TO HOME FCK YOU.

Slipped into port past midnight. The children are awake, they pelt us
      with
stones, they climb aboard, falling from the dark like bats.

What's your name? A child looks up at me. She wears the rags of a
thousand winters. I tell her my name. She wipes her nose with a
      clump of
hair, and asks again.

Philomene is the only elder come to meet us. The others are afraid.
      They
remember the mission ship: all it took was a single infected sailor,
      his breath
moving through the village like a spirit across the water, touching
      the living
and leaving the dead behind.

She was the child left to watch the corpses ripped apart by hungry
      dogs:

I was protected by a she-wolf.

And the priests had their magic. Death, they said, was life . . .

She leads me through the village. Lights drift across the sky, swaying
        like
shadows behind a screen, moss-colored, wind-bent like long grass.
        The
milky white trail of the dead sweeps low and touches down, here: on
        this
island, this village, this house.

Philomene stops and points to it. Strange shapes on a roof.
Where the girl lived, six years old.
Until she's buried, there will be fear.

Disease, you see, spreads here like a grass fire.

A child trails a toy boat made from a milk carton and a string.
What's your name? It is currency here, my American name.

We arrive at the mission, the bell tower without a bell.

Don't let them in, she says. They are poor as spirits and have no
        souls.
They've traded them in for shoes. It was the ravens taught them talk-
ing,
the lemmings asleep in their hair, and listen how they laugh like
        bears.

She touches a silver cross hanging from her neck.

The priest says, they live on lichen and crowberries and porcupine bones.

I sleep uneasily, the children tapping like moths at the windowpanes.
        A

crucifix dangles over me…Just on the other side of this wall, a child
        rests in
a coffin. Tomorrow they will cover her with alcohol-swabbed kisses.

Her things have been left for her on the rooftop of her house, her
        beaded
moccasins, a doll stuffed with tea. Her clothes still holding the
        shapes of
her knees and elbows, rumpled in a bag.

She will leave us tonight, trailing her dusty footprints across the sky. She
will want to take some of her things. She will want to take someone
        along—no one wants to die alone.

It's a strange thing, but here, no one ever does.

Philomene warned me not to look up at the aurora:

falling ashes of starbones,
threadbare empty clothes swaying over rooftops,
a wind on the water washing away our names.

1959

I thought I was storing it up. I guess I did.
I didn't know a thing.
I was a slightly fat, a slightly handsome kid,
sixteen, on a scholarship, away
from the new hegemon.
France was still coming to
—from the war and the war.

He didn't say World War
One or World War Two or World War
anything. He spoke of the *guerre de quatorze*,
which dismasted him. He drank up
what I'd bought him and he shuddered.
He adjusted his instrument
—some crude banjo-y thing—

on his stubbed right thigh. Badly and long,
he sang of the *guerre de quatorze*.
It lasted so long
and it was bad. An *idea*—suffering—
fired itself through my frame
like the *pastis* I'd ordered
             in my surprising good French.

If I could just stay right there like that on that bench.
Those slight waves lisping. That gravel strand.
St. Jean de Luz. That breeze and mollusky stench.
That sun melting on the far low Pyrenees.
If the people around me could just keep keeping quiet
like that—not because the music was good
             but because it was long and awful

and was his and was theirs and was soulful.

If that warmth could run down into both my feet.
If it could stay like that, just slightly rank and tearful.
If it could just be this light forever.
If every eye could be wet but mine
and that of someone's daughter, which kept shooting at me,
       though I couldn't determine whether to flirt or rebuke me.

To make a soul—I could *tell*! It would be so easy.

Evening Walk as the School Year Starts

When was the last lobotomy, I wonder?
Too late for Carl at least, whom it's all but hopeless
to dream of as that whipsaw of hateful passion
that would if it could have torn up his mother and father,
mild as they are; but that's what villagers say
of him before our time here, their smiles all rueful,
subtly shaking their heads. A raven, unsubtle,
grates from a hemlock as Carl steps into sight.

Familiar salutation: a jerk of the palm.
He's ageless as grass or gravel, his eyes still empty
from the old operation. He turns now: ninety degrees,
then ninety again like a sentry, the other way,
as he turns each evening—a kindergartner's totter
by the house of our mutual neighbor, who will not speak
to Carl's father. Why not? Neither must now remember.
We all should take the time to edit grievance.

It's some awful stink nearby that draws the raven,
but the rest of the world seems fixed on the morbid too:
a squirrel keeps pouring spruce cones down at me;
a gall-blighted butternut groans; the broadleafs wilt;
at my feet, a pair of toads that wheels have flattened
side by side, like cartoon icons of failure;
mosquitos strafe my flesh and a dragonfly,
one of the season's last, attacks a moth

so close before me I hear the fatal click.
The other day a son went off to college.
His mother and I are quietly beside ourselves.
We hug each other harder now, and vow
as one vows to love our children harder too—
gone so soon. The raven's dive is loud

as gunfire through brush to its putrid mess. I jump,
but Carl doesn't hear, it seems. I watch him scrape

up his family's drive—again that sure right angle.
We also believe a family thrives on order:
we rise to eat our 6:30 breakfast, then make
a certain sandwich for one of the daughters, a different
one for the other; we trek toward school at seven;
we gather the girls, prompt, at end of lessons.
Carl opens his door and shuts it—click—behind him.
It's after Labor Day, it's end-of-summer,

it's another season upon us. He still upbraids me,
that squirrel on his branch, his arsenal's store all gone.
Why me, dumb brute: I haven't done anything wrong,
I've got no grievance with him, nor with anyone really.
The darkness deepens, Lord with me abide.
The wishing star is not enough to light
the space around me, and this bit of hymn from my school days
plays again as day creatures crawl to cover

and night ones ponder, having no choice, the night.

Rodney Fallen: A Parable

Spring past, I'd cut much less than I thought for the shed,
and so one morning I called up Rodney Sweet,
never a man better named, though he's touched in the head,
some say, a Bible-thumper. Okay by me.

He does all right in the world with his "two big rules"—
Love God and your neighbor—which means his wood is good,
a cord's a cord, no popple or piss-elm, and fool
that I'd been, I felt lucky that Rodney Sweet still had

something on hand, and the whole of it fine rock maple.
He won't often sell by the half, but a half-cord would do,
for me, as I told Rodney. He calls me loyal,
and claims to like my trade for that, although

truth is I'm at best a doubtful, unsteady client.
Maybe it's just that we see most things eye-to-eye.
Speaking of eyes, his own are blue as heaven.
You notice that, right off, so when the ice

sent him arcing that noon, his feet straight up in the air,
till he crashed to hard ground and all but knocked out his brains
and lay gut-up like a drunk in some shitface bar,
the kind of place in which he'd never be seen,

and those eyes showed flat and sightless, it seemed the world
went down with him, and Lord-God how I worried
as I called to him over and over, "Rodney? Rodney?"—
like a life's most urgent question—and against my will

imagined nothing at all in that skyward gaze,
and then looked up myself, to where the awful

starlings fought the wind, and my goddamned trees
turned dark on the hills under sleetclouds that shuffled and mumbled

with only the juddering flags of beech and oak,
pallid and brown, making minimal gesture
against the shadows' grizzle, then back: on the snow,
his blood looked dimmer still, and all the other

colors leached breakneck away, and stupefied,
I contemplated Rodney, Rodney fallen,
till the blue eyes kindled, he looked at me, he smiled.
He spoke at last: "The Man up there's been tryin'

to pound some sense in that head for a long, long time."
O Jesus, I swear the first spring sun broke through
and the thaw began, and peace and warblers would come
because Rodney stood, and phoebes and vireos,

and there'd be moon and mice and love and deer
and courage, kestrels, warmth, another year.

Manifest

Litany: winter walk
In evergreens, wind-riven,
whose blaze-orange wounds
at limb and crown certify passion;
In the mitten-wool taste
of snow you scoop to your mouth
because—so you imagine—you thirst;
In illogical woodpeckers' laughter,
in their swooping flight,
that suggests assertion crossed by doubt;
In rough-frozen rims of tracks
the animals left in the dark preceding
nights, whose meaning needs no glossing;
In the hue of a beech
—neither quite somber gray
nor placid blue—that teases all sight and belief;
In the way this sun at solstice
jumps up from the hill
and asks no reading, but affirmation in the chill;
In the ermine who fough the owl,
resisting negation:
alone now, scarlet in snow—conspicuous, stiffened;
In the steam of your coffee at dawn,
pale testimony to addiction, harmless,
perhaps more so than others you want;
In one long-damaged knee
whose cartilage resists your walk, and warns
against a mock tranquility;
In the bland and sweet obedience
of your dogs, which raises questions
that touch on your worthiness, competence;
In the warmth (to which you'll return)

of shelter, so easily canceled should your fuel
withold its fire—a residue of the sun;
In fire, that has the power and glory
of "the things that have been made," as St. Paul saith,
commanding faith, however airy;
In warmth and shelter and fire,
to which of course you will return,
for which you are whetting desire;
In desire, whose quenching is life
and death, as poets used to say—
by enjoinder and designation: husband, wife;
In this cheery fall of siskins
to an earth that you'd thought barren: in their number,
that may be somewhere counted, their busyness;
In their vanishing
—before you can count them yourself—
that sermonizes vanity;
In the far waw of a power saw
that binds on a softwood's sap, congealed:
the logger swears profanely, we are not healed;
In the warming recollection of your children,
for whose sake you pray as you can for death
to have no dominion, that you are forgiven.

Small Waterfall: A Birthday Poem

Maybe an engineer,
stumbling on this small, all-
but-forest-swallowed waterfall—
a ten-foot drop at most—
could with some accuracy
say just how much energy
goes unharnessed here.

Enough, is it, to bring light
and heat to the one-room hut one might
build here at its foot—where,
piecing together the *hush*
in the current's *hurl* and *crash*,
a lone man might repair
to fix a shopworn life?

Enough, anyway, to light
one image in my head: this mist-
laced column of water's
as slim as a girl's waist—
yours, say, narrow still despite
the tumble down the birth canal
of a pair of nine-pound daughters.

Well, there's nothing for it but,
sloshing my way across the pool,
I must set whimsy into fact—
which is how, one blazing, cool
August day in New Hampshire, I
come to be standing with my
arms around a cataract.

. . . Nothing new in this, it turns out—

for I know all about embracing
a thing that flows and goes
and stays, self-propelled and -replacing,
which in its roundabout route
carries and throws, carries and throws
off glints at every turn, bringing

all it touches to flower
(witness those flourishing daughters).
Your reach exceeds my grasp, happily,
for yours is the river's power
to link with liquid, unseen threads
the low, far, moon-moved sea
and the sun's high-lit headwaters.

A False Spring

(She who'd been taken
hostage—when?—been bound
and drugged, kept in all things
in the dark, now at last found
she'd begun to waken.)

So gently that year did
January come on, it teased
out the crocus, half-hid
in snow, gilded the willows, eased
the forsythia into bloom.

(But a good hard blow
sent her blindly back under.
Escape? A mere dream,
and that the dream came in a glow
of green, of gold, no wonder.)

At the Windswept Cottages

They have just driven up from New York
to their three-room rental cottage in the mountains
where they sit on the cramped porch in the rising breeze.

He is reading a novel in his denim shorts,
feet propped on a pillow atop the rail.
The swimming pool glinting beyond his book
is empty of people. She has chosen
to wear the oversize pink tee shirt, tie-dyed
her long braid of gray hair also anachronistic.
Middle age, they both feel, has been cruel to their bodies.

They will soon decide to eat but not be hungry.
There is not one thing they have planned to do.
The guidebooks do not entice them.
For now the cool wind suffices.

In the course of the week in the beauty
of the mountains, each will remember summers
before they met. Colors persist.
The black pond full of fat sunfish.
Suntanned shoulders held in wet hands
at swim practice. Years later the blue chenille bedspread
on which naked delirious bodies lay
just after dawn in the farmhouse,
the sounds of cattle making a poignant singing.

But now they settle in, consider possibilities
of comfort, become familiar with the layout,
the textures of the brown furniture.

The Steam of Tea

a pot of tea
    that usual restaurant white ceramic
    with the single restrained dark green equator
in the spread yellow sunlight
    of the February morning
    centers the table with it's heat
as she remembers and tells him
    of her father, a pilot,
    taking her at twelve to Paris
how up on the Trocadero
    in the plaza of the Musée De L'Homme
    looking down on the Eiffel Tower
he suddenly took her wrists
      twirled her so fast
    that she became a straight line out
and she learned
    what he wanted her to learn:
    her complete freedom in the air
and how that brought her
    to a sumptuous freedom on the ground.
    Across the table, he listens to her
and looks behind her
    out the window at the rusted
    railroad bridge over the river
that drains, just here, into the bay.
    This is the ramshackle part of town
    old pilings, delapidated docks,
the broken hulk of a ferry
    that gives weight
    to his falling in love in February
        amid the seam of tea
        and the twirls of her voice.

Divorce

We've suffered a diminuendo of personnel,

Matthews quotes Mingus one night
when Mingus fired the pianist midset
and tonight, alone in the now larger house
on that now too friendly and too sympathetic
small town street, one of those nights
when he has the boys,
she adjusts to a solo, rephrases
the routines of her life.

Maybe dinner or maybe not? Maybe reading
or renting some foreign movie
that he would never watch?
In bed early and regaining some sleep?

How to go about the house,
mindlessly straightening or deliberately
straightening, remixing the bookshelves,
putting on some Ella and then leaving the room,
opening the refrigerator as if it held
ideas or other things to do, not lost,
not lost at all, but still fumbling a bit,
learning the tune, and finding somehow
more dynamics in the emptiness

and asking, asking the silent walls,
What key do I play this in? and telling them,
Hey, guys, feed me the tempo.

Small Geographies

Put to sleep in your parents' bed
you cross a magic stile.
Instead of leas of dark backyard

you're in a town, where streetlight slips
through windows gowned in white;
tall bars of yellow ride the walls

whenever cars go by. And you dream—
grids of silent light, floating formations
like chenille against a blackout sky.

Married, you move across the street.
The house you looked out from
becomes the view, the front room now is yours

but the sun rises wrong,
your head lies north instead of east.
The woman in the house has changed.

The mother still brings fresh baked bread
and Sunday pastries, but they taste
like a gift not yours by right.

Whole worlds hang on small geographies,
like a man moving from bed to a grave
only a mile away. Not even a mile.

Homage to Saint Cyril

Thessaloniki, Makedonía

It is the sound of water's footsteps:
out of the equation for a word,
a province so vast its center is nowhere,
an angel's language the blesséd tongue bespeaks.

Out of the equation for a word,
out of the shimmering river of speech,
an angel's language the blesséd tongue bespeaks.
A river of memory. A voluble silence:

out of the shimmering river of speech,
where stones drift and carry, particles of light:
a river of memory, a voluble silence.
From ash, lifted from a warmth that's past,

where stones drift and carry, particles of light.
Out of the south the incunabula rose,
from ash, lifted from a warmth that's past,
flowing north to Moravia, Serbia, and Russia:

out of the south the incunabula rose,
these silences I do not understand,
flowing north to Moravia, Serbia, and Russia:
a rhythmic hymn, rivering.

These silences I do not understand:
It is an illusion that thoughts are in our heads
a rhythmic hymn, rivering.
We are like the sea, and the stream

It is an illusion that thoughts are in our heads
We are whole only in our thoughts

We are like the sea, and the stream
Curving through the heart of the sea

We are whole only in our thoughts
Out from the shores of Thessalonika and Ohrid,
Curving through the heart of the sea
prophets carried the ikon of glagolithic runes.

Out from the shores of Thessalonika and Ohrid,
cresting the white arch of a wave,
prophets carried the ikon of glagolithic runes:
a love of words, eternal as wind.

Cresting the white arch of a wave,
to trap the voices of the wind in bars
(a love of words, eternal as wind),
he bonded fragments into a cage of letters:

to trap the voices of the wind in bars.
And the wild Khazars heard his prayer:
he bonded fragments into a cage of letters,
saw their offerings rise, like birds, and vanish.

And the wild Khazars heard his prayer,
a voice in song, pretending to be heard:
saw their offerings rise, like birds, and vanish.
Placing the last gold coin on his tongue, he died.

A voice in song, pretending to be heard:
a province so vast its center is nowhere.
Placing the last gold coin on his tongue, he died.
It is the sound of water's footsteps.

Jazz

for William Matthews (1942–1997)

Perhaps, when it comes time to catalog the pantheon
of those who stormed this way through our dark

century, you'll be remembered best by your grim
wit, that rind of soul you left behind. Death bides

its time and then eats straight through us. Why else
call it a body of work? You were a Horace for your age . . .

One could do worse. One could hardly do better
than to imagine you content on that Sabine farm

or indolent on Parnassus' slopes; instead, we'd see you
tilting back in your I'll-be-here-awhile slouch against

disorder, sipping a little Scotch, and drifting on
the cool riffs of blues you'll learn to love, again.

You'll light another cigarette. The afterlife (which you
once hoped "doesn't go on long") is easy: You just

push off from the heartbreak and go on to the sublime.
Time to play the high note, time to tell all you know

but won't be telling: the story of our lives. And just
remember this: like blind Homer, joshing to his faithful

dog the morning after of his wine-dark pee, life's sweet
secret is its predicaments. Dire time will hector all of us.

We'll see you there, with Mingus at the Showplace,
who'll snarl across the stage, "We've suffered a crescendo

in personnel." And he'll smile. Even in death, the poet
improvises. The band plays on. As if we had a choice.

Heron on the Dam

The cormorant across the water first catches the eye,
crescent wings held open to wind and sun—
perfect feathered cruciform—

then a slender shape off to the right
asserts itself like a statue
suddenly spied in a niched garden of the wealthy,
the perfect blend, like the tobacco mix
my grandfather sought in Amsterdam,

but the heron's gray, his thin legs a miracle
to hold him against the flow, and I turn

to look after my son—all this is taking place
in the middle of a perfect New England village—
and note how leaves on the mill pond have formed
an exact map of Surinam, where tobacco is harvested,
then shipped to Holland, where my grandfather
inspects it, before sending it on to Virginia

from whence it enters our feeble American lungs
troubled enough by this perfect Maine air
we're always hearing about, gilded today,

not like lilies, but like the light
in Old Master Renderings of the Annunciation,
the dove flying in nonstop on glory rays . . .

My son tugs at me, and the heron makes a perfect
one-hop takeoff, not disturbing a soul,
not even the cormorant, drying in the sunset,

as dark and radiant and perfect
as Christ forgotten on his perch on Calvary.

The Properties of Light

Isn't the whole world heaven's coast?
— Mark Doty

I come for the light, the artist says.
Dawn and again at sunset,
he goes to the Provincetown beach,
sets up his easel. At just the right angle,
he can catch that light on the canvas.

He uses words like *shimmer, glow, radiance.*
He talks about what our forefathers must have been
when they woke that first dawn just off the coast.
He darkens the room, lights up the wall
with his slides. We see
not the play of light against dark,
but the play of light against light.
We see it in the rocks, the beached whale,
the bones of dead fish.

In the last days of my father's life,
he kept calling me—Elaine, Elaine—
even though I was in the next room
or the same room and he didn't need
or want anything. He kept doing it.
If I answered, he'd know
he was still alive, and if I didn't,
he was dead.
The last time he called, he held out
his hand, all blue veins and bones now.
His head fell back, the skin
on his face smoothed out.

What I remember is the light,
how it slipped into the room and took him.

In that moment, the light was different,
and I saw my father as I had never seen
him before—young, full of wonder,
and in no pain at all.

To the Boy Saved from Drowning

So in the days
the moss had no stones
wild turkeys picked among
ruins of winter
deer browsed the brown margins

there was only the smoke
of my fire and the Milky Way.

From nothing,
from empty slumber
great blue the preacher
knee-deep in water,
tall in his tattered coat.

As it happened, I sunned
my young body on the wing dam
where the river swallowed a boy
whole and helpless as I was
at my own baptism.

I thrust my arm
into the rush of waters
and hauled him up,
dripping like a newborn
onto the thigh of the dam.

Three wives and at least
as many children, counting you.
Three bags of truth, I said.

And he rubbed his eyes,
glared at me as if I had

either pushed or fathered him.

You are the mud god himself,
he said. Now you know the truth.
Be silent. No talking.

The larger and small are singing.
The things will take it from here.

And we both
crawled off toward that
for which we had been saved.

Quiddity

I'll take the gentle cat
who wandered off into the snow
among abandoned carcasses
of trucks and cars over the hill
for what had been our love.

And what of the other one
who was too afraid to stray,
this pillow of a cat who still
lies next to me night after night
when I'm in bed?

This one adores me.
Lays her head against my chest
and combs my beard
with her claws.

She purrs and stretches,
and pretends she would never
kill me in my sleep.

The Language Animal

Because he can speak, because he can use his words, a whole headful
of them, he gives everything
names, even things calling themselves,
forever, something else.
Because he can speak he can efficiently lie,
or obscure with such brilliance
a listener with less language
is glad to lose more of it.
Because he can speak
he will be lonely
because those who speak back speak another language
of other derivations.
Because he can speak he speaks.
Because he can speak he can pray out loud.
Because he can speak the predators are drawn to him in the night.
Because he can speak
he invented the ear, then two, to better hear himself speak.
Because he can speak he thought he could sing.
Because he can speak
he has one more thing to do
besides searching for food
or hiding so as not to *be* food.
Because he can speak he draws a full breath
and speaks,
in sentences, each one beginning with a large letter
and ending with a period,
or the soon-to-be-invented marks
that indicate bewilderment and awe.

The Devil's Beef Tub

There are mysteries—why a duck's quack
doesn't echo anywhere
and: Does God exist?—which
will remain always as mysteries. So
the same with certain abstracts
aligned with sensory life: the tactile,
for example, of an iron bar
to the forehead. Murder
is abstract, an iron bar to the skull
is not. Oh lost
and from the wind not a single peep of grief!
One day you're walking down the street
and a man with a machete-shaped shard
of glass (its hilt
wrapped in a bloody towel) walks towards you,
purposefully, on a mission.
Do you stop to discuss hermeneutics with him?
Do you engage him in a discussion about Derrida?
Do you worry that Derrida might be the cause of his rage?
Every day is like this,
is a metaphor or a simile: like opening a can
of alphabet soup
and seeing nothing but Xs, no, look
closer: little noodle
swastikas.

Terminal Lake

Although they know no other waters
and have no creation myths,
the fish don't like it here: no way out,
no river to swim upstream or down.
Terminal Lake squats there,
its belly filled by springs, oh rain
and ice and snow. It's deep,
Terminal Lake, and no one's gone to the bottom
and come back up.
All's blind down there, and cold.
From above, it's a huge black coin,
it's as if the real lake is drained
and this lake is the drain: gaping, language-
less suck- and sinkhole.

Render, Render

Boil it down: feet, skin, gristle,
bones, vertebrae, heart muscle, boil
it down, skim, and boil
again, boil and skim
in closed cauldrons, boil your horse, his hooves,
the runned-over dog you loved, the girl
by the pencil sharpener
who looked at you, looked away,
boil that for hours, render it
down, take more from the top as more settles to the bottom,
the heavier, the denser, throw in ache
and sperm, and a bead
of sweat that slid from your armpit to your waist
as you sat stiff-backed before a test, turn up
the fire, boil and skim, boil
some more, add a fever
and the virus that blinded an eye, now's the time
to add guilt and fear, throw
logs on the fire, coal, gasoline, throw
two goldfish in the pot (their swim bladders
used for "clearing"), boil and boil, render
it down and distil,
concentrate
that for which there is *no*
other use at all, boil it down, down,
then stir it with rosewater, this
which is now one dense, fatty, scented, red essence
which you smear on your lips
and go forth
to plant as many kisses upon the world
as the world can bear!

Heaven
for Jack Wiler

I want to believe death is a simple relocation
when I pack up like I'm going for the weekend
but once arrive decide to stay because the afternoon

gin doesn't turn mean within my throat,
and the slant of light is fitting, almost blue,
and everyone who walks by the pool has long legs,

good calves, and I brown easily, never burn.
An extended holiday that turns to expatriation and only
wistfully do I miss what is left behind like that dress hanging

in my closet that I paid too much for but fits just right.
This will be the place where my bad habits and afflictions
do not follow—where I can walk into the sea without fear of sharks

because I don't even remember watching *Jaws* four times,
or fear of cutting coral since that scar on the bottom
of my foot isn't even there anymore—and I am barefoot,

cool sand for miles, and I swim for miles and get lost without worry
since I've already drowned in one form or another, and at night
sparrows nest against my throat and I won't be pecked like I was

when I was five and startled a mother Jay, and I'll be able to
remember that time because heaven is the kind of place
I can announce that I've let go of cumbersome fears

so those I meet who I don't remember, but want to remember,
can then say to me: *you've done so well.*

There's a Pig Outside

The waiter in here has a concussion from coming
onto another guy's woman says she slipped him her number
nothing he asked for but her boyfriend hit him over the head with a
      flashlight
knocked him out for thirty minutes and he looks bad today Sunday
      and I say *no wonder*
I didn't see you Friday when did it happen he says *Thursday night*
      went to the hospital
the next day my neck hurt from when I hit concrete steps and I think
      he really looks like shit
thought he'd been in a car crash and he goes on about the heavy
      flashlight and all
I can think of is Carrot the pig eating frozen yogurt outside this
      place
it's not every day one meets a slab of bacon intact slopping and
      burping off
a spoon so I ask the woman the pig's with *is it full-grown* she says
      he's ten I comment on dry skin
looks like your pig has dry skin she says *yes pigs are like that* I ask *what do*
      you do about it
she says *whatever any good lubricant* while I'm blown away because
the big she calls him
Carrot is snorting and grunting and I'm wondering what kind of a
      mess he'd make but she says
he's trained like a dog so I say *what do you feed him besides yogurt* she
      says *chow pig chow* and
proceeds to have him sit stay shake a leg rewarding him with a dog
      biscuit so I say *I've heard*
pigs are good pets she says *I don't recommend them* and I wonder why
      did she keep Carrot
all these years but guess it's like any pet one's responsible the
      moment one says

look, look at that cute piglet and now she has a two-hundred-twenty-
pound pig

not hog hogs are fatter I read that in some article and I say *I'm pretty
repulsed by your pig*

she chuckles says she understands it's like that whenever they come
to town for treats

and at that moment her girlfriend joins us drinking a cappuccino and
offers some to Carrot

the first woman says *come on Babe you know Carrot doesn't do well
on caffeine*

and I'm thinking I'm pretty sophisticated but a big pig with sparse
black hair dry skin and tiny

hooves resembling high heeled shoes and some bozo with a
concussion knocked out that pig

are just too much for one afternoon.

§

WILLIAM MATTHEWS

1942–1997

When William Matthews died in 1997 at the age of fifty-five, contemporary American poetry lost its shrewdest practitioner. In his poems and in his teaching (at The Frost Place and elsewhere), Matthews presented America with the gift of a deeply intelligent scrutiny that refused to take itself too seriously. As the translator of Latin poets such as Horace and Martial, he knew that worldliness was a long-standing antidote to self-regard. Indeed, Matthews relished the world (most expressively, perhaps, in his bittersweet poems about jazz) but he knew that no one gave a damn about ardor. It was more likely to give you heartache or a stomachache than a front row seat. Given this knowledge, his refusal to succumb to wry fretting is all the more impressive. He examined himself (and, at times, his society) and he let the often unhappy chips fall where they might fall. His wit, as another age might have said, was in service to his honesty.

Many readers consider Matthews's "On the Porch at The Frost Place, Franconia, NH" to be his signature poem. He lived a summer in that house and he had a good measure of Robert Frost's relentlessness in his own bones. In that poem he salutes Frost candidly and touches the actualities of Frost's environs (these swift / and aching summers") so as to see with his own eyes the "opacities" both poets treasured yet refused to indulge. Matthews, like Frost, was a thinker in his poems and respected the pure pungency of statement. Toward the end of the poem he writes that

"Frost's great poems
like all great poems, conceal
what they merely know, to be
predicaments."

Those lines refer to Matthews's poems too. He lives in his art, and this book, so full of moving poems, is an appropriate offering to two masters whose names deserve to be linked.

— Baron Wormser

107th & Amsterdam

A phalanx of cabs surges uptown in tune
to the staggered lights and two young black
men spurt across the dark avenue (two A.M.)

ahead of them: We're here, motherfuckers,
don't mess up. Three of five cabs honk: We're here
too, older and clawing for a living, don't

fuck up. The cabs rush uptown and the lights
go green ahead like a good explanation.
Everyone knows this ballet. Nobody falls or brakes.

Tonight I talked for hours and never said
one thing so close to the truculent heart of speech
as those horn blats, that dash across Amsterdam,

not to persuade nor to be understood but
a kind of signature, a scrawl on the air:
We're here, room for all of us if we be alert.

Mingus at The Showplace

I was miserable, of course, for I was seventeen,
and so I swung into action and wrote a poem,

and it was miserable, for that was how I thought
poetry worked: you digested experience and shat

literature. It was 1960 at The Showplace, long since
defunct, on West 4th St., and I sat at the bar,

casting beer money from a thin reel of ones,
the kid in the city, big ears like a puppy.

And I knew Mingus was a genius. I knew two
other things, but as it happened they were wrong.

So I made him look at the poem.
"There's a lot of that going around," he said,

and Sweet Baby Jesus he was right. He glowered
at me but he didn't look as if he thought

bad poems were dangerous, the way some poets do.
If they were baseball executives they'd plot

to destroy sandlots everywhere so that the game
could be saved from children. Of course later

that night he fired his pianist in mid-number
and flurried him from the stand.

"We've suffered a diminuendo in personnel,"
he explained, and the band played on.

Homer's Seeing-Eye Dog

Most of the time he wrote, a sort of sleep
with a purpose, so far as I could tell.
How he got from the dark of sleep
to the dark of waking up I'll never know;
the lax sprawl sleep allowed him
began to set from the edges in,
like a custard, and then he was awake—
me too, of course, wriggling my ears
while he unlocked his bladder and stream
of dopey wake-up jokes. The one
about the wine-dark pee I hated instantly.
I stood at the ready, like a god
in an epic, but there was never much
to do. Oh, now and then I'd made a sure
intervention, save a life, whatever.
But my exploits don't interest you,
and of his life all I can say is that
when he'd poured out his work
the best of it was gone and then he died.
He was a great man and I loved him.
Not a whimper about his sex life—
how I detest your prurience—
but here's a farewell literary tip:
I myself am the model for Penelope.
Don't snicker, you hairless moron,
I know so well what "faithful" means—
there's not even a word for it in Dog.
I just embody it. I think you bipeds
have a catchphrase for it: "To thine own self
be true . . ." though like a blind man's shadow,
the second half is only there for those who know
it's missing. Merely a dog, I'll tell you
what it is: ". . . as if you had a choice."

Writer-in-Residence

Blowsy geraniums, clay pots, stained here
by water and blanched there by Rapid Gro,
a restive cat with the idle in its throat tuned high . . .

No wonder summer is like a series of paintings:
it lacks verbs, though lacks is a verb, and is.
Time sags like a slack flag. But Shop N Save

has sold summer's last raspberry, and beyond
the topspinning rim of the horizon, dutiful
fall is kneading a squall of work and metabolic

dither. If time is money, teachers are shabbiest
of all the summer rich. The rest of the year we rejoin
the poor we refused to use our educations to escape.

I'm a swarm of pleasantries for my first class.
O syllabus and charisma! But chill is in the air,
and the old rage for work gathers against my indolence.

On the Porch at The Frost Place, Franconia, NH

for Stanley Plumly

So here the great man stood,
fermenting malice and poems
we have to be nearly as fierce
against ourselves as he
not to misread by their disguises.
Blue in dawn haze, the tamarack
across the road is new since Frost
and thirty feet tall already.
No doubt he liked to scorch off
morning fog by simply staring through it
long enough so that what he saw
grew visible. "Watching the dragon
come out of the Notch," his children
used to call it. And no wonder
he chose a climate whose winter
and house whose isolation could be
stern enough to his wrath and pity
as to make them seem survival skills
he'd learned on the ob, farming
fifty acres of pasture and woods.
For cash crops he had sweat and doubt
and moralizing rage, those staples
of the barter system. And these swift
and aching summers, like the blackberries
I've been poaching down the road
from the house where no one's home –
acid at first and each little globe
of the berry too taut and distinct
from the others, then they swell to hold
the riot of their juices and briefly
the fat berries are perfected to my taste,

and then they begin to leak and blob
and under their crescendo of sugar
I can taste how they make it through winter....
By the time I'm back from a last,
six-berry raid, it's almost dusk,
and more and more mosquitoes
will race around my ear their tiny engines,
the speedboats of the insect world.
I won't be longer on the porch
than it takes to look out once
and see what I've taught myself
in two months here to discern:
night restoring its opacities,
though for an instant as intense
and evanescent as waking from a dream
of eating blackberries and almost
being able to remember it, I think
I see the parts – haze, dusk, light
broken into grains, fatigue,
the mineral dark of the White Mountains,
the wavering shadows steadying themselves –
separate, then joined, then seamless:
the way, in fact, Frost's great poems,
like all great poems, conceal
what they merely know, to be
predicaments. However long
it took to watch what I thought
I saw, it was dark when I was done,
everywhere and on the porch,
and since nothing stopped
my sight, I let it go.

A Night in a World

I wouldn't have known if I didn't stay home
where the big dipper rises from, time
and again: one mountain ash.

And I wouldn't have thought without travelling out
how huge that dipper was,
how small that tree.

Fix

I.

I needle April into letting go:
out of a white all winter
we mistook for poverty, the world turns
suddenly indulgent, dealing

pinwheels and color wheels, springing
songbirds down buttered wires, waxing
the lips of women red, unrumpling all
the hearth-devoted dogs. The senses

split their pods—switchblades hatch
in the hands of the *nouveaux riches*.
The eye gets flashy with a superficial wit
and jets flock to the big blue bedroom,

trailing their ribbons of emission.
Green has made its inroads in your eyes:
you envy all of nature. But I unzip
your outerskin, and basketsful of pink

and white carnations flower forth. My hands
are full of health, they tremble on the verge of your
having, the one hooked eye to go, one undone rainbow,
prism of liquid, lip of spill—

II.

Far and away the strictest sun
is stationed overhead, its lashes
keep an eye on us. We don't look up
from loving. Therefore he,

held-bent on pleasure, readies
himself to come. He straps the fashionable
parachute upon his borrowed frame, and hums
a human tune. We hear him approach and then

we hear him hover there, for what seems hours,
in the season's wings, the near
obscene old god, revving and revving his
devil-may-care machine.

HEATHER McHUGH

Excerpt from an Argument with Enthusiasts, Concerning Inspiration

I agree that something
greatens us,
but intelligence doesn't enter into it.
At the moment I can calmly say
that we turn certain
switches, certain
lights go on; that there are rational
tricks to make
things go away and things arrive.

But with whatever brilliance in
the middle of the night
in whatever living-room we sit down and discuss
what dead men know, things
we can only intuit
breathe in the room. The curtain
fattens and collapses, swells again. Nobody
hears his own voice right.

The mind is flashy, yes, but take
the stupid wind away and say what's left alive.

Breathless is dead, however bright.

The Field

It was my day to study
in the field. I found
fences strung with glass beads,
small possessions of shock (signs of his
and hers). I couldn't make myself
at home. I lowed,
so the cow would,
but the cow looked up,
misquoted. When I got back to the house
my five hired fellow-specialists

were taping their abstracts
to the window. Soon it would be dark.

Intraterrestrials

The body alters more rapidly than a planet.
A hole in the lungs' upper atmosphere?
—no question of cause and effect. Here
a lover drowns in her own melt-off; here a brother
evaporates in the heat of his own atoms.
Everybody should almost die at least once
in a lifetime, my friend, the brain
tumor survivor, says. And it's true. In pain
the body is its own Mount Everest. Gobi of
the thorax, tropic of the abdomen, Antarctica
of the extremities. Yet there is no word
for *yes* among Pain's people. Even our dearest
bravest are involuntary explorers. Enough,
and the poles of the body reverse:
every wind blowing in the wrong
direction, the self can't find its feet. Thumb back
an eyelid, and the eye is all surface, its attention
concentrated on the depths. One thinks of the eyes
of fish. In there all fish are sharks. Off
with an arm, out with a belly. All flesh is meat
in the killer's ontology. Pain? Among sharks, only sharks
have feelings. As if on a distant planet
the ozone layer thins and thins.
Losing my hair was the most traumatic
experience of my life, complains a customer
in an ad for Rogaine. *Lucky him*,
whispers the man in bed B, between waves,
his body swelling wherever it doesn't shrink.
Odd what messages reach them.
There isn't another body in the world
that can feel my father's pain. Still as if our
feelings mattered, he strains to cover
his exposed testicles with his good hand.

Rather

Let us leave that one last clump
in the cat box undisturbed for them
to witness while they are ill, or that corner
of the bathroom mirror uncleaned,
let the flecks of toothpaste accumulate
there in flocks for them to notice, so
they cannot be missed, as we assist them
at the toilet or during their towel baths;
whatever the former duties of our ill,
let us do them well, yes, but not nearly so well
as they did when well. So too, let us not
assume our grown children despise us
when they leave that last bit of painting
or yard work undone, unfinished, though
we've long since paid them; rather
let us understand how much our loved ones
still need us to want us to need them.

Why We Need Poetry

Everyone else is in bed, it being, after all,
three in the morning, and you can hear
how quiet the house has become each time
you pause in the conversation you are having
with your close friend to take a bite
of your sandwich. Is it getting the wallpaper
around you in the kitchen up at last
that makes cucumbers and white bread, the only
things you could find to eat, taste so good,
or is it the satisfaction of having discovered
a project that could carry the two of you
into this moment made for nobody else?
Either way, you're here in the pleasure
of the tongue, which continues after
you've finished your sandwich, for now
you are savoring the talk alone—how
by staring at the band of fluorescent light
over the sink or the pattern you hadn't
noticed in the wallpaper, you can see
where the sentence you've started, line
by line, should go. Only love could lead you
to think this way, or to care so little
about how you speak, you end up saying
what you care most about exactly right,
each small allusion growing larger
in the light of your friend's eye.
And when the light itself grows larger,
it's not the next day coming through the windows
of that redone kitchen, but you,
changed by your hunger for the words
you listen to and speak, their taste
which you can never get enough of.

Love Handles

If the biker's head where the hair was
shines in the sun while he blows
into his helmet to get the heat out
of it, she doesn't mind. It's not him
with the bald spot, it's just him. And she likes
feeling the fleshy overhang in the front
when she climbs on behind and takes him
into her arms. How else could he carry her
up and up the wild, quick-five-
note scale that they float off on? Anyway,
who doesn't love a belly? Forget the revulsion
we're supposed to feel looking at the before picture
in the diet ad and remember the last time
you asked a good friend you hadn't seen in years,
What's *this*? patting where the shirt
stuck out. Or think of feeling somebody's
back, like the two old lovers laying in bed, she
turned away from him inquiring over her shoulder
with her finger, What's that, right there, is it
a bug bite or a mole? And he, the one trusted
with this place so private not even she
can see it, touching it, not skin or flesh
in this special, ordinary moment but something
else, something more, like the hand the hunched
old lady has in hers going across the fast-food
parking lot. Beside her an old man, the hand's
owner, is walking with what you and I
might think of as a sort of kick
over and over, but what they don't think of at all,
balancing each other like this so they can arrive
together to get a burger. The point is, you can't
begin to know how to hold another body
in your eye until you've held it a few times

in your hand or in your arms. Any ten couples
at the Fireman's Ball could tell you that. Put aside
your TV dreams of youth running its fingers
over the hood of a new car, or the smiling
faces of Tammy the weather girl and Bob on sports,
she with the unreal hair and he with the hair
that's not real, and imagine the baldies
with their corsaged wives under the whirling
chunks of light at the Ball. Think of their innocence,
all dressed up to be with the ones they've known
all their lives. See how after those years
of nudging and hugging and looking each other all over,
they glide, eyes closed, on love handles across the floor.

JACQUELINE MICHAUD

Looking West from
the Causeway

Maybe the light's what stopped me, the golden type we see
on summer afternoons that now was shimmering on flats tundra-like,
either side of the divide, turning them sweet shades of honey
between blue snow devils sweeping over

lunar-like mounds of white mud dunes. And off to the West,
where the water wasn't hard but open in patches, here and there
were heaps of fowl, white-dusted ducks huddled to keep warm,
though at first I thought they'd died of freezing

there in the middle of all the dazzling. And beyond were layers
of cold and warm light filtering through sea smoke of a silver
gauzed gray, and above that the deepest jade-green treeline
topped at its tips with thin strips of lavender and baby-blanket

pink pulled up to a babier-blue sky puffed by roly-poly clouds shot
through with hints of prismatic color. But, here's the thing:
one of those clouds became a diaphanous Dragon advancing
in slowest motion, from the mountainville side

to the sunshine side, his belly full of the sun glowing through,
and he was opening and closing his jaws, just gobbling up
the scenery—sea smoke me and all rising to meet him and, O,
it was so stunning! I wanted to cry, but knew

that would be a cheap thing to do, making emotion the meaning,
instead of just sitting there, quietly and letting sight be.
So I looked, and looked, and looked . . .
feeling happy no traffic came either direction.

And after a while I resolved to head home and write someone
who might conceivably care to know how afternoon sunshine,
in the midst of the causeway, in the middle of winter-
time goes.

King William Park

Flat on my back in the dead roses, I tried
to outstare the full moon's Sabbatarian
eye, and failed. Conscience is blackout—

the Rigger, my father, does my remembering,
dead-drunk in his neglected grave. At least
his guess, or anyone's, is as good as mine.

Little Alice was a victim of the cold war—
I swigged my brother's vodka and I shrank
and withered till I looked like a Methuselah.

When the barman barred me with a curse
I was the drink-witch who hexed his clientele,
plucking the Tampax from under my skirt

—that was when the bastard called the police—
and chucking it among the lunchtime crowd.
I was the shit who threw bleach in his face.

Daybreak's a throat scald, aftershave or schnapps.
That white eye hasn't slept a wink all night.
Memory's a baby cancer trying to grow up,

a skin graft or a transplant that won't take.
In daylight almost everything says DRINK ME.
The moon's policemen batter me awake.

Pietà

They carry him via the off-sales to the squat,
throw him down on somebody's mattress
and undress him. As he sprawls like a god

they unlace the calf-length oxblood Docs,
unstrap and peel off the three layers
of slashed and fraying bondage trousers

like a month-old bandage on a wound.
They raise him, gently, and draw up
the cutaway denim and the black tee shirt.

There's a red tattoo under the left nipple
and fading bruises all over his rib cage
from a kicking doled out in a boozer.

He opens an eye. Sinead swims into view
climbing uncarpeted stairs in bare feet,
already stripped down to her underwear.

Too stoned to stay awake, let alone fuck,
he goes under as she climbs on top,
and dreams of being a splinter in her heel.

Elementary School with Magnolia Trees

Tall chimneys
quad a memory across the sky,
years after the doors closed
shutting rooms where
our coats and lives lay knitted
in words and numbers; rooms
we parsed everyday
long into the afternoons.

That spring we planted
three magnolia trees, one
by the playground proper and two
each side the front walk,
that lead to the arched double doors.
A tree for each child
Olivia
Gail
and Tip,
killed Palm Sunday.
In a loud, horrific
instant of steel and glass
they were gone.
Mother
played organ and taught piano.

Grandmother
told fortunes and ghost stories
took every neighborhood kid
fishing and to the park.

Father
demon behind
the new car wheel.

That green and white
Oldsmobile, one of the first
after the war. He drove
it like a rocket, swooped down
the valley, tore up the hill and spread
them all like a new constellation
among the stars.

Mingei

Well, my darling, this mingei kimono's come pretty far, first
departure from some obscure prefecture in Japan, swooping
       nonstop
across the Pole on square wings to roost like a brooding
angular mantis in a chic little shop in Sag Harbor. Perhaps it dreams
of whales, or secret breasts nesting in basket-weave triangles.
There is no closure, no cincture to availability, although the
       Prada-clad
geisha is happy to supply a thin, blue belt.

I remember buying you this garment, in dark and light hope
that its triangles could poultice the sting of your daughter's contempt
for you and me and what we were up to.
You never wore it. It hung in sorrow on the back of your wardrobe
until one evening I put it on, solving my own equation. Fingering

this puzzle fabric now I think of the book of *shunga*, women
with high, lacquered hair and vacant expressions presenting their slit
       sex
between legs impossibly placed, reclining in inscrutable geometry
before their partners' giant phalluses curved and dangerous as war
       swords,
everything always about to begin.

Mingei: antique Japanese folk textile.generally dark blue and white
Shunga: 18th century Japanese erotic art

The Treaty

My grandfather, Frank Regan, cross-shanked, his shoulders in a moult,
steadies the buff
of his underparts against the ledge of the chimney-bluff
of the mud-walled house in Cullenramer

in which, earlier, he had broken open a bolt
of the sky-stuff
and held it to the failing light, having himself failed to balance
      Gormley's cuffs.
This Collins, Gormley had wagged, is a right flimflammer.

Cross-shanked against the chimney-bluff, he's sizing up what follows
from our being on the verge
of nation-

hood when another broad-lapelled, swallow-tailed swallow
comes at a clip through the dusk-blue serge
to make some last-minute alterations.

The Last Time I Saw Chris

In Amagansett, for crying out loud, setting the arm of his French
            helpmeet
towards a funky-as-it-gets exhibit in the Crazy Monkey,
a cross-cut saw
in the window not quite making up for this not quite being Long
            Island Sound,
the gobs of tar
on his and his buddy's pants

suggesting they might have been willing participants
in some recent keel-hauling. Blown, too, the opportunity to meet
and greet an incipient Jack Tar
or wannabe grease monkey
in an outhouse wired, for the love of mike, for sound.
When he turned away from me I could have sworn I saw

a woman on a seesaw
from the seventies, still flying a flag for the seventies. That's what
            was with the hotpants.
The politest way of putting it would be to say she and I'd been
            trying to sound
each other out, though it seemed unlikely ever the twain would
            meet.
She was just back from Benin. No monkey
business without an overcoat, for crying out loud. No losing the
            ship for a ha'p'orth of tar.

Not ship, I was treading water. Sheep. A sheep being the avatar
of no god we know of, always the best kind. For she was musing on
            an ancient saw
having to do with a monkey
and paying p(e)an(u)ts

to the guide, for the love of mike, who'd led her hunting trip. A
      hartebeest meet
summoned by a hartebeest bugle, a sound

that had barely the strength to resound
through the bush. Boots and saddles. The clench of Wright's Coal
      Tar
as she suddenly deemed it meet
to turn the other cheek, for crying out loud, looking back at me as if
      she saw that I foresaw
the needle-tracks just above the line of her pants
when her arms would set from years of firing up, as if I foresaw the
monkey

on her back (les ans, mon ange, les ans manqués),
as if I might look forward from an era in which we were all still
      relatively sound
in wind and limb to an era of night sweats, gasps and pants,
for the love of mike, now threatening to tar
all of us, straight or gay, with the same brush, the god who oversaw
our not knowing of him yearning now to mete

out retribution as the hartebeest pants for cooling streams,
      taratantara, taratantara,
our breathing indistinguishable now from the sound of a saw
through the breast of a monkey, for crying out loud, through
      monkey- or other bush meat.

Choice

We each owed allegiance to a demanding god.
Your god asked that you attach to nothing, to no one,
but the illusion of choice. When, in fact, you had no choice—

you were the one waiting for invitation, always. Then you
were given lives to create, convictions. I too lived in that illusion,
writing poems alone in the middle of the night. Without choice,
there is no knowledge, she said. This was our reward for our godly

devotion. To hold up, at the end of one's day, the semblance
of free act. But the image failed us. We should have drawn
strength from this tradition, we should have been blessed, but
we were sentenced to keep entering that same door, opening on

the first set of revelations: the man's face and the woman's—
                                        on fire, impassable.

Le Jazz Hot

At two in the morning, I opened the balcony doors.
It was there in the distance—ridiculous, unreal:
Eiffel Tower under a full moon. Across the boulevard,
the Metro: ST. GERMAIN des PRES (it)—there at the stop
a man playing a saxophone, back to me, petitioning the moon.

I swear that I understood the importance of what I was
being shown, though his improvisation offered choice after
choice I could not follow. For which did we long? (I
wondered as you slept) Grief or ongoingness? Go or stay?
Love or hate? The sax insisting, that dark averted face.

Dawn Mass, Past

Unstoppable courier, no news in her pack, she
plunges through the new drifts, opening a path.
It's dawn and twenty below, the Holy Spirit
flickers in a streetlamp's lantern, turns back
to glass as she passes, nine and fanatical,

blue-legged, in high boots. *Who made the cold?*
Satan made the cold: catechetical, depthless.
God was improvisational, less dependable:
Glassed-in orchids *here*, a tornado *there*.

Satan burned slowly along his great spine
of ice, turned away, meditating, as the sky
grew light. Thus cold was made cold by pure thought,
implacable, progressive as the idea of Self . . .

Who made you? God made me. But Satan made
the deep façade of longing—Satan made this day
wherein she stands alone on the snow-blocked steps
waiting for a sign—before her mittened hand

shatters the sheer thin surface, half-formed,
over the still water blessed in its marble bowl.

MIRIAM MÖRSEL NATHAN

We Will Find Out Later How to Catch a Whistling Bird

In a moment, a man will ride his bicycle
with branches of purple lilacs cascading

over the handlebars. He will send the flowers
to his beloved this morning. Later, he will

bring her a basket of gooseberries, and in the evening,
he will show her how to catch a whistling bird

with twigs and bananas. But for now, the man
rests his head on a flat stone in the forest and

opens his mouth to catch a waterfall of orchids.

Goliath

Another lynching. Madness grips the South.
A black man's hacked-off penis in his mouth,
his broken body torched. The terrorized
blacks cower, and the whites are satanized.
His students ask, in Carver's Bible class:
Where is God now? What does He want from us?

Professor Carver smiles. "God is right here.
Don't lose contact with Him. Don't yield to fear.
Fear is the root of hate, and hate destroys
the hater. When Saul's army went to war
against the Philistines, the Israelites
lost contact, fearful of Goliath's might.

"When we lose contact, we see only hate,
only injustice, a giant so great
its shadow blocks our sun. But David slew
Goliath with the only things he knew:
the slingshot of intelligence, and one
pebble of truth. And the battle was done.

"We kill Goliath by going about
the business of the universal good
which our Creator wills, obediently
yielding to Him the opportunity
to work wonders through us for all of His children.
That's all. Read Samuel I, verse forty-seven."

Live Jazz, Franklin Park Zoo

Kubie sobbed when a nearby jazz band stopped playing.
— Christian Science Monitor, 8/27/96

A tree grew. Oh, remembering gorillas!
O Orpheus singt! Oh, Africa in the ear!
The recluse, Vip, came out. Gigi sat still
and wide-eyed, black face pressed against the bars.

Kubie lay on his back, as he usually does,
vacantly staring. Then he turned over, hairy chin
on one huge leather palm; with his other hand
he scratched his head, contemplatively picked his nose.

The zebras' ears twirled. Behind their fancy fences,
the silenced animals listened to something new.
Suddenly their calls, even the lion's roar,

shrank in their hearts, as they knew something more.
And where there had been, at most, a nest of boughs
to receive it, music built a cathedral in their senses.

Like Princes of Serendip

for Nicole Boudreau and Arthur Papas
10/12/02

In the Ur-ancient Persian fairy-tale
about the Three Princes of Serendip
linguists find the etymological
source of the concept "serendipity."
The princes stumble onto fabulous
coincidence, as wonderful as love,
like the coincidence that introduced
two neighbors, worlds away from where they live.
What are the chances of meeting one's mate
on a beach in Aruba? In the world?
In life at all? Can science calculate
the probability that Art and Nicole
would be singled out for special blessings,
among which is the gift of second sight?

For there is evidence of second sight:
this public proof of their ability
to see, in the beloved's eyes, the light

of a future of possibility.
And by that light to see that something more,
grander beyond all apprehension, lies,
like a new-found Pacific, in the vow
their wondering hearts speak with thanks-giving praise.
We come as their guests to the sacrament
which changes ordinary love to wine
that overflows the cup of wonderment.
We feast on the consecrated cuisine
of bread broken as a special blessing
for each of us, fallen though we may be.

To each of us, fallen though we may be—
away from love, or out of the habit
of being thankfully surprised daily
that we once had love, or that we have it,
now, miraculously by our side—
Nicole and Arthur offer a Eucharist
of prayer and promises. As groom and bride
they are crowned with their individual pasts
woven together, making one of two
'til death, for richer, poorer, better worse.
As husband and wife they walk together into
the endlessly expanding universe
of serendipitous special blessings,
praiseful as princes in the ancient tale.

Priceless

I tackled my brother in slo-mo
into the mothball smell of the chocolate
velvet couch with springs weaker

than slinkies. He refused to fumble
even as I threatened to bite his fingers
like a mad wolverine. *Stop roughhousing,*

Mom said, walking into the rec-room
for her eight o'clock show, *The Galloping
Gourmet*, with lipstick kisses

around the rim of her wine glass.
She never took notes, never made the recipes.
She smiled too long at every joke,

saying, *That's priceless.*
Afterwards, she threatened to toss our smelly sneakers
left under the couch in the morning trash

and ordered me to pull the curtains.
Our neighbors must think we're running a nudist colony,
she said, even though no one ever walked naked in our house.

Drunk, she snored like a horse
upstairs in bed. My brother played Alfred Hitchcock,
smothering me with a couch pillow,

until I death kicked free and decided to teach him
how to drink wine in the basement. I checked the old freezer
for the purple cow heart bearded with frost that I had won

in third grade dissection class. Mom kept every prize
we brought home, saying someday we would thank her.
You could put that heart in a new cow

and it would still work, I said. *Would not*,
my brother said. What I really wanted to know
was why such a dumb animal had such a big heart.

We drank the sour wine and pissed
off the back porch under the yellow bug lights.
My brother sprayed farther because he's fatter,

but he wasn't happy. *I hope the yard's dry*
when Mom wakes up, he said. *Forget it, dogs piss
here all the time*, I said.

Yeah, but she doesn't like them, either.

In Unison
for David Keller

Take the body
as subject, David: body
of knowledge, of isolation
by which I am made precious,
known as myself,
as you, human friend
are made precious and recognized,
the creature markings telling your story:
the crazy eyes and the hair standing up wild,
your square feet. These are not
insults, David. No! They are how
the Portuguese Captain,
ten miles out to sea, knows
the slow arching rise of the humpback
out of the blue grey currents and
names the heavy beast by her torn fin,
by the white speckled patterns on her face
before she sounds the water and is gone.

She is recognizable as are we.
The body names us—all
the organs in their glistening membranes
revealing themselves as you or me.
Our sheathed and separate lives
surfacing, cresting in the air to their own
undoing. All that is within us and without
expresses something that continues
to explode into matter. Glorious,
David, this fleeting saga of the body,
the way we must know ourselves and each other
by the skin's devotion to limits:
a living tension stretched

over the rim of the self as the skin
bends over the hollow gut of the drum
wanting finally to be open enough
to be free—so resonant as to sound
its solidarity with vastness:
deep calling to deep.

Woman Crossing Bridge

Heat rises up three stories of frost-scoured vines.
She knows few people, sits close to the classroom door,
Far from the thrust-open windows' screened drop.
Sweat bleeds into the armpits of corroded wool.

She remembers the counselor's eyelids at half-mast.
Words like skinned fists scrape her ears.
"What would you do if you felt like
Hitting the baby?" "Leave." "Leave where?" "Leave
The apartment." "What would you do...what would you do. . . ?"

She closes her notebook and pulls her coat tight.

She shoulders her way across the bridge.
Walks as far as she can from the chipped, enameled rail.
A mummy in lavender scarf, green coat.
"I don't think I love you anymore," her husband had said.
His words, with a marksman's accuracy,
       bull's-eye her disarmed, forsaken heart.
Too late to don a bulletproof vest.

"Breathing hurts," she replies to her vanished husband,
and her words disappear
in rib-aching arctic air.

It's cold in her tank of a car.
Her breath's frost obscures the windshield.
Her mittened hand swipes feverish circles.
Petra watches him at the daycare and at her family home at night.
Petra is the 'rock' of her name. Petra lets him sleep
In her closet-sized room in a bed of folded blankets.
Petra doesn't worry how she'll get through a sweat-soaked coward's
       "death-defying" day.

Petra doesn't worry how easy it'd be
        to wipe the smile off a baby's face.
Smoke billows like sleep-thick breath
        out the tailpipe's poisonous hole.

She pulls into the daycare's snowbank-bordered lot.
A gasp of warm air escapes out the cold metal door.
She draws his lung-filled heat into her arms.
Presses him to her unprotected chest.

The Class

We say things in this class. Like why it hurts.
But what they say outside of class is different; worse.
The teacher hears tales from the combat zone
Where the children live, conscripted at birth,
In dynamited houses. Like all draftees,
They have one job, survival,
And permit themselves some jokes.
Like my father hits the bottle. . .
And my mother. In my office a sofa,
Books, prints, disorder on the desk.
Everything paid for, chosen, they know that.
I've put myself in a drug rehab program
Or *I know I'm anorexic* or *The sonofabitch*
Was raping me for years and now
I'm so frightened for my little sister
But she refuses to talk to me.
Their nervous eyes glide over printed poems
I hand them, but nothing exactly sticks –
The black student pulled apart by his loyalties
Whose bravado breaks like a shoelace
At a cleaningman's curse, *you fucking Oreo.*
The homosexual drummer tapping out
A knee tune, wagging his Groucho brows.
Hey, you ought to meet my mom real soon.
Cause when I tell her, she's gonna die.
Abuse, attempted suicide, incest,
Craziness, these are common stories,
This street-to-street fighting
Yet these children are privileged.
They're eating.
They have their own beds, and they go to college.

The teacher's job is to give them permission
To gather pain into language, to promise
The critics are wrong, the other professors are wrong
Who describe an art divisible from dirt,
From rotten life. *You have to,*
Of course, you have to write it. What the hell
Do you think Emily did, Walt did, Hart did
Bill did, Sylvia did. Write for our own sake,
Write for the sake of the silenced,
Write what makes you afraid to write.
The teacher hates the job. She'd like to make
The classroom a stopping-place in a pilgrimage,

Poetry itself a safe-house
Between slavery and freedom

Since that is impossible,
Since freedom is another word
Like foot and ankle to the amputee,
The teacher helps them descend to hell.
Where she cannot reach them, where books are ashes,
Where language is hieroglyphs carved in walls
Running with slime, which they'll have to feel for
In the steamy mist, while the whip opens their backs.
They'll write about that, or nothing.
Against evidence, the teacher believes
Poetry heals, or redeems suffering,
If we can enter its house of judgment.
Perhaps it is not the poet who is healed,
But someone else, years later.
The teacher tells herself that truth is powerful.
Great is truth and mighty above all things,.
Though she would never say so in a class.

The Nature of Beauty

I can only say, there we have been; but I cannot say where.

— T. S. Eliot

As sometimes whiteness forms in a clear sky
To represent the breezy, temporary
Nature of beauty,
Early in semester they started it.
Lisa read in her rich New Jersey accent,
That mixes turnpike asphalt with fast food,
A sexy poem that mentioned "the place
Where lovers go to when their eyes are closed
And their lips smiling." Other students grinned,
Thinking perhaps of the backseats of Hondas.
Instead of explaining "place" as a figure of speech,
The teacher wanted them to crystallize
Around it as around the seed of a cloud.
You all understand that? You understand?
The place we go to? Where we've been? They got it.

All semester they brought it back
A piece at a time, like the limbs of Osiris.
Mostly from sex, for they were all American
Nineteen-to twenty-one-year-olds
Without a lot of complicated notions.
But Doug got it from the Jersey shore,
Foam stroking his shins, his need
Leaping in fish form. Robin
One time from dancing
With a woman she didn't
Have sex with, once from her grandmother
Doing the crossword puzzle in pen.
Kindly David from a monstrous orange bus
Whose driver amazed him by kindliness
To passengers who were poor and demented.
Dylan from a Baptist church when song

Blent him into its congregation, sucked him
Into God, for a sanctified quarter hour,
"There's no separation at that height,"
Before it dropped him like Leda back to earth
And the perplexity of being white.

The vapor of the word collects,
Becomes cloud, pours itself out,
Almost before you think: the small
Rain down can rain.
A brief raid on the inarticulate
Is what we get, and in retreat we cannot
Tell where we've really been; much less remain.

When I Was Asked How I Could Leave Vermont in the Middle of October

I did not want to be dependent on autumn
I wanted to miss it for once   drop into
another latitude where to show that beauty
well known I wanted to show that beauty
can be held in the breath just as we breathe
grief and betrayal they don't always
have to be happening in the living minute

Look there it is now our own golden
wine-colored world-famous Vermont fall green
as summer to begin with and then the sunny
morning draws mist out of the cold night river
the maples are sweetened there's a certain
skipped beat a scalding as you live that
loyal countryside ablaze trembling
toward its long winter nobody should have
to bear all that death-determined beauty
every single year this aging body knows
it can't be borne

How to Tell a Story (My Method)
(Most of the Time)

Now prose

Find the paragraph to
hold the poem steady
for six or eight pages

the teller is waiting
her voice her throat
is still narrow help
help she'd cry if she could

she may be frightened by
those arts invention and
memory solitude's heat

what is her language try to
assemble her mother's
whispers her father's way
of lifting a sentence
then silencing it which
of the world's years freed them
to speak to strangers why
are they laughing

don't let her lose the poem
in the telling of day by
day because the subject
is time the place is only
paper the story is still
a puzzle the teller
knows why

ELISE PASCHEN

House through Leaves

They raised the house through leaves
which flared and burned blood-red,
topaz, magenta, plum.

They raised the house. She was
a house where he would live
and pile the logs, the branches.

Around the house he staked
out earth before the sun
slipped down, although the leaves

shone through the night dark as
her hair which tumbled dusk-like
about her open face

by whose light he would labor.
He planted his fence, post
by post, before the leaves.

Before they fell. Before
the sap, the bud, the shoot.
They raised the house through leaves.

Farewell

Still there is light, and stands of trees,
though nettles cut, and sun may burn,
though you are gone deep in the earth,
still grass, still wings, still there are trees.

Though you are gone deep in the earth—
I dig the dirt, I dig the dirt—
it's caught beneath my nails, the dirt,
deep in the earth. And you are gone.

Out on the road, under the sun,
though nettles cut and then will burn,
you're in the grass, you are the sun.
We share the light. Forget the night.

But let me breathe. Are you in air?
I smell the dirt. The earth is still.
I walk the road: you are not there.
The night comes down. I breathe in still.

Genealogy

Great-uncle Henry Farrell was just sixteen
when he was killed in a fall from a turnip truck.
The wheel hit a pothole and he tipped
headfirst onto the Kildalkey Road.
They laid him out on the green settle bed
where four or five children slept each night.
He is buried like all the Farrells
under a cross in Kildalkey churchyard.

Edward Swords, a great-uncle on the sailor side,
turned twenty-eight in Northeast China.
It was just luck to land in the first battle
of the war to end all wars. A stray shell struck
the mainmast of his ship, braining Edward
for good measure. His grave has a number
instead of a name. The mothers who wept
over Henry and Edward have been dead
these donkey's years. Death dates have been added
to their birth dates in the family annals.

A hundred years ago when the first moving-picture
was shown to rapt audiences, journalists
were jubilant. "We have defeated death," they said.
But the journalists too have gone the way of all flesh.

My son was married under the great medieval clock
in the old town square of Prague.
A skeleton marked time as the twelve Apostles
paraded past the window above our heads.
Memento mori while Japanese tourists clicked

their cameras, freezing our lives for an instant.
Perhaps our beaming faces will appear years hence
in some Japanese home video or photograph album.
Children will ask our identities and heads will be shaken.
Who were those people and what are they to us?

Thatch Pub, 1958

It was Grand National Saturday
and our father, never a betting man,
had put a shilling each way for the four of us
on a horse called Oxo. After his dinner
we trailed him to The Thatch to see the race
running a gantlet of cap-shadowed glances
as the men looked up from their pints
to gawk at the strangers.

I think the world was completely brown then.
The smoke-filled air. The dun-colored caps
of the drinkers. The dark oak of the bar
and deeper dark of porter
chased with a swirl of whiskey.
The smell you'd sometimes get
in the early morning after it rained,
when you walked over a metal grating
and caught the waft of stale ale
and Woodbines rising up from the depths.

Our father, thin as a whippet among
stout-fattened neighbors, beckoned the barman
while we clung to his coattails. He brought us
Orange Crush poured sideways into tall Harp glasses,
and *Tayto* crisps tasting of smoke and beer.
The television blared from among
the dusty bottles on a corner shelf.
All eyes were glued to Oxo when our sister,
nervous as a thoroughbred,
clamped her teeth down hard and bit a piece
from the fluted edge of the glass.

The Fare

Bury me in my pink pantsuit, you said—and I did.
But I'd never dressed you before! I saw the glint
of gold in your jewelry drawer and popped
the earrings in a plastic bag along with pearls,
a pink-and-gold pin, and your perfume. ("What's this?"
the mortician said . . . "Oh well, we'll spray some on.")
Now your words from the coffin: *"Take my earrings off!*
I've had them on all day, for God's sake!"
You've had them on five days. The lid's closed,
and the sharp stab of a femininity
you couldn't stand for more than two hours in life
is eternal—you'll never relax. I'm 400 miles away.
Should I call up the funeral home and have them removed?
You're not buried yet—stored till the ground thaws—
where, I didn't ask. Probably the mortician's garage.
I should have buried you in slippers and a bathrobe.
Instead, I gave them your shoes. Oh, please
do it for me. I can't stand the thought of you
pained by vanity forever. Reach your cold hand
up to your ear and pull and hear the click
of the clasp hinge unclasping, then reach
across your face and get the other one
and—this effort could take you days, I know,
since you're dead. Let it be your last effort:
to change my mistake and be dead in comfort.
Lower your hands in their places
on your low mound of stomach and rest, rest,
you can let go. They'll fall
to the bottom of the casket like tokens,
return fare fallen to the pit
of a coat's satin pocket.

Why I Am Not a Buddhist

I love desire, the state of want and thought
of how to get; building a kingdom in a soul
requires desire. I love the things I've sought—
you in your beltless bathrobe, tongues of cash that loll
from my billfold—and love what I want: clothes,
houses, redemption. Can a new mauve suit
equal God? Oh no, desire is ranked. To lose
a loved pen is not like losing faith. Acute
desire for nut gateau is driven out by death,
but the cake on its plate has meaning,
even when love is endangered and nothing matters.
For my mother, health; for my sister, bereft,
wholeness. But why is desire suffering?
Because want leaves a world in tatters?
How else but in tatters should a world be?
A columned porch set high above a lake.
Here, take my money. A loved face is agony,
the spirit gone. Here, use my rags of love.

Lunchtime at Ocean Point

The sun, dumb to its own dangers, lasers through
the saltspray atmosphere. The wind, reckless as
a fool, pays scant attention to what it disturbs.
The Atlantic, that loud bull, pounds the shore,
beleaguers whatever the reef. Behind a close-by
dune, youngsters insist on flying a cloth-tailed
kite. It tears into bits like a well-worn flag.
Up against the horizon but out too far, fragile
sailboats, as if in a flotilla, take on the sea.

The penetrating screeching of a gluttonous gull
competes with the deep-toned drone of a foghorn
bellowing out at nothing. Against the backdrop
rise & fall of surf having its way with rock or
sand: the recurrent ka-boom of an Air-Guard jet
breaking barriers of unearthly sound, off-color
hooting, hollering of football-happy schoolboys,
the boom-box blare of beachside lovers, mouths
on fire, tongues in tune to popular rock-n-roll.

One can imagine the old-money rich in privileged
homes, fortressed in no small comfort, away from
the seaside conspiracy of noises, of sun & wind,
munching on crisp greens, sipping on choice tea.
Whatever conventions they subscribe to, whatever
cotillion, up-scale boutiques, the country club,
were they to limo by they'd chance on no one but
themselves if only as family dishing out salads
forked with plastic, coffee cupped in Styrofoam.

May Evening

some of us trim	*on a day I remember*
the lawn	*warm then as now*
some of us look	*a day like body temperature*
for our wallet	
some of us wipe	*a forlorn wind*
the dishes	*stirred the leaves*
some of us	*buds still tight*
walk the dog	*and white green*
some of us	
have a bone scan	*I heard a car door*
some of us yawn	
and check our watches	*slam*
some of us	*they are going somewhere*
have radiation	*without me*
for the second time	*a punishment*
in the cities	*I am going*
may blossoms fall	*somewhere too*
on concrete sidewalks	*sitting in my window*
wondering	*and never coming back.*
what's the next step	

Angels of Self-Abandon

To be diminished into divine love
by a maelstrom of fatigue where, at rest,
angels speak of an outcast poverty
of the soul, how they yearn to breathe
despair, breathe the wild surrender
of the body.
    Oh they may adore spare grace
in the wrecked ribs of the starved, count
bone above bone with such deliciousness.
Answer the call of inexhaustible pain.
    Angels would lick the lather
of tubercular phlegm, brace scars
upon flesh if they were fleshed, carry
red-wound amulets, victoriously humbled.
    Lovers of self-abandon, cordoned in
a gimbal to the stern of heaven, they
fixate on decimation.
    But who among carriers of the body would
bear such saintly weight when ground falls under
the lapsed dome and we are uprighted into holiness?

Dinner with the Poet Laureate

Dissatisfied with the conversation, the four-year-old
keeps poking the tip of a peacock feather into the faces
of the guests; later, slowly eats the rest of the seeded
rolls brushed with egg and baked till golden earlier in the day
by the less good poet, who was nervous both before

and after the guests arrived, thinking of Tennyson's
glossy laureate beard, nails sticking out of the sheetrock,
not enough chairs, and the probability that the four-year-old
would find something along the lines of a peacock feather
with which to terrorize the guests: as when he informed her inlaws,

over cocktails, that he planned to be gay when he grew up.
The painter and the photographer begin some chat about galleries
that the poet laureate and the less good poet listened in on,
the less good poet squirming in her chair, self-conscious
about her restlessness. In a Kate O'Brien novel, the mother

superior of an Irish girls' school, well read in the poetry
of Henry Vaughan, subdues a sense of internal chaos by keeping
her hands quiet at all times. Is this an impossible task?
The physical self is so willful, shamelessly following its bad habits,
while the mind is like an anxious, second-guessing parent.

Because the poet laureate asserts that he doesn't like the music
of Merle Haggard, the photographer has chosen Etta James,
who says she would rather be blind, boy, than see you
walk away from me, babe; sure true about more than one thing
the less good poet can think of: the whole reason the poet laureate

has wedged himself at her kitchen table (she hopes); though she
    worries

they have nothing to say to each other over the second kind of
        tomato
soup he's had today, which the four-year-old is deliberately spooning
down the front of his pajamas. Nothing goes as planned;
think of a sonnet unleashing its skewed logic down the page,

careening around every turn. The Burden of the Mystery,
Keats called this beetle-browed unease she feels, wishing
for pleasure, for confidence in a situation that seems close to tears,
for Etta vanished, the painter trying to explain the odd path
her career has taken, the photographer a father wiping soup

off the four-year-old with a dishcloth.
The less good poet pours out the last of the Riesling.
All the ways the mind works, folding in on itself—
John Berryman with those poems about Chris, falling-down
drunk in her capri pants on a ratty hearthrug; and here,

four people eating dinner with a child whom the photographer calls
the Boy Tyrant when he's lying in bed with the less good poet
smoking a bowl and rehashing the evening; and she reminds
him of the poem in which she imagines having thrown
the four-year-old off a bridge, an exhilarating aspect of the art,

like being possessed by a kind of honest evil spirit,
a sort of longing for the truth of the matter, something analogous
to what she feels now, propped up beside the photographer,
his face shadowed under the dim lamp, broad-boned and mercurial;
the desire that overtakes her for vision—

to be able to take in everything and align it in some stately
Spenserian array, heavy as alabaster and ivory, remote as heaven,
in a poem that uses the word *crimson* in a way that really works.
The problem with being a good poet is the triviality that arises,
like fog spreading over a window. Just when she thinks she's run up
        against

something really important, her thoughts stage-dive into the crowd.
What does a real poet imagine over the dish pan?
Did T.S. Eliot idly vacuum the same section of carpet twenty times,
let the rhythm of a line circle around him like a fish,
hum a tune in the key of the motor while Vivienne

broke things in the next room? The less good poet cannot
manage to put herself into anyone else's shoes: the whole
world seems fixed on herself, the center of a tiny Aristotelian
universe plagued by the malignant orbit of the four-year-old,
paid employment, and laundry. Asleep, the photographer

emits a small snore, emblematic of the calm order of his own
more Galilean universe, where steady hard work produces
superior results and nothing keeps him awake, not even
a less good poet looking for love, whose mind is a castle
honeycombed with a thousand passageways—

climbing and twisting, falling into endless loops and permutations;
and there is no way out, no way at all. But she wants him
to know she's here, as she wants to believe that the painter
has left this house in the country to sit in the dark passenger
seat of a reliable Subaru, mesmerized by the windshield wipers

sweeping back and forth in their dark mirror, a sweetness
like tires hissing down a wet street; that the poet laureate reads
Pope as woodchucks browse in his kale and cats do nothing
to stop them; that Snow White and Rose Red wander
through the forest hand in hand, but no beast dares touch

one hair of their heads—that there is a way to compose
these pieces into patterns of great beauty and precision,
as a clock ticks, as a falcon flies over a woodland edge,
crying its hunger in heroic couplets. The world conflates into
      Milton's
royal image, but didn't Keats wrestle with exactly this pain?

When the four-year-old wakes in the morning and puts on his
      cowboy mask
with a smile, the less good poet will dish out yogurt and orange juice,
while Shakespeare brews more coffee and the diminution of space
points their love as sharp as a needle, the image rocking her back
on her heels as if it were her own. At another dinner, the painter

and the poet laureate, even the buzzing four-year-old, might hear
those words ringing off the countertops, off the bones of her skull;
the photographer, on his way to hunt out that Merle Haggard tune
about Roman sandals, stopping to listen—every sound a chime,
a thought, a heartbeat; each phrase a life lived over and over.

The War Statue

My great-grandfather fought for the Union
through the whole Civil War
and lived to continue his study of his classics.
He convinced his hometown to erect,
at the terminus of their Decoration Day parade,
a memorial statue of a Union Soldier
made entirely of wood.

When a boy I marched to it during WWII
and noticed its severe weathering.
The bayonet and part of the rifle barrel were already gone.
And the wheezing soldier before his WWI bronze statue
vilified the Germans who gassed him.

When thirty I marched to the statue again
as the Korean War was winding down.
The face was disappearing
and the hands had no fingers.
And the armless sailor before his WWII marble statue
vilified the Japanese who sent the kamikazes.

When I was fifty, I journeyed to Greece.
How wise of the ancient Greeks to dictate
that their grave memorials be made of wood.
Only a tumulus of dirt remained at Marathon.
And the legless vet before his Korean War fiberglass platoon
vilified the Chinese who laid the land mines.

At seventy, I visit the statue alone.
Crows caucus loudly in the evergreens.
A cold winter rain drenches us both.
I no longer can discern
the Union uniform and cap.

Snow Men

That winter . . .

Snow on the pines,

chickadee songs.

The air sharp and clean

and as vivid as ever.

But they all died.

One after the other.

The winter the family

melted like snow.

Karakorum

That sunny dome! Those caves of ice!
— S. T. Coleridge

For social studies, I show my old
slides of Mongolia.
The five of us entering
Ulan Bator's Hotel B
where flies blacken the breakfast
but ignore the white yogurt.

My family by the propeller plane
on the sandy runway.
A student asks, Is that really you?
and I answer, Yes.

The yaks and Bactrian camels
in the Gobi, where sun never reaches
the snow and ice in Yolyn Am,
Valley of the Eagles.

Then, the slide of my son
on a Mongolian horse,
only vast desert and the owner's felt
and canvas yurt in the background.

This very spot where Marco Polo
came to Karakorum—Kublai Khan's
pleasure-dome, the palace garden
angel fountains offering wayfarers
honey, yogurt, milk, water and vodka—
only a stone turtle left to mark the place.

I tell how these high-cheeked people
may have crossed a land bridge to America.
A student asks, Is that the son who died?
and I answer, Yes.

Dogwood Alarm

By pairs and threes they crash
and spin to the shoulder, drivers
stunned, unable to keep their eyes,
wheels, the tingle in their fingertips
from bark and open drifts of silk,
and looseblown momentary bloom.

April. They pass, retreat sideways,
floating away from the little accident.

A specimen tree in a suburban yard
is one thing, fertilized, gravid, buds
popped out all over, azaleas snapping
at its knees. But the woods at the edge
of plowed fields are another story, a waltz
at the dogwood diner, the dance that slays us:

Four or five flowers hover over a branch,
crossed, notched, whiter than this world allows.

GERI RADASCI

Building Stone Wall

Your father puzzled together this dry wall, then passed
on, himself a kind of riddle. He used no mortar,
trusting the rocks to bind by gravity
and the shifts of frost. He believed

in boundaries. If this wall, a lichen-encrusted
fable, could grab and lead us by the hand,
connect us to the builder,
we would see

your father's red hands, bare
in unfriendly weather to save the expense
of gloves. You could strike a match on that skin
and his eyes would not blink, because he was so entranced

with bad memories: the harrowed ground where bodies
lay—seven Nazi boys—he himself once killed
and left in cold plots, in Belgium, somewhere.
I made it, he'd growl harshly, meaning,

perhaps, this rock buttress or the distance
he had run through the rubble of open eyes.
And, because he understood the conditional
truth of stones, he'd say, *To make an almost indestructible*

wall, never think of beauty, never taper
the wall too finely. It might tip over.
The idea was to gird in
your land securely, protect your rights

of detachment, separate road from the enigma
of wild fields. The trick was to stack stones
in such a way that each new row
always casts a shadow.

Sick Sister

You called.
You were just like yourself
although I know you're

still off—
I was supposed to ask
if you're taking your Navane please
try to see the doctor

but we talked about your new bike
instead   it's real
lightweight   you said
                              you can fly

The Bounty
for Gerald Stern

Dear Gerry, While you and your Pittsburgh buddy, the great Jack
        Gilbert,
were reading to poets gathered in that same city,
I was walking the aisles of COSTCO with Jonah and Gabriel. Have
        you ever
been there, or in one of these warehouse food chains, stores of the
        Alice "eat me"
variety, everything enlarged, larger than life, at least my life with its
        city cupboards,
but, also, stores where my all-American—albeit first-generation—
        appetite
for purchase is born and born again in the next aisle where a fork-
        lift pulls out
a crate of Dunkaroos? The boys scream for everything big.
You, with grown children, what do you know from Dunkaroos?
And my God, the austere Jack Gilbert, what would Gilbert think of
        the double-sized
cart overfilled with thirty-six rolls of Charmin and bulk-wrapped
        Bounty,
twelve for eight dollars and seventy-nine cents, and the cases of
        Juicy-Juice
juice boxes? Food chains with not a thing in my cart from the food
        chain.
But you understand, Gerry, the deals, Gerry, the deals.
Gilbert, with his mountain and his poem "Hunger" that I read to
        students
to take them to that line, "going beyond the seeds," what would
        Gilbert think
of Jonah and me filling to overflowing the over-sized cart, and
        Gabriel piled high

in the cart, holding a two and one-half pound box of cheddar
    goldfish.
Did he read that poem "Hunger"? Did you read your song of the
    green willow?
Or was it all new poems and in our hometown, too.
I would have liked that, too, to be childless in Pittsburgh,
among poets, even with my shyness of poets.
Instead, there was enough French's Mustard to squirt the boys
    through childhood.
But the deals, Gerry, and I have the receipt to prove it.
That's thirty-six rolls of toilet paper at twenty-four cents a roll and
    the twelve for
eight dollars and seventy-nine cents comes to seventy-three cents a
    roll of paper
towel and so on and on up to two hundred eighty-eight dollars and
    fifty-seven
cents. With not a vegetable or fruit in the cart.
I remember my first time, not in COSTCO but in B.J.'s,
which is the same but with a different name.
Jonah, maybe just two months, woke with a raucous hunger.
I nursed sitting on stacked crates below the stocked warehouse
    shelves.
The shoppers gave me terrible looks. I tried to write that B.J's poem
    but got stuck
with a fake Whitman love of the things and a true highbrow hatred
    of glut
without even a mention of Jonah's delicious suck.
This time there was also a frenzy of sucking, the kids wanting to eat
    and drink
everything in the car and both boys screaming,
"There's nothing at all here to eat." What's left?
I got lost on ninety-five, brought Jonah late to his violin lesson,
waited out front with Gabe asleep in back.
That's when I had the chance to think of Pittsburgh, of poems,
of you and your friend. Imagine Jonah with his quarter size violin.

Imagine Dunkaroos. His small fingers, his wrist held just right to
      bow.
The bounty of your music. Gilbert's strict beauty. Gabe sleeping
      through it.
And, this, my happiness, Gerry, the whole heartbreaking
      deal.

Food

At first there is no blood. At first
there is only the blessed, born naked and blind,
six months fatted on hand-picked grasses, rabbit
that Juan Del Peral is grateful is stupid
like all rabbits and easily lulled into feeling
the plucking of its ears as sign to relax.
Because Juan Del Peral wants to be an honest man,
he picks up the rabbit by its hind legs –
letting its slack body hang—pats it across
the head, pulls the ears until they fall
close to the skull and never turns away
from the others. Let them see, he thinks,
that the man who cleans their cages and sings
to them his best love songs, will strike them down
with not too much effort and less regret. It is true, too,
that the hand that comes down on the soft place
where the ears and neck meet is quick and light,
a lighter hand, for instance, than a man might use
on the body of an erring child. But about regret,
Juan Del Peral is only partways true.
With the rabbit hung to be bled, he sits back
to whet the skinning blade. The rabbits seem jittery.
He thinks how he has watched their twitchy sleep, and how
he has opened a rabbit, held the testicles in his palm before
dropping them in the bucket, how he has pinched
and then pulled back their skin, yanking and
yanking until he wonders if this time
it is his own skin that will go, and how he has bled
the necks, catching the first blood to save for cooking. There,

there, he says to his rabbits,
though he knows that one by stupid one
with short pulls he will convince them of his love
until the ears relax and with a skilled soft rap
he will strike the next beauty down.

New Poem

He stopped calling
and then I stopped calling
and for those of you thinking
"girlfriend tell me something new"
this poem will be a problem.
This poem is old and hates loud music.
This poem has big hair and tight jeans
and is sitting on public transportation snapping
gum. This poem is sipping Budweiser from a bag
with the guys, top button undone
voices all loud and full of themselves
saying *fuck* like they're the first to think of it.
This poem doesn't mind how ugly that sounds.
This poem thinks everything tonight is ugly.
"See, what did I tell you? Nothing new," says
this poem while waiting for a phone call
this poem on hold with a customer service representative.
Tired poem that's been turned down for tenure,
denied a mortgage, whose car needs new brakes.
Sad poem who's eating pretzels for dinner;
poor poem who ran as hard as she could
to catch this train.

Ugly Poem

It could be the bus to anywhere, but it's the 74—
running the same route as the 76
none of us coming from anywhere but work,
maybe a job we hate or just the place
that wears us down, and there on the platform's the 74—
lit like our dreams of home.
No one has to wait in the cold;
nobody's baby is crying.
We shuffle on and then we hear
this bus isn't going anywhere
this bus won't leave til 9:40 and
this is how home can turn on you,
this is how little it takes:
the stupid baby that won't shut up
the badgering old man who speaks for all of us
when he whines did the driver know
and why didn't he tell us
when there was still time
to catch the 76; the driver
who turns the ignition off because
he doesn't have to take this crap.

I am fed up with rage, I am tired
of cranky angry folk. I am sick and tired of meanness:
the lovely fawn-colored pit bull
my neighbors have taught to kill cats.
The ugliness of my other neighbors
with their trash cans overturned
to save *their* parking spaces on the street.
The vacant lot that used to sway with chicory
and Queen Anne's lace in a blue-white sea
that's graveled over now and full
of repossessed cars.

I have a friend who has cancer.
Last time she went for radiation
she walked out because of the technicians.
Maybe they were telling tasteless jokes
more likely they were talking
about where to call for takeout
marking "x's" across her torso
Tic-tac-toe "we had Chinese
yesterday" "I'm here" she says
"I'm on this. You must talk to me."
On her way home she stops for gasoline
she leans against her car
and doesn't want to die.
"People like you will burn in hell,"
says the man who takes her money.
She doesn't see the broken cross
tattooed on her neck
until she gets home.

It Being Forbidden

to excuse oneself from table
before each morsel is chewed and swallowed;
it being forbidden to laugh
unless he conducts, pitch and duration,
his arms raised, our sisterly heads shamed
downward; it being forbidden
to invite another to that table who dares
to be more handsome and charming than he.

It being commanded to worship
that occupier of the armed-chair,
carver of pheasants, rabbinic imposter,
tweed-suited weekend gardener,
peddler of diamonds to the ghetto

and we do worship him
for plentiful is his table,
joyous the summer camps,
vast the Canadian forests,
the Caribbean Sea.

He who orchestrates with knife and fork
pulls us to our knees
and we pray with him who whispers
do you love me
and we cry with him who whimpers
no one loves me
and we kiss him on his temple
no one touches me
and we remain in his house
longer than we ought, for he prophesies

even you shall leave me
and when we do leave him, as we must,
we transplant lilacs and peonies from his garden
to ours so that he shall bloom
beneath our windows.

Elegy

My body given away, parts
flown to other parts—a child
receives my eyes, another
my heart, the diseased organs
remain, benign now.
In death I am waiting
for my soul to arrive
that I may divide it equally
among frightened neighbors.
In death I pursue a man
younger than my father
ever was in my life.
In death I am a mother
who disowns her children
in a market parking lot.
In death a ghost lies
under me, pregnant. In death
I unbury myself and try
to extract my soul surgically;
it will not release, will not;
I discover there is no one else
this soul wishes to be.

Youngstown, Ohio, 1952

I climbed the hill on my green Schwinn bike
at dusk when the air lifted enough
for me to see the orange flush
of the open hearth on the horizon.
Tomorrow, it would rain ashes on
our '52 Chevy. Later, on a field trip
to the mill, I walked on a catwalk
above the open mouth. The runoff
hardened into steel squares,
moved across the floor on rollers.
The men in hard hats were so close,
their sweat turned to powder
on their faces. The cast off heat
rose and billowed our skirts out
in small, suspended parachutes.
On summer afternoons I floated
on a blanket in the backyard,
in the haze that wanting makes,
lifted off beyond the yard,
beyond the gray sun, imagining
a clear trajectory, a blue sky.

Harvest Time

Evening sun and wild geese going south;
Trees tired of leafy fullness, shedding
Fields full of treasures;
It's time for harvest.

And I too, wheezing here with chalk dust lungs,
Halt-footed from some fifty years of classroom marathons,

Dim-eyed, squinting against the misplaced modifier
      and the setting sun,
Long for the harvest.

Forsythia

From the hall I watched him shatter the orange dishes
my mother thought unbreakable—
slamming them against gray tile
as she crouched, denying milkman, mailman,
all who came to the house while he was at work,
who heard quick breaths between her words,
appraised her body.

Each night
I set the table and when it was time
we all sat for him to lead us in grace,
careful to keep our elbows off the cloth,
careful to eat everything so he wouldn't say
how ungrateful we were for the food on our plates
and then, with his leather belt, teach us manners.
But when he smashed those dishes I ran.

It was still light so it must have been spring,
yes, May, because I crawled through wands
supple as whips but studded with blossoms
to get inside the forsythia cave.
I looked as hard as I could:
each stem was a tight green throat,
each mouth tongueless gold entered by bees
whose furry bodies spun back out
dusted with pollen, carrying nectar
in pouches on their spindly legs,
                              and watching them
I almost forgot the sounds inside the house
until my mother slammed the windows down
and my ears filled with buzzing.

Huddled in the damp earth beneath forsythia,
straining for silence, I watched night
billow up from the dirt, sapping the flowers.
When the crashes stopped,
she called for me: *Come in. Come in.*

Song of the Magdalene

Her dark hair half-hiding her slender face,
she sits in shadows and
stares past the light of the oily lamp.
She remembers the men held in her fragrant arms.
Strong men whose bodies
glistened after the fierce dance.
Quiet men who brought their needs
and left gold coins that she kept in
a box beneath her bed.
She smiles with sadness at forbidden thoughts, for
all her memories have been forgiven, now
her past is a foreign place.
Chosen and sinless,
She cannot return there.
Holiness becomes a lonely state,
A halo, a clumsy adornment.
Mary Magdalene, bride of the morning, rises.
braids her hair before a clouded mirror,
binds her garments tight against her breasts.
Gathering her ointments and her faith,
she joins the women waiting in the Garden.

Ash Pit

It thumped my sister's skull—
this concrete backyard ash pit—
and changed her face into a flag
of red, branching rivulets

that stopped our game of tag
and her screeches of delight
because she hadn't been it
and she hadn't been caught.

How quick she would have felt,
this nimble girl of ten,
if her big brother had lunged
and missed her again.

But this time he did not.
The coals in the basement bin
chuckled among themselves
at what the furnace thought.

MICHAEL RYAN

A Two-Year-Old Girl in a Restaurant

Your delight, which is contagious,
has been occasioned by
the twinkling point of a steak knife
about to liquify your eye.

so when your father swats it
from your prehensile fist
you squinch your blooming face
tight as a blastocyst

as if all the world's pain
had conceived inside your skull
and you, the prima diva
of the coloratura wail,

go deep into your soul
to sing how such pain feels,
and we remember well
and smile or do not smile.

Reminder

Torment by appetite
is itself an appetite
dulled by inarticulate,
dogged, daily

loving-others-to-death—
as Chekhov put it, "compassion
down to your fingertips"—,
looking on them as into the sun

not in the least for their sake
but slowly for your own
because it causes
the blinded soul to bloom

like deliciousness in dirt,
like beauty from hurt,
their light—*their* light—
pulls so surely. Let it.

MICHAEL RYAN

In the Sink
Paul H. Ryan, 1909–1964

Tiny red spider, in your weird world
of instructive vibrations and spikes of heat,
you're spread like a *nerve-end* naively unfurled
as if a touch would be a treat.

You're safe for now, at least from me—
although your utter otherness
jolts my not being what I don't want to be,
which, in your case, should be obvious

since you're the one stuck in a porcelain bowl
where any drunk who wants a drink
could send you swirling down a hole
and never see you in the sink.

Influence is too pale a word
for how a father lives in his son.
Rejoice you're not his drop of blood.
I'd flick this faucet and go on.

Giving Answers to Questionnaires

Two parts of the body.

Strong, aged hands. The caress of their lined movement.
Hair the color of frost on a morning's windowpane.

A hero.

One who does not depend on the moment's popularity.
All the little fathers and saints of the Church.

A time of day or night.

Twilight. The season of neither fall nor winter.
But the exact, naked point in between.

A totem animal.

The great bruin in hibernation. The stillness of that hairy strength.

An abstraction.

Loyalty and betrayal. The summer you depend on to stay.

A landscape.

The distance of the Theban desert. The plural city that holds
yourself and yourself.
The tawny ghost of a land alive.
My own small soul yearning for the gold breadth of Thebes,
the sight of that expanse.
If I could but see the dust of the hands of Saint Anthony.

An astrological sign.

Zero.

The irrelevancy of a choice other than my own.
The whiteness of that.

A color.

Rust. The inventions that outlive us.
Rust. The warmth of the southwestern earth.
Rust. The intense life of that aridity.

A phrase you have heard all your life.

Kyrie, eleison.
Lord, have mercy.

The Father of Hands

I have always been in love with your hands,
the two expressions of you that never hit a child
but held me close to your paternal breast. I imagine

the memory: my miniature fists clutching your index fingers
as I balanced first steps, pulled into your heart. Like that,
I have spent the whole of my life walking toward you.

I have always been in love with your hands,
the silver dusting of hair on your forearms
like an American prairie, shaping the expanse of me.

They held the world firm. And I was borne
in the harbor of your arms, the fine, gold
parchment of your skin, manuscript of years.

I am the definition of your hands, whose mirrored
shape I give back to you. Your sleeping, father hands
I held in the hospital bed, through the silver bars.

Time never withered your broad, muscled arms. For a time,
my hands held yours to this world, pulled into my heart,
the strength that always held me in strength and belief.

The anchors of my hands, which are your hands,
those two expressions of you I have always been in love with,
holding me close in this pulsing warmth of grief.

Abraham, Isaac and . . . Sarah

How faithful must a son be
To lie bovine beneath the blade?
The wind whimpers and the bough bends.

Here is a father who believes,
A son who chooses to obey.
As told, this is a man's story.

But, at a distant hearth, alone,
A mother kneads her bread and grieves
Tears that crack the crust of Heaven.

Personal History

I was born in a garden of
artificial roses.

My mouth was stuffed with dollar bills that
bought my silence.

I covered myself with words
to keep warm.

In school the report card said A+ in
Careful.

One day I spoke
and the house burned down.

My sister left me standing
in the train station.

My brother climbed down from the mountains
and offered me his ropes.

I fell in love with three children
I would one day bear.

One of them went away, taking wit and grace.
I collected Vulnerability.

My daughter taught me to love lipstick
and poetry.

My son imbibed my fears and
guzzled music.

I am writing a love poem that is so long
it has taken me thirty years.

Still, I go to sleep, afraid of wolves. But I will wake,
with milk full, for the mouths hungry in my bed.

Autumn Equinox

The morning glories
continue
knowing nothing,

but such a caprice,
this lavish clambering
toward—what?
Only sunlight.

For that they open, every day.

Believe me, the grief
I feel cannot be
explained.

In moonlight, broad
as the sprawled land we look across,
the blossoms are closed
like miniature umbrellas,
our clothes on the line colorless
yet bright beneath a round white
platter of mercury,

whatever takes place
in the world surrounding us,
where dear friends
will die.

These nights we hear transports
from the airbase upstate.
These days I hear fighter jets
going east
at ungodly speeds.

Autumn chill,
a stream of piss streams
in golden-gray thatch.

The morning glories are
—what colors?
"Blue as our girl's eyes," or bluer.
Tinted rose, as wishful thinking is said to be.
Wrinkled slightly like crepe paper,
with white centers,

with avid greed vines that climb
whatever we do,
defying all
but
the killing frost.

Clio

How many do you greet, Grace,
with *Sweetheart?* with
Darling? Your fledglings,
innumerable. I could not know
the world as I do, careening in space,
without you—speaking as one
of countless. That day on Wall Street,
amassed in a blockade at the stock exchange.
You recall the stilt-walkers—three,
with bass drum and tattering snares,
who defied the actual gravity
of our presence in that place,
striding east towards an armored line
of mounted police who forced
three horses to charge 100 yards
of clattering pavement and crash
squealing in to the dancers' legs
gruesome as the smell of mace
so they toppled upon the crowd
and were lowered carefully down.
There are those who hate us
for merely believing. Your face

is inseparable by that phrase
of Tranströmer's: *We have not*
surrendered, but want peace. You
live in multiple, overlapping realms,
disparate neighborhoods, a traveling case;
I can't know all the others, but this one
we share. Smarts Mountain commences
as though at the foot of your garden rows,
rising in layers from your windowsill
and from ours as well. This time of year

bright ice crests the peak, startling
delicacy upon spruce and rock, a lace
spun from frozen immaculate droplets,
now acidic as vinegar. Yet gorgeous.
Chickadees stitch thin loops between
feeder trees: almost needless to say,
at moments one imagines a globe
where the agony is effaced,
where the families are okay,
the jobs are fine, international relations
are steadily improving with the season
which has grown large, like a vase
filled with unimpeded light—*grace*.
The maples and ash trees now childlike
in their naked lack of leaves with snow
arriving wide and cold and clean to sight.
This storm is quiet as slumber, without a trace
of violence or strain. By evening, townsfolk
assemble not to protect or demonstrate
but as parishioners, approaching the church
on the hilltop village green for vespers,
a carol recital by candle-glow. Meanwhile
a circle of our friends will gather to say,
Happy birthday. Dear Grace.

The Village of Philosophizing Dogs

While one is pestering the evening sky
In its aloof majesty,
Another acts upon a mysterious hint
As he trots down the road,
Stopping and retracing his steps.
Like someone solving a puzzle
Or trying to divine how

It all adds up—if it adds up at all?
Who said that? I growled into the bushes.
There was no reply, of course.
The naked woman who came down the stairs
Holding a glass of red wine
Had other things on her mind:
Like, has anybody in this house
Thrown the trash out today?

Everything gets a kick out of frightening us,
The village dogs yelped in unison.
It's like one of those lizards who may not blink
All summer long
As they sun themselves on a rock.
What I'm saying honey is, there are plenty of clues
But no answers as far as I can see.

Wonders of the Invisible World

Wine that bloodies the lips and tongue,
Then a half-whispered tale
Of how young witches
Used to ride married men
Through the sky at night.

The stars were like lit candles
That had wandered away on their own,
And the misty woods
Were a floating white nightgown.
It seemed only yesterday
Old Scratch tucked us into a bed of dead leaves.

You let a snake crawl around your legs,
Except it wasn't really a snake,
And it was closing time.
A beat-up old van with four bald tires
Waited for us in the parking lot.

Invitation

We are going to serve a late lunch
In the garden for a few friends.
We'll start with cold squid salad,
Minced scallions, garlic and parsley,
And a pot of black and green olives
And homemade bread to wipe the oil,
When we are not sipping the wine.

And if some bird graciously assents
To sing for us after the roast lamb,
The cheese and the fresh strawberries,
We'll raise our glasses high and toast
The invisible bird, the golden light,
The shadows lengthening,
And keep them raised till its song is over

Stiletto-Heeled

I go stiletto-heeled,
    The leather minis
        Mothballed, the garters

a weeping woman, sleepless,
            compost receding
                    rage and sorrow

I like to think
            no harm comes
                    to the animals

Spelunking dry and wet
            leaves on trees
                    caught fantasy

Shepherds howl, dark night,
            soul. In the fog,
                    we take no photos.

Slipping Out

I could be you or the one-eyed
Korean lady who picks her teeth
under the freeway. Or the three-
fingered man bent double all day

over the strawberries, shuffling
bills into the teller's hands on pay
day. That way his wife in Playa
de Tortulla can buy mud bricks.

The mind is almost transitive
so we all but slip behind our
children's eyes, all but occupy
our lovers' neurons and sentient

skin. The old woman with calcified
knuckles, grins and flushes
like a mother suckling her baby.
Her grandchildren eat her eel

and pickles at her table. She
thinks, *These small ones will
still walk here, still chew,
still hear the tower's bells*

by the hour. And that's enough.
A whole life of back pain
and fire and still it's enough.
Or the bitter man, lashed

by angina, the one who spits
out the names of all the gonifs
he's ever known. He almost dies

one night and comes to, teary

and strange. Claiming he turned
into light and inhabited his wife,
he weeps all day—*sorry, sorry,*
so very sorry squeezes her hand

with astonishing gentleness. We
could be him, or the bewildered
wife with her embarrassed but softening
smile. What of the self, you say—

its famous cell and lost key?
Of course, each has one tongue,
one unavoidable terror, and countless
thirsts. Of course, the mind clangs

and clangs like a warning of invasion
or fire. But don't be so sure the bell
won't crack and the soul slip out.

TOM SLEIGH

Raft

Dr. Pepper and the Bible on the shelf together, a tricycle
                    laying tracks through
the rare snow of a Texas winter, a new green Plymouth Valiant
with fins and a V-6, a drive-in theater screen, blacks to the left,
                    whites right,
        ripples on water like the damned being
                    winnowed from the saved;
            oh black-browed history, on your raft
we float, your raft cobbled from dead languages, bones, fires,
        dust-hung fields sprouting pylons, towers, domes,
from rivering taxis, radio waves, wide pre-reflecting eyes channeling
            through the city's circuit-woven brain
enwound with subway vaults and girdered catacombs
                while Lethe's waters open
                    to swallow
                us, languorous, taking their time . . .
As boys, my brothers and I found logs strapped with fraying rope
        and drifting on a pond, Tony's Grove—
                the mountains fell
            sheer into still water that trapped
feathers, leaves, berries, bark, fishbones, beaver bones,
the heaviness of water dragging it all down:
                Sharp-eyed presence,
buoy us up on this raft once made of logs but now
            only of words, from traces
of woodsmoke and frying pan, from saplings chewed by beaver
                and beaver stuffed
and staring back from dim vitrines, from huts and treasure hoards
                hidden in
        back alleys of apartment buildings crumbling
the way aqueducts, temples, menhirs, dolmens crumbled
            and were scavenged
for cornerstones to celebrate new gods and ward off
            demons and mad souls

trapped in trees, from TV warriors noble as the Roman
Marius and barbarian Jugurtha, from Cassius Clay
        who rose up
Muhammad Ali once Liston from
the Lewiston Penitentiary went down, taciturn Liston moving
stolid in the ring, from dynasties of Yankees
      Ford, Mantle, Maris,
        from Giant Mays of the basket catch
and Willie McCovey the slugger and the high-kicking windup
      of fastballer Marichal
while the basement bombshelter in hushed silence attends
        devotions of
      canned goods gleaming on steel shelves,
from wires crisscrossing, sparking, fusing in the overloaded brain,
oh gone and battered traces all lashed together with intricate knots
       memory now fumbles to untie:
        Again we step
onto the raft riding low under our weight, the logs' gaps
    letting water seep through that rots the rope
even as we splash one another, wrestle, dive . . . sit drifting on
the raft, a chill on the ripples as sun feathers
      behind a peak and the pond
reflects our faces peering over the raft's edge, our faces
       so calm—
      faces of brothers
unconscious of past or future, who lie on a raft
    in cool negligence of each other's presence,
adrift, absorbed, our swimming suits drying, then dried.

TOM SLEIGH

Speech for Myself as a Ghost

"Whoever I was, whatever I may have done, speaks to me
and you now in the voice of this rainy light carrying us back
to where moments ago I *was* the steam rising from your coffee

and then further back to a room made shadowy by sunlight,
a Murphy bed covered by red curtains, and bottle brush blooms
that hummingbirds needle with such appetite;

and then to a wheelchair where your father sits and stares
not knowing that we're there, and back further to when
hot milk scalds my tongue, an air raid siren blares,

mosquitoes buzz grainy as newsreel bombs
that fall in clusters in the drive-in's dark, the projector's beam
wavering through those bloodsipping swarms

—and back to where the doors the dead enter so freely
it's as if they hadn't died opens to orchard rows
of cherry trees whitening the air as crows, flocking, fly

branch to branch, a stick beats time to *caw caw caw caw*,
an irrigation ditch fills while the promised land
brims over its reflection until it swamps the window

so that now we hear what throbs in each marrow bone:
a phantom heartbeat that, slowly counting down,
echoes in the iced-over sectors of the brain

where ghosts crowding to hear that fading pulse
meld with one another mist into mist
and melt back into the wash of uncreated Chaos

(. . . that place in which nothing gestures to nothing else,
least of all this voice straining to reach you widowed
by these words that suddenly ring false)

—your coffee gone lukewarm as under dormant boughs
a trash fire ignites a drop of rain
coolly transparent through migrant shadows."

BRUCE SMITH

Groove and Break: His Voice at Fifty

1.
There were do-it-yourself kits they assembled, my parents,
        and stained a maple and varnished and steel wooled
and varnished, it would be our style—reproductions
        of the old and valuable, the American primitives,
worked on, worked up. Having no past, my mother made my father
        stop for a dry sink or a deal on a hutch. The warped boards
of the table meant the blood from the roast collected
        on my plate like a stroke at five o'clock,
a puddle in the lower lobe. I learned quiet and eat and *family*
        hold back, speech as mastication, too many syllables,
a mouth full, and a low growl, as outside a mongrel
        snapped at its own balls, maybe fleas, maybe
the soul in torment in paradise he guarded, curled
        back on himself at the entrance to the gates
of Philadelphia, nineteen-fifty, I'm four, and the dog
        must have had the mange, and in the rabid itch
and fang and bark at nothing but itself
        the voice that is my birthright.

2.
And always the music that was not my own
        beyond the bore of the engine and the El's metal on metal,
the boy's heart, not my own but a bristling thing
        like a pine cone or the fur of an animal
that would carry the spoors off by wind
        or friction. From the basement uncle with a highball
splitting the rent, listening—to sharpen himself to cut the off
        hours or dull himself to forget—to the opera.
La Traviata it was, the fallen woman who would account
        for the taste of the soul, the trace of something
like fluoride in the water. Upstairs, a baby alligator uncle
        brought back from Florida. It snapped at pencils

and ground beef and thunked its tail when it would turn
       around or turn into something at night. For the boy
two minds both pink mouthed and cat-eyed and thickening
       silently. I slept with the transistor like a sister
I never had who whispered the voices of the Black singers.
       Said: *Ooo, child.* Said: *Take me, Shake me.*
Said: *Just another little piece of my heart, now baby.*

3.

I listened in the Valley of Too Much Rain
       where the orchids were pink-mouthed divas
for my voice. I listened in the climax forest
       and in the anechoic chambers of old growth.
I heard the muzzy barge horns coming down the gorge,
       burr and drawl of log trucks, April,
and the rain like the singers with their cargo
       of legato and bliss. I heard my voice
in the beloved's and it was a hound that wanted
       out of the body or *below* or *above*, anywhere
but here. I heard the child's cry, a father stitch,
       a mother scald, the voice of the Coach Huntress on loss.
Others had their talk around the table, their stories
       like light they'd carry with them in the next life
I had a sore throat.

4.

Brilliant outside. The window a voice. Red a C
       F a pale green. G is blue. Silver the groove,
black the breaks. The window said something
       I could only know by choking back
all that was not me to speak silently
       the chewed-on, midweek song of the dying.
Friday, pay day. Saturday, the bridge.
       Said: *Can you take us to the bridge?*
James Brown to his saxophonist who used the ax
       to split my tongue. I barked back,

I was anxious. Uncle dreams of the veins
      in the throat, the light in the shot glass.
Said: *Bliss is what breaks*. Said: *Who's on bass*?
      Said: There is always a mad dog defining
one end of speech, the border of teeth,
      the other end catches and trembles
and this is my tongue.

In the Blue Room

1. Just As I Had Signed Away My Life

in the event that I was held hostage
and learned to rat my way through the portals,
corridors, and locks of the penitentiary, I saw the last jags
of a man who had fallen and shriveled into the fetal
position on the floor after drinking most of a tin
of duplicating fluid from the mimeograph machine.
He held himself and thrashed like a grunion,
waterless, on the granite of the B-wing tier of Education . . .

Later is a Babylon I write from where I can say
he failed to copy himself out and died a dull-purple,
pre-evolutionary thing. I write and rewrite his body
but fail the literal. No hammer, no will, no craft
can repeat the heart's distressed elegy,
our suicide note, the first and final draft.

2. Two Men, Rampant

On another day that is hermetically
preserved for me as if in tins, I could see
from a deep blue distance the fake Florentine tower
where the guards held guns, discreetly, and the power
of the architecture was to be archeology
every life held in its amber, in its prehistory
of stone, bronze, iron of the walls, shields, and locks
in which I found an exact measure of our lack
of civilization. I open to the day

in question, a beaten silver and hot.
The ruins I uncovered of the riot
were the heraldic figures of two men, joined at the hip,

head-locked, hunched, and white-lipped
and perfectly still in their grunts to kill each other.
They looked as if they were looking carefully down
for something lost in water.

Flight

I'm an accountable someone taxied down runways indicated
by small sapphires of light and contraindicated

by the city's heart condition, cataracts, and scum.
My inroads on the night are assisted by Valium

and are carried out at great heights by uniformed
men with well-modulated voices I've spent my entire life

to this belt-tightening, oedipal juncture hating. I'm off
and flawlessly yawed toward you, lover,

that you may love me to *Beast of Burden*, or better,
Daddy, You're a Fool to Cry, with its emotionally sleek,

sympathetic identification with all those who strive, seek,
come home from work, sleep—slower for all those whose rock

and roll is dance of hurt and release, hurt and release.
A voice I don't believe tells me *our ground-time here will be brief.*

Old Woman Dreams

In those early times,
pretending to study the sleeping dog,
I watched the old: my grandmother,
toothless, her teeth on the bed table in a glass,
how she ate her cake like that,
all gums, *dunking it*
my father said, her son, who still had teeth.
And it went somewhere, to the same place,
dreams go in the morning.

Old women liked it that way, vanished cake.
I tried to imagine him born from her,
Ancestors, my father born from his mother,
the umbilical cord that connected them.
I had seen the dog give birth,
chew the opalescent sacs pups are born in.
Once in the car, twenty or twenty-one,
playing as if in a dream, Twenty Questions
with friends who knew the family,
no one could guess umbilical cord: animal.

And now again I dream in Old Lady,
as if I could speak the language perfectly,
understood all the thoughts
that needed to be brought to air.
What is with me are not the toothless gums,
diapers and forgetfulness, rude joints and noises,
but only the long country traversed, the century.
How the colors of the afghan I knitted,
though I never have, run together,

like years, children's laughter
blending with grandchildren's,
their faces awake, asleep,
happiness in gardens.

On the Possession of Horses

Their heads hunker forward when they canter
as if only one direction were possible
and they don't understand fire.
They gallop back to a burning barn.

Nothing about horses compels me now,
though once I wanted to be one.
What do horses have to do with love,
the flowering limbs of their bodies,
their hearts chiseled from stone,
and riders cling to them
as if just this holding on,
this staying on could be everything?

Once an entire village banned horses.
You couldn't blame them after all the trouble.
One minute normal, and the next
the children were possessed,
leaving their comfortable beds at night
cavorting with horses from all around
under the laden apple trees.
No one knows how they planned it.
They rode horses by moonlight,
bareback and bare-assed
even in thunderstorms.

When horses trot and canter,
their hooves clatter, their bones
chime like funeral bells, like clappers.
They knock against the earth, their heavy
hooves beat against the earth.

Love Tale

1

Somewhere near Avignon a woman sits
   at a wicker vanity, bathed in first
light of the season. A promise of sun
   warms wormwood shining onto glass.

She thinks she can reach out
   to the man standing in a field.
His field is plowed, black earth
   groomed almost as smooth as her mirror.

If she called to him
   her voice would blend
with the mourning doves
   passing like grey puffs in weighted light.

2

A leaf grazes his face.
   He walks along soft red lanes.
Blooms of red poppies
   whole fields of them.

He is a boy taking leave,
   rotating his fingers in a wave,
He remembers waving to his father
   remembers following calling to him.

Is it a dream? He watches
   as an SS officer
points a revolver at his mother's breast.

The man wants to talk, wants to begin
    everything again
tell a woman deep in her own grief
    about death, about marriage.

3

She does not move from the vanity.
    To walk away is simple.
It takes practice to wait,
    to conceive an imaginary pause
moving like dust motes
    silent as an unopened book.

Someday life will come towards them
    in a sleek boat
on a river smaller than the Rhone.
    It will be an afternoon in summer.
They will have lives to live again.

Passing the Gene to Jane

Grandfather says Jane inherited the talking gene
from Nonnie; she's on the phone most of the day,
started with all those sisters talking to each other
and then a whole gaggle of women heard about it
and now there's all this jabbering, in one ear and
out the next mouth and then it swings around
back through the whole passel of women again,
telecommunicating the whole damn town.

Nonnie says she's listening and trying to help
figure things out with people, somebody has to do it
and since he sits in the kitchen eating peanuts
and just happy to be alive this has turned out
to be her job, one of her jobs at any rate, besides
some people think she has a knack for it, some even say
she's the best listener in South Dartmouth,
people get paid for this who aren't half as useful.

Jane, who's three, says she may not understand perfectly
but she always gets the drift and she's going to keep on
talking, probably a lot, it helps her figure things out
and besides, she's good at it and she knows that
and (*new word! gentle! men!*) would gentlemen
please understand she's making order in her mind
and the world and that's called *thinking*,
a business she intends to be in, like Nonnie.

Why I Wake Weeping

after dreaming I pass my son while he is hitchhiking

Admittedly
points of red
are little clue, the form
one with the darkness.
so the deer
are not seen in the field
or the soft worlds of clover
at their feet.
what should be grand clues
are only as the dot on the "i"
barely a word enough to
identify.
so, it is no wonder
that I wake weeping
for the image of a
young man at the side of the road.
backpack, cap down to his eyes—
all my life I have missed
the things I love most
driven
by my fear.
So now, when I do not
recognize the face,
the half smile
like the waning moon,
i pass him by,
do not stop.
he never tells me
of that night when
everyone passed him by
when arriving home so late
no lights would light

for him,
the fire would not kindle.
he accepts it somewhere
within himself, like
barbed wire on fence
grown into the tree.
it has become a silence
between us,
his knowing I know,
neither of us saying it.
beyond recognition
all those days growing like
yeast in bread:
why should I have known?
such an immediate, ambiguous task
to always be the one giving life.

I wake weeping
for the slow configuration of days,
weary and accumulative of grief.
I wake weeping for the boy
I passed by on a journey,
too fearful to stop
for the stranger in us both.
I wake weeping
for all those days
eaten quickly like
morning bread,
for the nights I saw
no figure
beyond the points of light.

Hooking Rugs and Ice Fishing

He volunteered with a dying patient
expecting to go through the five stages of grief
at the first meeting. Instead
she talked about hooking rugs:

the needle, the thread, the cloth,
the rhythmic movement of the hands.
He tried other matters in conversation—
she talked of hooking rugs.

On the next visit she spoke of the intricacies
and hardships of ice fishing that her husband
had done before his death. Week after week,
hooking rugs and ice fishing.

Angered, he said to friends,
"I can't go on with this
interminable hooking rugs
and ice fishing."

One day as they sat
in the hospital cafeteria,
she going on, he bored and vexed
with hooking rugs and ice fishing

the room
went silent, air turned
a luminous shade of green, hooking
rugs and ice

fishing shopped. She leaned over and said,
"I could not have done this

without you,"
then on again with hooking rugs

and ice fishing. Soon after she died. At the funeral
relatives said to him, "Thank you,
all she ever spoke about
was you."

Buck

Cockeyed speculation, his old lady called it
when he said in his next life he'd return
as a deer. "Young buck with a big rack
of horns?" she smirked. He grumbled a deep cough,
shuffled out with the care arthritic limbs demand
and stepped off the deck. Inside, later
a chill hovered. He grabbed the shirt
over his heart and twisted. Pulseless
he slumped to the floor like the bags of potatoes
he'd stacked his whole life, wrinkled and soft
as the last sack in spring ready to split and seed.

The death simmered down, people went home
and she settled back in the house by the pond.
"I miss the old guy to haul wood. By Jesus,
this house leaks as bad as a pail left
two years on a stump." She was warmest
in the upstairs bedroom, heat rising
from the kitchen below. Sun once in a while
beamed through the dormer that looked
at night like a one-eyed fool winking
over the lake at those "ice fishing idiots,"
she, alone, stitching on a quilt.

One night she's about to snap off the light.
"Clomp, clomp" on the deck, so she flips the switch
and gazes down on the boards streaked with moon
reflected off the snow. The buck looks through
the glass dining room doors, woodstove
crackling red flame around its draft. Damn.
He turns by the kitchen door, makes

a feeble clumsy hop on the steps and ambles
down the shoreline, picking his way,
an old man, head high, half blind
and hungry, out for fresh air and a smoke.

JEAN VALENTINE

The Hawthorne Robin Mends with Thorns

Talking with Mary about 1972

like a needle

through my 25-years-older

breast my years thinner rib: 1972:

a child life

away from my children:

"but you couldn't have been different

from the way you were"

but I *would* to have been different

Can You Fix Anything?

My granddaughter's sorrows, no.
My sorrows,
your end of life sorrows, no.

There was a past life I can't fix,
a future life I can't fix,
neither the red nor the green.

I couldn't fix the stovepipe.
Get heat. Can you
fix anything?

ELLEN BRYANT VOIGT

Winter Field

The winter field is not
the field of summer lost in snow: it is
another thing, a different thing.

"We shouted, we shook you," you tell me,
but there was no sound, no face, no fear, only
oblivion—why shouldn't it be so?

After they'd pierced a vein and fished me up,
after they'd reeled me back they packed me under
blanket on top of blanket, I trembled so.

The summer field, sun-fed, mutable,
has its many tasks; the winter field
becomes it adjective.
                        For those hours
I was some other thing, and my body,
which you have long loved well,
did not love you.

Long Marriage

Forward his numb foot, back
her foot, his chin on her head,
her head on his collarbone,

during those marathons
between wars, our vivid
Dark Times, each dancer holds

the other up so he,
as the vertical heap barely
moves yet moves, or she

eyes half-lidded, unmoored,
can rest. Why these, surviving
a decimated field?

More than a lucky fit—
not planks planed from the same
oak trunk but mortise and tenon—

it is the yoke that makes
the pair, that binds them to
their blind resolve, two kids

who thought the world was burning
itself out, and bet
on a matched disregard

for the safe and the sad—*Look*,
one hisses toward the flared
familiar ear, *we've come*

this far, this far, this far.

ELLEN BRYANT VOIGT

Anthropology

The large dog sprawls in the road, remembering
his younger triumph over passing cars.
Here comes one now; it swerves, blares it horn,
and his littermate, a smaller quicker dog
trolling the suspect mole, slinks to the porch.
This fails to shame, or teach, or galvanize,
since he would rather be envied than admired—
he holds the road as lion would his rock,
walrus his floe.
                        I knock on the windowpane;
he looks toward me, then turns his thick neck back
to look at the road. I knock again; he looks
at me, then heaves his body up, strolls
to the house with plausible irony: he's not
accountable, who woos whatever traffic
sidles past; whose sleep is comatose
and not disturbed, like hers, by the tick of the hunt;
whose head happens to reach to the willing hand—
my hand rubbing his crown, her currying tongue,
all of it costs him nothing. His one job?
To wag his tail when the Alpha Male comes home.
Meanwhile his busy sister patrols the yard,
chases after thunder out in the field,
bites midair in winter the snow-detritus
shuffling from the eaves—she knows she's a dog,
knows what dogs do:
                        hope to please, and plunge.

Plaza del Sol

This is a veterans' ward, here by the pool
in Florida, where every chaise is taken, every frame
stretched out to full extension, the bodies just removed
from cold storage, exposing to light and air
the wound, the scar, the birthmark's crushed grape,
contiguous chins undisguised by pearls,
pitted shoulders plumped or scapular, flesh
pleated under an upper arm, a vast loaf rising
out of the bathing bra, or chest collapsed
and belly preeminent, spine a trough
or a knotted vine climbing the broad cliff-wall.
Down from this pelvic arch five children came;
that suspicious mole, his mother kissed;
but who will finger such calves, their rosaries?
Here's a brace of ankles like water-balloons;
here's a set of toes shingled with horn.
Here is the man, prone, whose back is a pelt,
and the supine woman whose limbs are Tinkertoys,
and the man whose tattooed eagle looks crucified,
and his brother with breasts, and his wife with one—
a woman tanned already, dried fruit arranged on a towel—
and her pale sister, seated, bosom piled in her lap,
oiling the lunar landscape of her thighs.
The hot eye over them all does not turn away
from bodies marooned inside loose colorful rags
or bursting their bandages there at the lip of the cave—
from ropy arms, or the heavy sack at the groin,
or the stone of the head—bodies mapped
and marbled, rutted, harrowed, warmed at last,
while everyone else has gone off into the sea.

My Ex-Lover Comes Back into My Life

as a dog   A sad-eyed nameless mutt
I invite in out of pity   who pees

in every room and is not ashamed when
I push his nose in it   shrugging

it off as soon as I let go   to grab towels and soak up
the stink and embarrassment   Leaving me again

to wonder why I let him in in the first place   or
what thug of a father hurt him   when he was a sorry

boy   cursing him from his life to the next saying
he was not man enough   So now here he is

head in his paws   eyes gooey with anguish   or there he was
digging another Budweiser from my fridge   Life so bright

and certain in the cans below the butter dish   their all-American
colors calling   one skinny-anxious loner

galumping hopelessly homeward his leather jacket
not thick enough to hide   a puppy heart at seventeen

He was stupid and brave and loyal   the kind of straggler
who might just win you   limping in as he did

with his woebegone blues   behind
an overhang of hair   A kiss just when

and where I needed it most   And how many years
is a dog year anyway   and if a man hush-whimpers

beside you while you sleep   is he lost or wounded
or innocently dreaming   I wasn't savior enough

I let him go   without so much as a good luck
fuck   I kicked him too   unrepentantly

so he's come back to me   a wayward runt
who Life begs to toss off a bridge   and I am trying

to remember his true name   Buster   or Prince
Teddy2   or Champ   and as he circles the floor

three times before settling down   I pretend he is
looking for forgetfulness   or forgiveness   the secret

scent that transmutes one day to the next   And if tomorrow we go
together on his favorite car ride   the wind will lick

his floppy ears   He will open his mouth in what seems
to be a smile   And this time I'll hold the door for him

he'll believe me when I say   *good dog   attaboy*
go home now   and then I'll drive away

Adagio

If we come to the crest of the hill & look down   into the river   deep
      slow moving water
  do we see cloud sky descend   a single plover   circling through
      riffled blue
shrieking *kill-dee-eu kill-dee-eu* to its mate shuffling
at the shore's edge   wing outstretched   feathers stroking air
engaged in a game of ruse & fret   while trees come into themselves
slender & strong limbed   so earnest & confident—
(convinced the world is theirs   to do with as they will)
greensweet leaves   held close to bodies   like hundreds of lovers
willow hair   tangled with mystery   ready to give up secrets
      embrace the pooled water-light below

sun floating up   out of nowhere   insistent beautiful mindless
      impotence
   holding neither memory nor desire   being the same always
heated white strobe   engaged in argument   jousting with the day
      moon
each laying claim to a momentary space   & now morning's spring
      sheen
the damp field draped in shine grass splendorous as it sways its way
down the slope   past woods & moss & rock & stone wall   a dance
      into daydream—
this miniature   fixed   mesmerized by its own form & shadow
even crickets   think they are angels humming   the three noisy
      blackbirds
grasping the fence   as the lone pine   picking up groundwind
bends into the trill of light   the meadow which sighs comfortably
each stem & blossom   every sepal petal   sure of its necessity
& the river   wise & ingenuous   knowing the truth   laughs & winds
      off
         branching out like mind opening . . .

& you? breath sweet caught in throat   hushed voice on the rise   like
    smoke
      spun into air   laughter suspended pianissimo   the lover's
      face
by yours   otherworldly   luminescent   moving close closer to the
    silent eddy
each gesture   feature   alive in the moment   believing in the next
reaching for the idea of future some small sense of permanence
& river reeds   speak quietly   keep on with their slap slap . . .
      sotto voce—
& do you see? birdcall killdeer sky cloud   all memory
tree & leaf   gone   sun & willow drift   past pine & moon & meadow
blackbirds   toward a new place   every bough   wind & flower follow
even as hands dip into water   mouths & sound   eyes & sight
fragile as crystal shatter   mosaic of thin shimmer & glimmer
this fine ballet   on the slow cold pull of the current   a'flutter –
      gone . . . but *where?*

Have we been here before? *Seen. Realized.* A flash of river flint & the
    world
    we know   caught in the instant stopped & held   a sudden
    reflection   something? . . .
what was & will be   tapestry woven into the *now* time   held & let go
blue meadow   crickets in grass wingbeat-studded sky   faint birdsong
the lost performance   closing scene   & only water still sings: *the*
    end   the end
all of it elsewhere   rush & color   twitch & trig   & riversong
    becomes prayer
(yes unanswered   our deities make no concessions   especially not here)
& you your face desolate   slow current of blood   cooled skin   grey
    flesh
struggling under weeds & mud   you breathless   remembering   in
    slow motion
      left with absence   lament for want & loss

In the instant   the river shudders once   flows on   out of epitaph &

elegy

waterfilm takes frame after frame to nowhere—

we turn in mid-air   gaze at the image   meeting the light   a nearby
distance

slow & sure   press on going tenderly   to what is dream   but not
dream

discovering   what is   *now & here*   has already gone

only the living past   as real as ripples on the surface   stays

Daily Grind

A man awakes every morning
and instead of reading the newspaper
reads Act V of Othello.
He sips his coffee and is content
that this is the news he needs
as his wife looks on helplessly.
The first week she thought it a phase,
his reading this and glaring at her throughout,
the first month an obsession,
the first year a quirkiness in his character,
and now it's just normal behavior,
this mood setting in over the sliced bananas,
so she tries to make herself beautiful
to appease his drastic taste.
And every morning, as he shaves
the stubble from his face, he questions everything--
his employees, his best friend's loyalty,
the women in his wife's canasta club,
and most especially the wife herself
as she puts on lipstick in the mirror next to him
just before he leaves. This is how he begins
each day of his life--as he tightens the tie
around his neck, he remembers the ending,
goes over it word by word in his head,
the complex drama of his every morning
always unfolded on the kitchen table,
a secret Iago come to light with every sunrise
breaking through his window, the syllables
of betrayal and suicide always echoing
as he waits for his car pool, just under his lips
even as he pecks his wife goodbye.

Gravedigger's Birthday

We had only dated for three weeks
but there I was, burying her cat.
To top things off, it was my birthday,
but I knew the cat's death trumped it
so into the ground I went,
never having dug a gravae before
but knowing I should know how.
Such an ancient, simple action,
as if our bodies evolved to do such work—
opposable thumb to dig and dig
deeper into the earth, and standing erect
to toss soil from our graves. I remembered
something from somewhere—boy scouts
or horror movie—delve deeply enough
so raccoons can't stir up the corpse.
I did it all quietly with a sudden solemnity
not for the cat—I barely knew it—
but for the motion, the first ancestral thing
I had done in years, aware this was traffic
with old gods. The indifferent stars pinned
the lips of the grave open, and I lifted up
that solid eggplant of a body, and lowered her
carefully into the soil, as if the cat could feel it,
or the earth could. Ridiculous.
Then I lifted up that shovel, again
knowing what to do—load upon load
into the earth, back onto that body,
returning it but also casting it out
of my modern life where I would soon take
the short walk from the grave to the house,
eat some meat without thinking
of eating the meat, get in bed
next to my new, warm, mourning girlfriend

on a mattress imported from far away, some speck
of the grave's dirt rising behind a fingernail
as I lie awake, the faint next click
of my life's odometer there in the darkness,
living and dying at the same time,
thinking how so much motion and instinct
lies inert in the earth next to the swing set,
and how the ground's new toothless mouth
settled into closure without pomp,
temporary and permanent at once.

The Body of My Brother

First it belonged to my mother
or seemed to,
stuffed into her
like a foot in a sock.
Then it took care of itself
for a while, filling out
into home runs, high jumps.
There were times
it must have been afraid
hiding in a bunker
in South Viet Nam
having happen to it whatever it was
that makes bodies years later
jump out of bed in the middle of the night
not awake
sweating and shouting.
Last time I saw it
it was older than mine,
thinned out
by too man cigarettes
and favors given away.
Now they've taken it
from the hospital bed
where it gasped out his last punch line
and put it in a box
that no one will ever see again
though now we stand around it
observing gestures even death cannot remove:
head tilt, wry smile,
hands the same as my hands

crossed over his chest
like they never were in life,
a few pictures and mementos
scattered around it
as if they were crumbs of a happy life.

Volunteer Award

With great pleasure and deep regret I must
inform you of the highest
merit your son while serving
his flag in disregard of
in recognition of others your years
painlessly accompanying the body a detail
and a monetary award he fell
in battle your selflessness giving
generously your time a plaque and your son
was a credit and comfort to those less
fortunate the remains will be transported
it is people like yourself who give this
sacrifice as a ceremony in vain
in your honor will be laid to rest
enclosed find check to cover meals
the casket and your hours of service
in a horse-drawn dignified looking
forward for freedom and justice
congratulations again

Hunting Blind

Sit on the knoll.
Watch the valley spread out all around.
Think how wonderful it all looks.
Think about the sun,
the quality of light,
the light scud or clouds,
the small cars on the highway.
Isn't that a little red barn over there.

Turn away my friend!
This is how the world seduces you.
This is satan in the desert,
Christ looking at the heart of darkness.
This is not the way things are.
Things are mean;
you ought to know that by now.

Think about it.
That barn: aren't there rats in it?
And isn't that the house where the guy at the bar lives?
The guy that kicks the shit out of his wife every weekend.
It's an ugly fucking world.
Don't let it kid you brother.

Wake up you simple fool.
Those aren't clouds.
That's not a road.
That barn is rotten with beetles and dung.
That forest hides a pit,
in the pit are dozens of rotting cows.
They're swollen with the heat,
ripe to bursting

and deeper in the woods there's a dirty old black bear,
raising its head a little now in the breeze
catching the scent of putrefaction,
licking its chops and turning to amble off to the pit.
At the head of the pit, high in a tower,
is a man with a 30/30 and it's loaded
and in an hour or so the bear is going to be strung up
on those lines, his guts running out into the gravel and weeds,
and flies will be swarming all around the man
and he'll swat at them and finish gutting the bear
and carve it up into steaks and bones
and sell the bones to other men in cities and eat the steaks with
some catamount beer and click on the tube
and watch another episode of cops or married with children or the
         freaking
nature channel
and belch and get up and swat his wife like the bear swats a cub or a
         trout
swimming happy in a cold stream and she'll fall down and maybe sob
         a little it's
been like this for so long. Then he'll waddle into the bedroom
         bounce off the
wall once losing his balance, take off his shoes or maybe only one,
         he's really
drunk tonight, and then he falls asleep, snoring, big gut gleaming up
         at the
moon and she walks in with that 30/30 and blows his stupid head off
         and if you
looked out the window you'd see that cloud zip across the moon and
         it's the
same one that the world is using to trick you now

It's all illusion
It's the magician with nothing up his sleeve
pulling the coin behind your ear,

your big flapping stupid ear.
It's just another day in hell.
The sooner you wake up the sooner we can get back to work.
Your vacation's almost over.

Holding the Egg

I scratched with my fingernail onto
the arctic-cold windowpane
removing the patterns of ice.
Clearing a spot the size
of a dime, I peered into
the blue and white landscape.

"Here, hold this," my mother said,
handing me the red-checked napkin
with the warmed egg.
Ice-tingling hands round
it and life spread through
my fingertips.
It is the holding, rather than
the eating that counts.

The storm last night
silenced heat and lights
with a knockout punch.
I light the sterno, knowing winter
has a way of bringing things together.

With tilted head, listening
for wind sounds,
my little one sits, solemn, content,
her hands cupped, holding an egg.

Going Home

There is no going home
as usual
the vehicle stalls
in reverse gear
in mud tracks

as essential as
the flat fields, the blades
of shadowed pines over the drive,
the sun bleeding
from the west.

On the rise the house,
painted clapboard, the color of cream,
is rented now like bodies
of water and minerals made
living by some miracle

which is to say some process
we don't understand.
Someday we'll have a
different owner,
a different lover,

like pine trees and whirling wind
that primitive communion
like a new testament
of each generation.
All going home is never going back—

there may be ruin, and mud tracks
deep to make wheels spin. The only way
is slogging on,

or else walking
on water.

Or yet it may be dry
the sand flying in your nostrils
but you must breathe, must go, must go
on, which is to say, go on making
required visits, like stations

of a cross. It is a way
of finding what we'd lost
or never had, or learning we were only
renters, and making new covenants,
of going where we belong.

PETER WOOD

What Luck! A Little Jingle for David Hall
down where the people are
— Richard Eberhart, August 1980

Muttly and a flaky bitch
part Irish setter, featherbrained,
are hanging out these days around the inn.
This inn.
The place I'm hanging out myself.
The owner's Swiss. He's pissed
that local mutts can use this place.

I'm waiting in the shade
for the handyman's truck
so I can borrow a wrench
to fix my bike. Some drunk
must have run the wheel into a wall.
But thanks to David Hall,
all I need is a wrench. What luck!

To pass the time and try to turn
low culture high, I light a joint.
The bitch sniffs as if to say
to Muttly, This guy's a mutt like us.

They walk up and lie down,
upwind but close. I say
What luck, Muttly! Let's get nice.
I swear, he puts all paws in the air
and wriggles on his back.
That's mutt talk for *What luck!*

This Year's Muttly

By what right do we call ourselves poets?
— William Matthews, August 1981

In 1981 some luck's been grim.
Armand, the Swiss, went broke,
ran off and got snuffed by gangsters
for his debts. Maybe that's just talk.
Anyway, the inn he owned is shut.
Tough luck. And this hut here, this barn's
in danger too. Here we scrunched
in buggy fog pondering authority,
the loss of poets' lucky bucks of public funding.

I thought of Muttly. He might cheer us up.
Breaking out my smoke supply
and tying on my biking shoes,
I set out to fetch him, cruising
for a hot bitch in a cool location, knowing Muttly.

Most dogs I saw were pedigreed or else employed
as watchdogs or companions—a pair of spaniels,
two swell dalmatians, a couple of beagles. But Muttly?
No such luck . . . I need to find some trick.
As "poet" I promised to deliver
one Muttly poem Tuesday (That was Monday).
Now, however, it is Tuesday and Muttly
is still missing. No trick attracts him,
unless, between you and me, some trick
can be worked by a lucky tongue.

BARON WORMSER

Explication du Texte

One midwinter night in the tacky
But cozy grad club after a beer
Or two and the usual chat about
Our overbearing, neurotic profs
You emerged from a musing silence
To announce that as a lapsed Catholic
The only heaven for which you could muster
Any fervor was Wallace Stevens's:
"Consider (you said), it is piquant
Yet amiable, voluble yet courtly.
Delirious with chatter
And bewildered grace. What
(You asked) was the Christian heaven but
An insipid smile, an anaesthetic
That Stevens cheerily challenged,
Fashioning his own cock's crow of sublimity
From his proudly pagen taste.
The best of heavens is implied in
The imagination's zest. Unblessed it is blessed."

I felt far away from any heaven
In that sealed tomb of cigarettes
And denimed *philosophes* though
That didn't keep me from skewing
The insurance-man poet as being "in reality"
(A favorite, all-purpose, idiot phrase
Of mine) an armchair fascist and fantasist,
A cold-blooded Prospero who summoned
Elegancies because he couldn't abide
The contingent pain of mere flesh.
His heaven as the leisure class's wallpaper.

"Don't give me that pissed-off, working-class jive,"
You said, looking aggrieved and bleary at the same time.
"Stevens despised the wisdom of wariness.
The man sang joy from the grayest air."

I wouldn't bend. Frost held me that
Year like an instructive nightmare.
His shrewd gravity was my longed-for
Compass. We fenced half-heartedly,
Downed our Buds, eyed the clock
Donated by a local realtor for the minute
To repair to our bookish cells.

Awkward hurt spoke in your gentle eyes.
When on earth would our words have lives?

The Novel of Alcohol

After the clamor of invention subsided—
The spurious heat of the authoring self,
The idealist arrogance of insight,
The brooding that makes an honest book—
There was the bottle.
Typically misrepresented by those
Who believe in the duty of meaningful works
That amber fire mimed for an hour or two
The greater awakening, the personal sun
That once rose, so spectacularly
To quicken the veins of the stoniest morning.

That too subsided into complaint, silence,
A listing belligerence that amused some
Of the locals on the plaza and bored the rest.
"The great gringo"—another fool, more or less.
Still, those onlookers rarely pursed their lips.
They had their own ruined gods
And they grasped in their calm way, the whole
Sorriness of the artist's volcanic light. Bound
To flicker and faint, they might have said.
Bound in its Odyssean urge to visit too soon
The uncanny land of the wordlessly dead.

On the Lawn of the Kinsman
(1996)

A full moon in early August:
It sits amid the needling stars
Softly startling, a child's emblem
To admonish all sublunar
Beauties, to gild the dark.

The gathered writers sit
On the dewy lawn in the small hours
Exchanging tales of words,
Endurance and fitful powers.
For a northern night, it's warm

And the moonlight is balm.
Longing forgets to fret
As their articulate pleasure
Winds above the crickets,
A lulling, human music.

There's an answering aura in
The weak light, the murmur rising
Into the quicksilver of second sight.
The tableau sings
Like the cold moon, a painted ring

Of frail eternity. The voices
Hum on. Make a wish—
But this would be that end
When love is shrewd yet moonish,
When we accept our gifts.

Acknowledgements

Every effort has been made to trace the ownership of copyrighted material and to secure the necessary permission to reprint the selections in this book. In the event of questions about the use of any material, the publisher, while expressing regret for any inadvertent error, will be happy to make the correction in future printings. Thanks are due to the following for permission to reprint the material listed below:

Resa Alboher: "Wild Onions" is previously unpublished and is reprinted with permission of the author.

Edith Aronowitz-Mueller: Parts of "Poems from the Fat Girl" have appeared in *Kalliope* and *Sojourner* and are reprinted by permission of the author.

Renée Ashley: "Where You Go When You Sleep" was first published in *Chelsea*. It was also published in the book *The Various Reasons of Light*, (Avocet Press Inc.), and is reprinted by permission of the author.

Joan Baranow: "Beautiful" is previously unpublished and is reprinted with permission of the author.

Jeanne Marie Beaumont: "I Brake for Animals," copyright 2001 by Jeanne Marie Beaumont, first appeared in *DoubleTake* (Fall 2001) and is reprinted by permission of the author. "The Plenty," copyright 2000 by Jeanne Marie Beaumont, first appeared in *Barrow Street* (Summer 2000), and is reprinted by permission of the author.

Sheryll Bedingfield: "Back to Zero" is previously unpublished and is reprinted with permission of the author.

Philip Cioffari: "Racing the Uptown Express" was originally published in *Worcester Review* and is reprinted with permission of the author.

Amy Clampitt: "Iola, Kansas," "Amaranth and Moly," and "Syrinx" are all reprinted with permission of the publisher, Alfred A. Knopf.

Cathleen Cohen: "Beautiful Feet" is reprinted with permission of the author.

Wyn Cooper: "Postcard from This Place" and "Postcard from Harmony Parking Lot" originally appeared in *Secret Address* (Chapiteau Press) and are reprinted with permission of the author.

Sidney Creaghan: "Salt of Surrender" is reprinted with permission of the author.

Jimmie Cumbie: "Angler" is previously unpublished and is reprinted with permission of the author.

Christopher Cunningham: "Cows at the Salt Lick" is previously unpublished and is reprinted with permission of the author.

Mary DeBow: "New Hampshire Farm" is previously unpublished and is reprinted with permission of the author.

Mark DeFoe: "The Summer List" first appeared in *Poet Lore* and is reprinted with permission of the author.

Jessica G. de Koninck: "Footprints of the Stars" is previously unpublished and is reprinted with permission of the author.

Catherine DeNunzio-Gabordi: "The Doily" is previously unpublished and is reprinted with permission of the author.

Karin de Weille: "Potter" is previously unpublished and is reprinted with permission of the author.

Margaret Diorio: "From a Phone Booth" is previously unpublished and is reprinted with permission of the author.

Susan Donnelly: "The Gospel Singer Testifies" appears in *Transit* (Iris Press, 2001) and is reprinted by permission of the author.

Martha Andrews Donovan: "The Nearness of You" is previously unpublished and is reprinted with permission of the author.

Catherine Doty: "Eggs" and "Outboard" were first published in *Endless Mountain Review* and are reprinted with permission of the author.

Karen Douglassa: "Crow's Daughter" is previously unpublished and is reprinted with permission of the author.

Juditha Dowd: "The Marriage Bathroom" is previously unpublished and is reprinted with permission of the author.

George Drew: "The Old Boy" is previously unpublished and is reprinted with permission of the author.

Stephen Dunn: "Dismantling the House" was first published in *Poetry*. "Monogamy," "Turning to the Page," and "Achilles in Love" are previously unpublished. All four poems are reprinted with permission of the author.

J. K. Durick: "Taken" is previously unpublished and is reprinted with permission of the author.

Lynn Emanuel: "Like God," "Dressing the Parts," and "Elsewhere" have been reprinted with permission of the author.

Joan Cusack Handler: "Gravy" and "Psychotherapist with Black Leather Binder Sits in White Oak Chair That Came Through a Fire" were first published in *GlOrious* (CavanKerry Press, 2003) and reprinted with permission of the author.

Sandra Handloser: "Christmas in Florida" is previously unpublished and is reprinted with permission of the author.

Jeffrey Harrison: "Arrival" is from *Signs of Arrival* (Copper Beech Press, 1996) and is reprinted with permission of the author. "Family Dog" is from *Feeding the Fire* (Sarabande Books, 2001) and is reprinted with permission of the author.

Siegfried Haug: "Ploughing in Fall" is previously unpublished and is reprinted with permission of the author.

Allen Heggen: "That Afternoon in Harvest" appeared in *Northern Woodlands Magazine* (Winter 1997) and is reprinted with permission of the publisher.

Hugh Hennedy: "Pietà in Camera" is previously unpublished and is reprinted with permission of the author.

Lois Hirshkowitz: "Darkfall" is reprinted with permission of the author.

Deming Holleran: "Trash Day" is previously unpublished and is reprinted with permission of the author.

Paul Hostovsky: "Conversations with My Son" is previously unpublished and is reprinted with permission of the author.

David Huddle: "April Saturday, 1960" is previously unpublished and is reprinted with permission of the author.

Sydney Lea: "1959," "Evening Walk as the School Year Starts," "Rodney Fallen: A Parable," and "Manifest" are reprinted with permission of the author.

Brad Leithauser: "Small Waterfall: A Birthday Poem" and "A False Spring" are reprinted with permission of the author.

Robert Lesman: "At the Windswept Cottages" has been published in the chapbook *Sky Reports* (2001) and is reprinted with permission of the author.

Howard Levy: "The Steam of Tea" and "Divorce" originally appeared in *SouthWestern Magazine* and are reprinted with permission of the author.

Betty Lies: "Small Geographies" was previously published in *Kelsey Review* (2000) and is reprinted with permission of the author.

P. H. Liotta: "Homage to Saint Cyril" previously appeared in *The Ruins of Athens: A Balkan Memoir* (Garden Street Press, 1999). "Jazz" appeared previously in *Connecticut Review*. Both poems are reprinted with permission of the author.

Carl Little: "Heron on the Dam" originally appeared in *Main Progressive* and is reprinted with permission of the author.

Diane Lockward: "The Properties of Light" originally appeared in *Wind Magazine* and is reprinted with permission of the author.

Daniel Lusk: "To the Boy Saved from Drowning" originally appeared in *Louisville Review* and is reprinted with permission of the author. "Quiddity" is reprinted with permission of the author.

Thomas Lux: "The Language Animal," "The Devil's Beef Tub," "Terminal Lake," and "Render, Render" are reprinted with permission of the author.

Nancy Richardson: "Youngstown, Ohio 1952" is previously unpublished and is reprinted with permission of the author.

Mary Columbo Rodgers: "Harvest" is previously unpublished and is reprinted with permission of the author.

Susan Roney-O'Brien: "Forsythia," winner of the first prize in the Worcester County Poetry Association annual contest, and which first appeared in *Worcester Review*, is reprinted with permission of the author.

Patricia Rose: "Song of the Magdalene" is previously unpublished and is reprinted with permission of the author.

Michael Ryan: "Ash Pit," "A Two-Year-Old Girl in a Restaurant," "Reminder," and "In the Sink" first appeared in *American Poetry Review* and are reprinted with permission of the author.

Nicholas Samaras: "Giving Answers to Questionnaires" and "The Father of Hands" are reprinted with permission of the author.

Lois Sargent: "Abraham, Isaac, and . . . Sarah" is reprinted with permission of the author.

Nina Schafer: "Personal History" is previously unpublished and is reprinted with permission of the author.

Jim Schely: "Autumn Equinox" is previously unpublished and is reprinted with permission of the author. "Clio" first appeared in the chapbook *One Another* and is reprinted with the permission of Chapiteau Press.

Charles Simic: "The Village of Philosophizing Dogs," "Wonders of the Invisible World," and "Invitation" are previously unpublished and are reprinted with permission of the author.

Jane Simon: "Stiletto-Heeled" is previously unpublished and is reprinted with permission of the author.

George Singer: "Slipping Out" is reprinted with permission of author.

Tom Sleigh: "Raft" and "Speech for Myself as Ghost" are reprinted with permission of the author.

Bruce Smith: "Groove and Break: His Voice at Fifty," "In the Blue Room," and "Flight" have appeared in *The Other Lover* (University of Chicago, 2000) and are reprinted with permission of the author.

Elizabeth Anne Socolow: "Old Woman Dreams" is reprinted with permission of the author.

Margo Stever: "On the Possession of Horses," originally published in *Chelsea* and which also appeared in *Frozen Spring* (Mid-List Press), is reprinted with permission of the author.

Harriet Susskind: "Love Tale" is previously unpublished and is reprinted with permission of the author.

Jean Sinclair Symmes: "Passing the Gene to Jane" is previously unpublished and is reprinted with permission of the author.

Jennifer Thomas: "Why I Wake Weeping (after dreaming I passed my son while hitchhiking)" is previously unpublished and is reprinted with permission of the author.

Parker Towle: "Hooking Rugs and Ice-Fishing" and "Buck" are reprinted with permission of the author.

Jean Valentine: "The Hawthorne Robin Mends with Thorns" and "Can You Fix Anything?" are previously unpublished and are reprinted with permission of the author.

Biographies

Resa Alboher is a Frost Place Festival and Seminar participant and an American living in Moscow, Russia. The poem "Wild Onions," from a collection-in-progress of Russia-inspired work, was written at The Frost Place in 2002.

Edith Aronowitz-Mueller teaches at the University of Massachusetts–Boston. Most recently her poems have appeared in *Massachusetts Review* and *Connecticut Poetry Journal*.

Renée Ashley is the author of three books of poetry: *Salt, The Various Reasons of Light*, and *The Revisionist's Dream*. Her novel, *Someplace Like This*, was published in July 2003. She has received creative writing fellowships from the New Jersey State Council on the Arts and the National Endowment for the Arts and is on the faculty of Fairleigh Dickinson University's MFA in creative writing program.

Joan Baranow's poems have appeared in journals such as *Paris Review* and *Spoon River Poetry Review*. She has two books, *Living Apart* and *Blackberry Winter*, as well as a collaborative CD of poetry and jazz. She lives with her husband, poet David Watts, and their children in Mill Valley, California.

Jeanne Marie Beaumont is the author of *Placebo Effects* (Norton, 1997) and *Curious Conduct* (forthcoming, BOA Editions), and coeditor of *The Poets' Grimm: 20th Century Poems from Grimm Fairy Tales* (Storyline Press, 2003). In addition to The Frost Place, where she has served as a resident faculty member several times, she has taught at Rutgers University and the Unterberg Poetry Center of the 92nd Street Y. She lives in Manhattan.

Sheryll Bedingfield works as a psychotherapist and marriage and family therapist. She is sensitive to aspects of spirituality in human growth and relationships. Her poetry appears in *Proposing on the Brooklyn Bridge*, *Poems about Marriage*, a collection edited by Ginny Lowe Conner, and *Poet Works* (Grayson Books).

Marvin Bell was born in New York City in 1937 and grew up on rural Long Island. He holds a bachelor's degree from Alfred University, a master's degree from the University of Chicago, and a Master of Fine Arts degree from the University of Iowa. He is the author of fifteen books.

Elinor Benedict won the 2000 May Swenson Poetry Award for her collection *All That Divides Us* (Utah State University Press). She has previously published five chapbooks of poetry and several short stories in journals. She served as founding editor of *Passages North* literary magazine. A native of Tennessee and later a resident of Ohio, she has lived in the Upper Peninsula of Michigan for twenty-five years.

Terry Blackhawk is founder and director of Inside Out Literary Arts Project, a nonprofit writers-in-schools program, serving students in Detroit's public schools. She is the author of *Body & Field* (MSU Press, 1999); a chapbook, *Trio: Voices from the Myths*; and *Escape Artist* (Bookmark Press, 2003), which was awarded the 2001 John Ciardi Prize.

Billie Bolton is a native Georgian. She first came to The Frost Place Poetry Festival in 1996 and found it so welcoming and inspiring that she returned in 1997, 1999, and 2001. She is indebted to many talented poets who have taught at The Frost Place.

Laure-Anne Bosselaar grew up in Belgium and then moved to the United States in 1987. Fluent in four languages, she published poems in French and Flemish. She is the author of *The Hour Between Dog and Wolf* and of *Small Gods of Grief*, which won the Isabella Gardner Prize for Poetry for 2001. Both books were published by BOA Editions.

Among other publications, her poems have appeared in *Ploughshares*, *The Washington Post*, *AGNI*, and *Harvard Review*, as well as in numerous anthologies. One of her poems won the National Poetry Contest, sponsored by *I.E.* magazine.

Kurt Brown is the author of five chapbooks and two collections of poetry, both published by Four Way Books: *Return of the Prodigals* and *More Things in Heaven and Earth*. The editor of several anthologies, he teaches in the graduate writing program at Sarah Lawrence College.

Eloise Bruce's first book of poetry, *Rattle*, was published by CavanKerry Press in 2004. She is a member of the poetry group Cool Women and has worked in Theatre for Young Audiences as a director and playwright. She received a fellowship in poetry in 1998 from the New Jersey Council for the Arts. She serves on the advisory board of The Frost Place.

Julie Bruck is the author of two collections of poems: *The End of Travel* (1999) and *The Woman Downstairs* (1993), both published by Brick Books. Her work has appeared in such magazines as *Ploughshares* and *The New Yorker*. A former Montrealer, she lives in San Francisco.

William Byers is a retired nuclear submarine officer. He received his MFA from the University of Maryland-College Park and currently works as a substitute English and mathematics teacher in the county high schools.

Claudia Carlson was born in Bloomington, Indiana, and has published poetry in *Heliotrope*, *Space & Time*, and *Fantastic Stories*. She is the co-editor of *The Poets' Grimm: 20th Century Poems from Grimm Fairy Tales* (Storyline Press, 2003). She works as a senior book designer at Oxford University Press and lives in Manhattan with her family.

Robert Carnevale's poems have appeared in *Paris Review*, *The New Yorker*, and other magazines and anthologies. He has received two poetry fellowships from the New Jersey State Council on the Arts and is currently sharing a National Endowment for the Arts Literary Translation Fellowship with Russian-literature scholar Carol Ueland.

William Carpenter lives in Stockton Springs, Maine, and teaches at the College of the Atlantic in Bar Harbor. His latest book is a novel, *The Wooden Nickel* (Little, Brown, 2002).

Carli Carrara lives in Hebron, NH. She has had poems published in *Phoebe, Appalachia, Sojourner, Onion River Review, California Quarterly,* and *Underwood Review.* She is currently working on a book of poems.

Hayden Carruth was born on August 3, 1921, in Waterbury, Connecticut, and was educated at the University of North Carolina at Chapel Hill and the University of Chicago. For many years, Carruth lived in northern Vermont. He now lives in upstate New York, where until recently he taught in the Graduate Creative Writing Program at Syracuse University. Noted for the breadth of his linguistic and formal resources, influenced by jazz and the blues, Carruth has published twenty-nine books, chiefly of poetry but also a novel, four books of criticism, and two anthologies.

Teresa Carson works for Verizon Communications and is an MFA student at Sarah Lawrence College.

Helen Marie Casey's poetry has been published in literary journals including *Laurel Review, America, Christian Century, Connecticut Review,* and in the anthology *Mischief, Caprice,* and *Other Poetic Strategies.* She was a semifinalist in the 2001 "Discovery"/The Nation contest.

Karen Chase lives and teaches in the Berkshire Mountains of Massachusetts. Her poems have appeared in *The New Yorker, New Republic,* and *Yale Review,* and her book of poems, *Kazimierz Square,* was short-listed as the Best Poetry Book of the Year 2000 published by an independent press. Recently her work has been anthologized in *The Norton Introduction to Poetry* and Billy Collins's anthology *Poetry 180.*

Tim Churchard teaches full-time in the education department at the University of New Hampshire and coaches part-time with the hockey and football programs there.

Philip Cioffari's fiction and poetry have appeared in magazines and anthologies including *North American Review*, *Michigan Quarterly*, *Northwest Review*, and *Southern Poetry Review*. He teaches creative writing at William Paterson University in New Jersey.

Amy Clampitt is author of *The Kingfisher* (1983), *What the Light Was Like* (1985), *Archaic Figure* (1987), and *Westward* (1990). *A Silence Opens*, her last book, appeared in 1994. The recipient in 1982 of a Guggenheim fellowship, and in 1984 of an Academy of American Poets fellowship, she was made a MacArthur Prize fellow in 1992. She was a member of the American Academy of Arts and Letters and was a writer in residence at the College of William and Mary, visiting writer at Amherst College, and Grace Hazard Conkling visiting writer at Smith College. She died in September 1994.

Cathleen Cohen is a painter and teacher in the Philadelphia area. She is the director of the Interfaith Youth Poetry Project and a recipient of a Pennsylvania Council on the Arts grant. She is the author of *Poetry and Jewish Prayer: A Handbook for Teachers*.

Wyn Cooper's newest chapbook is *Secret Address* (Chapiteau Press). A CD of songs and poems he cowrote with the novelist Madison Smart Bell was released by Gaff Music in 2003. He was a resident faculty member at The Frost Place in 2001 and 2003, and recent poems have appeared in *AGNI*, *Poetry*, *Crazyhorse*, and *Vermont Magazine*.

Sidney M. Creaghan, a Louisiana native, is a Jungian psychotherapist, watercolorist, mimic, wife, and mother, but not necessarily in that order. She is an observer, a listener, and a devotee to the well-being of our globe, especially our animals, trees, waters, and crops.

Jimmie Cumbie is a playwright and poet living in Chicago. His poems have appeared in *Spoon River Poetry Review*, *Spout*, *Poetry Motel*, and *Nexus*. His plays have been produced at several Chicago theaters including Curious Theater Branch's Rhino Festival '02, Stage Left, and Footsteps.

Christopher Cunningham holds a BA from Stanford University and a PhD from Duke University. His critical essays have appeared in *Arizona Quarterly* and *Mississippi Quarterly*; his chapbook *Good Coffee* is a finalist in the Center for the Book Arts Chapbook Competition. A high school English teacher, he lives in New Jersey with his wife and children.

Mary Debow Florio has taught English for over twenty years. Her work has been published in several magazines, including *Paterson Literary Review*, *Lips*, *English Journal*, among others. She has won several prizes for her poetry, including second place in the 1997 Allen Ginsberg Poetry Competition (as Mary DeBow). In addition, she is one of the founding members of Hill Poets and a member of No Retreat, a woman's writing collective.

Mark DeFoe teaches literature and writing at West Virginia Wesleyan College. His work has appeared in four chapbooks and in *Poetry*, *Sewanee Review*, *Paris Review*, *Yale Review*, and *Kenyon Review*. He is the winner of two fellowship grants from the state of West Virginia.

Jessica G. de Koninck is both a Festival and a Seminar participant at The Frost Place. Her poems have appeared in *Jewish Women's Literary Annual*, *Bridges*, *Exit 13*, and elsewhere. A New Jersey resident, she has two children and works for the Department of Education as director of legislative services.

Catherine DeNunzio-Gabordi lives with her husband and children in southeastern Connecticut, where she teaches high school English. She attended The Frost Place Poetry Festival in 1998.

Karin de Weille has taught literature at the University of Toronto and the New School and creative writing to children. She is currently teaching at John Jay College in Manhattan. She received a BA in economics from Princeton University, a PhD in literature from the University of Toronto, and an MFA from Sarah Lawrence College. Her poems have appeared in the journals *Big City Lit* (March 2002) and *Lurnina* (2002) and in the anthology *A Time of Trial* (2002). She has recently completed a book on modernist experimentation in literature and the visual arts.

Margaret Diorio was born in New York City in 1925 and studied at Columbia University. From 1973 to 1983 she edited and published *Icarus, A Poetry Journal*, and she coordinated the Baltimore Arts and Peace Poetry Festival until 1995, when her Parkinson's condition made it impossible for her to continue. Her work has been praised by such poets as Robert Penn Warren, Marianne Moore, and May Sarton, who said of her poems, "You have such a special, original voice. . . . The images of violence are terribly haunting . . . but always the images of nature are there to nourish."

Susan Donnelly's poetry collections are *Transit* (Iris Press) and the Morse Prize winner *Eve Names the Animals* (Northeastern University Press). Widely published in magazines, anthologies, and textbooks, she lives and teaches poetry in Cambridge, Massachusetts.

Martha Andrews Donovan is a Frost Place Festival participant and an assistant professor of writing at New England College. "The Nearness of You" is part of a series of poems centered on the death of her mother. Two other poems have been published in *Potpourri* and *Green Mountains Review*.

Catherine Doty's poetry is widely published in journals and anthologies. The recipient of fellowships and prizes from the New York Foundation for the Arts, the New Jersey State Council on the Arts, the Academy of American Poets, and other organizations, she has long taught poetry in schools and writing workshops.

Karen Douglas lives and writes in Maine. She holds an MA from Georgia Southern College and an MFA from Vermont College. Her books include *Red Goddess Poems* and *Bones from the Chimney*. Her work has appeared in many quarterlies and magazines, and she is currently at work on a collection of creative nonfiction stories.

Juditha Dowd lives and writes in western New Jersey. She spends a lot of her time watching the seasons change along the Delaware River.

George Drew was born in Mississippi and raised there and in New York. He is the author of *Toads in a Poisoned Tank*, a collection of poems; and *So Many Bones*, a bilingual chapbook published by a Russian press. He has been published in journals such as *Antioch Review*, *Mississippi Review*, and *Southern Poetry Review*.

Stephen Dunn is the author of twelve collections of poetry, including the recent *Local Visitations* (Norton) and *Different Hours*, winner of the 2001 Pulitzer Prize.

J. K. Durick lives in South Burlington, Vermont, and teaches writing at the Community College of Vermont and SUNY at Plattsburgh. His poetry appears in such places as *Vermont Literary Review*, *Northern New England Review*, and *Delta Epsilon Sigma Journal*.

Lynn Emanuel is the author of three books of poetry: *Then, Suddenly*—(University of Pittsburgh Press, 1999); *The Dig* (1992), which was selected by Gerald Stern for the National Poetry Series; and *Hotel Fiesta* (1984). Her work was included in *Best American Poetry 1995*, edited by Richard Howard, and she recently co-edited the 1994-95 volume of *The Pushcart Prize Anthology* with David St. John. She has received two fellowships from the National Endowment for the Arts and two Pushcart Prizes. She is a professor of English at the University of Pittsburgh, where she directs the writing program.

Martín Espada is the author of seven poetry collections, most recently *Alabanza, New and Selected Poems, 1982–2002* (Norton). He is a professor in the English Department at the University of Massachu-setts–Amherst.

B. H. Fairchild grew up in small towns in the oilfields of Texas, Oklahoma, and Kansas. He has been awarded fellowships from the Guggenheim and Rockefeller Foundations and the National Endowment for the Arts. His third book of poems, *The Art of the Lathe* (Alice James Books, 1998), was a finalist for the National Book Award and was given the Kingsley Tufts Prize and the William Carlos Williams Award. *Early Occult Memory Systems of the Lower Midwest* (Norton, 2003) received the National Book Critics Circle Award in Poetry.

Patricia Fargnoli's book *Necessary Light* (Utah State University Press) won the 1999 May Swenson book award and was a semifinalist for the Glascow Book Award. Her latest book is *Lives of Others* (Oyster River Press). A former Frost Place resident faculty member and participant, she was a Macdowell fellow and has published in *Poetry, Ploughshares, Southern Poetry Review*, and *Prairie Schooner*.

Barbara A. Flaherty is an artist of many talents, but finds the written word to have the most color and depth of presentation. Her poetry has been described as narratives on transition and appealingly instructive even for those inexperienced in poetic forms. Barbara's most recent publication, *Beach Rain*, a book of poetry and photography published in May 2003, along with her previous volume of poetry, *Memory and Metaphor, Collected Poems*, are available through Amazon.com.

Florence Fogelin lives in Vermont and has spent many summers in Littleton, New Hampshire, near The Frost Place. Her chapbook is *Facing the Light* (Redgreene Press of Pittsburgh, 2001).

Nan Fry teaches in the Academic Studies Department at the Corcoran College of Art and Design in Washington, D.C., and is the author of two collections of poetry: *Say What I Am Called*, a chapbook of riddles translated from the Anglo-Saxon; and *Relearning the Dark* (Washington Writers' Publishing House, 1991).

Allison Funk is the author of three books of poems: *The Knot Garden*, *Living at the Epicenter*, and *Forms of Conversion*. She has received a fellowship from the National Endowment for the Arts, the George Kent Prize for Poetry, the Celia B. Wagner Prize from the Poetry Society of America, and the Morse Poetry Prize. She is Professor of English at Southern Illinois University—Edwardsville.

Douglas Goetsch has four collections of poems, including *First Time Reading Freud*, winner of the 2002 Permafrost Award. He teaches creative writing to incarcerated teens at Passages Academy in The Bronx.

Dana Gioia was born in Los Angeles in 1950. He received a BA from Stanford University. Before returning to Stanford to earn an MBA, he completed an MA in comparative literature at Harvard University, where he studied with the poets Robert Fitzgerald and Elizabeth Bishop. In 1977 he moved to New York to begin a career in business. For fifteen years Gioia worked as a businessman, eventually becoming a vice president of General Foods. In 1992 he left business to become a full-time writer.

Barbara Goldberg is the recipient of two National Endowment for the Arts grants and is the author of six books of poetry, most recently *Marvelous Pursuits*. She is the translator, along with Israeli poet Moshe Dor, of *The Fire Stays in Red: Poems by Ronny Someck* (University of Wisconsin/Dryad Press). The mother of two sons, she lives in Chevy Chase, Maryland.

Edith Goldenhar has taught for several summers at The Frost Place as a resident faculty member. She lives and writes on the North Fork of Long Island, New York.

Sarah Gorham is the author of *The Cure* (2003), *The Tension Zone* (1996), and *Don't Go Back to Sleep* (1989). New poems and essays have appeared in *APR*, *Virginia Quarterly Review*, *Poetry*, *Poets and Writers*, *The Journal*, and *Prairie Schooner*. She is cofounder and editor-in-chief of Sarabande Books.

Melanie Greenhouse lives and writes on the outskirts of a small fishing village in Connecticut, where she has been inspired to write, produce, and direct two plays. Since 1994 she has coordinated a literary and musical series in Mystic, Connecticut.

Shaun T. Griffin's last book of poems, *Bathing in the River of Ashes*, was published in 1999 by the University of Nevada Press. He directs a rural nonprofit agency that serves children and families, and for many years he has taught a poetry writing workshop at the local prison. When funding allows, he publishes an annual journal of their work: *Razor Wire*.

Andrey Gritsman, a native of Moscow, Russia, emigrated to the United States in 1981 and works as a physician. He is a poet and essayist who writes in English and Russian and is the author of four volumes of poetry in Russian. *Bilingual View from the Bridge* was published in 1999. His new collection, *Long Fall,* is forthcoming from Spuyten Duyvil Press. Poems and essays have appeared in *Manhattan Review, New Orleans Review, Poetry New York,* and *Berkshire Review,* among others, and were anthologized in *Modern Poetry in Translation* and *Crossing Centuries: The New Generation in Russian Poetry.*

Luray Gross, a poet and storyteller, works in schools and communities as a teaching artist. She received a poetry fellowship from the New Jersey State Council on the Arts and is the 2002 Bucks County (Pennsylvania) Poet Laureate. Her second collection, *Elegant Reprieve,* won the 1995-96 Still Waters Press Poetry Chapbook Award.

Stephen Grosso has published two books, a story about a crippled beggar, and a book of stories about people of great religious faith. His poems have appeared in various journals.

Holly Guran is employed in an urban community college and is published in *Noctiluca, Phoenix, Connecticut River Review, Late Knocking,* and elsewhere. She coordinated a local reading series, Working Poets, and is currently assisting the editor of *Noctiluca* with their upcoming issue.

Elizabeth Hahn, an editor of *Cumberland Poetry Review*, has published poems in journals in the United States, Canada, and Great Britain. Her work has received several Pushcart Prize nominations. (Nightshade Press, 1992) was followed by a chapbook, *Kindred* (1998). A collection of boating anecdotes, *Hustled Aboard*, was published in 2001. A professor of English, she lives in Nashville, Tennessee.

Donald Hall was born in New Haven, Connecticut, in 1928. He began writing as an adolescent and attended the Bread Loaf Writers' Conference at the age of sixteen—the same year he had his first work published. He earned a BA from Harvard in 1951 and a B. Litt. from Oxford in 1953. Donald Hall has published fifteen books of poetry, most recently *The Painted Bed* (Houghton Mifflin, 2002) and *Without: Poems* (1998), which was published on the third anniversary of the death of his wife and fellow poet Jane Kenyon's from leukemia.

Joan Cusack Handler's poems have appeared in *Boston Review*, *Poetry East*, *Southern Humanities Review*, and *Worcester Review*. She has received awards from *Boston Review* and the Chester H. Jones Foundation and has served as a resident faculty member at The Frost Place. Her first book of poems, *GlOrious*, was published in 2003 by CavanKerry Press.

Sandra Handloser mixes writing with her career designing sets and costumes for film, theater, and television, including episodes of *The Sopranos*. A memoir that blends her mother's stories of 1920s Russia with her own experiences of the 1960s is in progress.

Jeffrey Harrison is the author of three books of poetry, most recently *Signs of Arrival* (Sarabande Books, 2001). He has received fellowships from the National Endowment for the Arts and the Guggenheim Foundation, and his poems have appeared in many magazines. He was a participant at The Frost Place Poetry Festival in the early eighties and since then has taught at both the Festival and Seminar. He also serves on the Advisory Board.

Siegfried Haug grew up in rural Germany and lives in Connecticut. What he knows about poems is this: they are healing magic.

Allen Heggen, after a couple of peripatetic decades, lives and writes in Newark, Delaware.

Hugh Hennedy's poems have been published in many periodicals and some anthologies, among them recently *Tar River Poetry*, *Portsmouth Unabridged: New Poems for and Old City*, and *Ice: New Writing on Hockey*. His books of poetry are *Old Winchester Hill* (Enright House) and *Halcyon Time* (Oyster River Press).

Lois Hirshkowitz is a founding editor of *Barrow Street* and has taught at the Writer's Voice in New York City. She has published three books of poetry: *Nurture & Torture*, *Marking Her Questions*, and *Pan's Daughters*. Her work has recently appeared in *Paris Review*, *Crazyhorse*, and *Manhattan Review*.

Deming P. Holleran lives in Hanover, New Hampshire, and is a founding member of the Still Puddle Poets workshop there.

Paul Hostovsky's poems have appeared in magazines including *Carolina Quarterly*, *Berkeley Poetry Review* and *Spoon River Review*. He won first place in the Comstock Review's 2001 Poetry Contest judged by Mary Oliver and has been nominated for a Pushcart Prize. He lives in the Boston area, where he works as an interpreter at the Massachusetts Commission for the Deaf.

David Huddle is the author most recently of *La Tour Dreams of the Wolf Girl*. He teaches at the University of Vermont and the Bread Loaf School of English.

Deborah Hughes has been a grateful participant in The Frost Place Poetry Festival in both 2000 and 2001 and in the Seminar in 2002. This is her first published poem. She lives in New Jersey and works in Manhattan.

Sophie Hughes, a seventy-five-year-old poet, was born on a farm in Houlton, Maine, and holds a BA from Barnard College and an MA from Columbia Teachers College. She retired in 1984, having taught Art at the Lexington School for the Deaf for twenty-five years. She lives in Manhattan.

Cynthia Huntington is the author of three books of poetry: *The Fish-Wife* (University of Hawaii Press, 1986), *We Have Gone to the Beach* (Alice James Books, 1996), and, most recently, *The Radiant* (Four Way Books, 2003), which won the Levis Prize. She is also the author of a prose memoir, *The Salt House*. She directs the creative writing program at Dartmouth College.

Kathie Isaac-Luke's poetry has recently appeared in *Connecticut Review*, *Montserrat Review* and *Sarasota Review of Poetry*. She edits *Caesura*, the journal of Poetry Center San Jose.

Gray Jacobik's book, *The Double Task* (University of Massachusetts Press, 1998), received the Juniper Prize. *The Surface of Last Scattering*, (Texas Review Press, 1999), was selected as the winner of the X. J. Kennedy Poetry Prize. *Brave Disguises* (University of Pittsburgh Press, 2002) won the AWP Poetry Series Award for 2001. She is a distinguished professor of literature at Eastern Connecticut State University and was The Frost Place poet-in-residence during the summer of 2002.

Nancy Kerrigan Jarasek is a Frost Place Poetry Festival participant whose poetry has appeared in the anthologies *Nantucket: A Collection* and *Proposing on the Brooklyn Bridge*. Educated in Chicago at Loyola University and St. Xavier University, she is a New England transplant working as a marriage and family therapist.

Phyllis B. Katz is a classicist who teaches at Dartmouth College in the Women's and Gender Studies and the Master of Arts in Liberal Studies programs. She lives in Norwich, Vermont, with her husband and two Springer spaniels, Telemachus (Max) and Peisistratus (Pi).

Meg Kearney's collection of poetry, *An Unkindness of Ravens*, was published by BOA Editions, Ltd. in 2001. Her work has appeared in such publications as *Ploughshares*, *Gettysburg Review* and the anthologies *Where Icarus Falls* and *Urban Nature*. She is associate director of the National Book Foundation in Manhattan.

David Keller's most recent book is titled *Trouble in History* (White Pine Press, 2000). He is director of admissions for The Frost Place Festival of Poetry and lives in Lawrenceville, New Jersey, with his wife, the poet Eloise Bruce.

Jane Kenyon published four books of *poetry: Constance* (1993), *Let Evening Come* (1990), *The Boat of Quiet Hours* (1986), and *From Room to Room* (1978); and a book of translation, *Twenty Poems of Anna Akhmatova* (1985). In December 1993 she and her husband Donald Hall were the subject of an Emmy Award–winning Bill Moyers documentary, "A Life Together." At the time of her death from leukemia in April 1995, Jane Kenyon was New Hampshire's Poet Laureate. A fifth collection of Kenyon's poetry, *Otherwise: New and Selected Poems*, was released in 1996, and in 1999 Graywolf Press issued *A Hundred White Daffodils: Essays, Interviews, the Akhmatova Translations, Newspaper Columns, and One Poem*.

Galway Kinnell is the author of ten books of poetry, the latest of which is *A New Selected Poems*. He has also done translations of the poetry of Yves Bonnefroy, Francois Villon, and Rainer Maria Rilke. He lives in New York and Vermont.

Judith Kitchen is writer-in-residence at State University of New York–Brockport in upstate New York. She is the author of two collections of essays, a critical book on William Stafford, and a novel. In addition, she is poetry reviewer for *Georgia Review*.

Mary Kollar's poems have appeared in various literary magazines. She codirected the Center for Capable Youth at the University of

Washington until her retirement. She currently lives in Seattle, where she writes, cares for her grandchildren, and works with her family at A. J. Kollar Fine Paintings.

Barry Koplen's poems have been published locally and a few regionally. Since attending The Frost Place Poetry Festival his work has been influenced by Baron Wormser. Chapbooks published prior to that include *Exposed, Broken Hearts Broken Homes,* and *Father's Day Canceled.*

Christine Korfhage was born in Albany, New York, grew up in various places around the world, and now lives in Sanbornton, New Hampshire. She received her BA from Vermont College and her MFA from Bennington College.

Joan S. Krantz has been teaching high school English in public schools in Connecticut for twenty-nine years. She has been writing poetry for forty years and lives by the maxim "Life is too short to wait and to waste."

William Kumbier teaches writing and world literature at Missouri Southern State College in Joplin, Missouri. He has participated in The Frost Place Poetry Festival in 1995, 1998, and 2001 and has co-edited two anthologies of participant poetry.

Elizabeth Kuhn, originally from Germany, is an associate professor of linguistics in Virginia Commonwealth University's English Department. Her poems have appeared in *International Poetry Review, Paterson Literary Review, Formalist, Hollins Critic* and others.

Maxine Kumin is the author of thirteen books of poems, including *The Long Marriage*, the memoir *Inside the Halo and Beyond*, and three essay collections. Among her numerous awards are the Ruth Lilly Award and the Pulitzer Prize. She and her husband live on a farm in New Hampshire.

Alexis Lathem received the 1999 Chelsea Award for Poetry and is a 2003 AWP Intro Award nominee and an MFA candidate in creative writing at Vermont College. Her poems have appeared in *Beloit Poetry Journal*, *Spoon River*, *Chelsea Review*, and *Texas Observer*. She is an agriculture and environmental journalist and activist and lives in New Haven, Vermont.

Sydney Lea founded and for thirteen years edited *New England Review*. He is the author of a novel, a collection of naturalist essays, and seven collections of poetry. His sixth book, *New and Selected Poems*, won the Poets' Prize, and his most recent, *Pursuit of a Wound*, was a finalist for the 2001 Pulitzer Prize.

Brad Leithauser is the author of five previous *novels—Equal Distance, Hence, Seaward, The Friends of Freeland*, and *A Few Corrections*; four volumes of poetry—*The Odd Last Thing She Did, Mail from Anywhere, Cats of the Temple*, and *Hundreds of Fireflies*; and a book of essays. He is the recipient of many awards for his writing, including a MacArthur fellowship. An Emily Dickinson Lecturer in the Humanities at Mount Holyoke College, he lives with his wife and their two daughters, Emily and Hilary, in Amherst, Massachusetts.

Robert Lesman was born in Indiana and now lives in Virginia in the northern Shenandoah Valley. His poems have appeared in such magazines as *Maelstrom, Artemis, Distillery*, and *Northern Virginia Review*. He has published two chapbooks, *Thinking of Animals* (1993) and *Sky Reports* (2001), and is currently working on a translation of poems by the Polish poet Boleslaw Lesmian.

Howard Levy's first book, *A Day This Lit*, was published by CavanKerry Press in 2000, and his poems have also appeared in such magazines as *Poetry, Paris Review, Threepenny Review* and *Gettysburg Review*. He has been very proud to be a resident faculty member at The Frost Place Poetry Festival for a number of years. He lives and works in New York.

Betty Lies is a Geraldine Dodge poet and a Distinguished Teaching Artist for the New Jersey State Council on the Arts. Her poetry has appeared in many journals, and she has published four books, the most recent being *Earth's Daughters: Stories of Women in Classical Mythology*. She is a member of U.S. 1 Poets' Collaborative and Cool Women Poets.

P. H. Liotta has lived in Iran, the former Yugoslavia, and Greece and has published fourteen books, including academic texts on Balkan disintegration, three poetry collections, a novel, and two memoirs. His work has been translated into fourteen languages, and he has received an National Endowment for the Arts fellowship in poetry as well as the Robert H. Winner Award from the Poetry Society of America.

Carl Little holds a BA from Dartmouth College, an MFA from Columbia University, and an MA from Middlebury. His books include *Edward Hopper's New England*, *The Watercolors of John Singer Sargent*, and *The Art of Maine in Winter*. His poems have appeared in *Paris Review* and *Hudson Review*. He lives on Mount Desert Island and is director of communications at the Maine Community Foundation.

Diane Lockward's first book, *Eve's Red Dress*, was published by Wind Publications in 2003. She is also the author of a chapbook, *Against Perfection* (Poets Forum Press, 1998). She is a poet-in-the-schools for both the New Jersey State Council on the Arts and the Geraldine R. Dodge Foundation. She received a 2003 poetry fellowship from the New Jersey State Council on the Arts.

Daniel Lusk's poems and stories have appeared in many literary journals including *American Poetry Review*, *New Letters*, and *North American Review*. He is the author of two books, *Homemade Poems: A Handbook* and the novel *O, Rosie*, and three poetry chapbooks. He has twice been awarded literary fellowships from the Pennsylvania Council of the Arts and in 1995 was winner of the Gertrude B. Claytor Award of the Poetry Society of America. He is associate dean for academic programs in the Division of Continuing Education as well as Director of the Summer Writing Program at the University of Vermont.

Thomas Lux has recently released a new book called *The Cradle Place*, published by Houghton Mifflin.

Maura MacNeil is a New Hampshire poet who has published in numerous literary journals. She is the editor of *Entelechy International: A Journal of Contemporary Ideas* and works as an assistant professor of Writing at New England College in Henniker, New Hampshire.

June Coleman Magrab lives in Bethesda, Maryland, and Grantham, New Hampshire. She has been a MacDowell Colony fellow (1995, 1997), a fellow at the Virginia Center for the Creative Arts (1996), a Frost Place Poetry Festival participant (1992-2002), and was awarded a grant from the Vermont Studio Center (1997). She has published in *New York Quarterly, Oxford Magazine, Caprice*, and elsewhere.

William Matthews won the National Book Critics Circle Award in 1995 and the Ruth Lilly Award of the Modern Poetry Association in 1997. Born in Cincinnati in 1942, he was educated at Yale University and the University of North Carolina. At the time of his death in 1997, he was a professor of English and director of the writing program at the City University of New York.

Heather McHugh has taught at the University of Washington in Seattle since 1984, and in the first low-residency MFA program (now in Asheville, North Carolina, at Warren Wilson College) since the 1970s. Her newest collection of poems, *Eyeshot*, will be available from Wesleyan University Press in August 2003.

Jo-Anne McLaughlin a longtime college writing instructor and community arts activist. She most recently taught in The Frost Place Masters Seminar series. Her latest book, *JAM*, was published by BOA Editions.

Wesley McNair is a recipient of grants from the Rockefeller, Fulbright, and Guggenheim Foundations. His most recent books are *Fire*, a collection of poems, and *Mapping the Heart*, essays on place and poetry.

Jacqueline Michaud moved to Maine in 1974, following undergraduate studies in medieval French literature at Catholic University of America in Washington, D.C. In 1984 she opened an independent consulting firm, and from 1990 to 2001 she was development director of the Haystack Mountain School of Crafts, an international artists' retreat.

Martin Mooney's poetry, short fiction, reviews, criticism, and cultural commentary have been published in Irish and British periodicals. He has four collections of poems: *Grub, Bonfire Makers, Operation Sandcastle,* and *Rasputin and His Children.* He has twice served as a resident faculty member at The Frost Place Poetry Festival and currently lives near Belfast, Ireland, with his partner and their two children.

Ruth Moose is a member of the creative writing faculty at the University of North Carolina at Chapel Hill. She has two collections of short stories, *The Wreath Ribbon Quilt* and *Dreaming in Color;* and four collections of poetry, *To Survive, Finding Things in the Dark, Making the Bed,* and *Smith Grove.* She has been awarded a North Carolina Writers fellowship, a MacDowell fellowship, and five PEN Awards.

Bliss Morehead is a writer and editor with poems published in numerous journals and is the coauthor of a collaborative poetry/painting book, *Sightlines,* (Frogpond Press, 2002). She is currently a candidate for an MFA in poetry at Warren Wilson College.

Paul Muldoon teaches at Princeton. His most recent books are *Poems 1968–1998* and *Moy Sand and Gravel.*

Carol Muske-Dukes has published seven collections of poems, most recently *Sparrow* (Random House, 2003). The founding director of the graduate program in creative writing and literature at the University of Southern California, she writes a regular poetry column for the *Los Angeles Time Book Review.*

Miriam Mörsel Nathan's poetry and essays have appeared in *Daughters of Absence* (Capital Books, 2000), *From Daughters & Sons to Fathers: What I've Never Said* (Story Line Press, 2001), *Gargoyle*, and elsewhere. She was a fellow at the Virginia Center for the Creative Arts in 2001 and 2002.

Marilyn Nelson's most recent book is *Carver: A Life in Poems* (Front Street Books, 2001). She recently retired from the University of Connecticut to accept a position at the University of Delaware. She is Poet Laureate of Connecticut.

Will Nixon has published two chapbooks: *When I Had It Made* (Pudding House Publications) and *They Are Laughing* (Pavement Saw Press).

Gunilla Norris lives in Mystic, Connecticut. Her collection of poetry is *Learning from the Angel* (Lotus Press).

Debra Nowak is a Minnesota native living in New Hampshire. Her work has appeared in *The Ledge, Underwood Review, Sidewalks,* and the book *Teaching the Art of Poetry: The Moves.*

Alicia Ostriker has published eleven volumes of poetry, most recently *The Little Space: Poems Selected and New* (2000) and *The Volcano Sequence* (2002). She has received the William Carlos Williams Prize, the Paterson Poetry Award, and the San Francisco State Poetry Prize, among others. She teaches English and creative writing at Rutgers University.

Grace Paley was named Vermont State Poet in 2003. She is a writer, teacher, feminist, activist, and sometimes publisher. *Just As I Thought,* is a collection of her personal and political essays and articles. Her *Collected Stories* was a finalist for the 1994 National Book Award, and *Begin Again: Collected Poems,* was published in 2000. She lives in New York City and Vermont.

Elise Paschen is the author of *Infidelities* (Story Line), winner of the Nicholas Roerich Poetry Prize, and *Houses: Coasts* (Oxford: Sycamore Press). She is co-editor of *Poetry in Motion* (Norton), *Poetry Speaks* (Sourcebooks), and *Poetry in Motion from Coast to Coast* (Norton). The former executive director of the Poetry Society of America, she teaches in the writing program at The School of the Art Institute of Chicago.

Angela Patten is a native of Dublin, Ireland, now living in Jonesville, Vermont. The author of *Still Listening* (Salmon, 1999), her work has appeared in journals including *Literary Review* and *Prairie Schooner*, and in *The White Page/An Bhileog Bhan: Twentieth Century Irish Women Poets*. She teaches poetry writing at the University of Vermont and is development director of the Vermont Arts Council.

Molly Peacock has published six books of poems, *And Live Apart* (1980), *Raw Heaven* (1984), *Take Heart* (1989), *Original Love* (1995), *Cornucopia* (2001), and a collection of her poetry entitled *New and Selected* (2003); and two prose books, *Paradise Piece by Piece* and *The Private Eye*. She was also co-editor of *Poetry in Motion: 100 Poems from the Subways and Buses* (1996), and is the poet-in-residence at the Cathedral of St. John the Divine.

Gus Pelletier retired as a professor of English at the State University of New York at Delhi. He earned a BA and MA from Siena College and a Doctorate of Arts from State University of New York at Albany. He did postdoctoral work at University of North Carolina at Chapel Hill, Cornell University, and Yale University. His published work appears in many journals, quarterlies, and anthologies.

Peggy Penn was the director of clinical training and education at the Ackerman Institute for the Family from 1985 to 1993 and now directs a project investigating the uses of language and writing in family therapy. She teaches throughout the United States and Europe. She is a coauthor of *Milan Systemic Family Therapy: Conversations in Theory and Practice*. Her poetry is published in *Paris Review, Beloit Journal, Western Humanities Review, Southern Poetry Review*, and so forth. She has won two prizes for poetry and was included in the Emily Dickinson anthology published in 2000. In September 2001 she published *So Close*, a book of poetry (CavanKerry Press, 2001).

Jenny Pierson teaches at George Washington University and leads a poetry workshop for retirees at American University. She is at work on a new collection of poems entitled *Sin Eaters*.

Dawn Potter lives in Harmony, Maine. Her first book of poems is forthcoming in spring 2004.

Sherman Poultney lives in Connecticut, has a PhD in physics from Princeton, and works at a high-tech company. His poems have appeared in *Heartbeat of New England*, *Tiger Moon*, *The Signal*, and elsewhere.

Carol K. Powers wrote from ages seven to eighteen, winning a couple of national awards for her short stories; then college, marriage, and family came along during the Stepford fifties, and she wrote nothing for forty years. Recently she decided to start again (with grave doubts), but the good news is that apparently the rule of "Use it or lose it" doesn't apply to those in the arts.

Wanda S. Praisner is a recipient of a poetry fellowship from the New Jersey State Council on the Arts and three fellowships from the Geraldine R. Dodge Foundation to the Provincetown Fine Arts Work Center. She has been nominated twice for a Pushcart Prize. Her first book is *A Fine and Bitter Snow* (Palanquin Press (USCA), 2003). She is a poet in the schools for the New Jersey State Council on the Arts.

Margaret Raab lives in Chapel Hill, North Carolina, teaches in the creative writing program at the University of North Carolina at Chapel Hill, and works as communications director for a global health project. Her book, *Granite Dives* (New Issues Press at Western Michigan University, 1999), won the Roanoke Chowan Award.

Geri Radacsi has been a journalist, English teacher, and corporate communication specialist. Currently she is associate director of university relations at Central Connecticut State University. Poems have appeared in *Southern Humanities Review* and *Sycamore Review*. In spring 2000 a collection of poems, *Ancient Music*, won a national poetry contest and was published by Pecan Grove Press.

Jane Rawlings graduated from Smith College, Bread Loaf, and Iowa's summer writing program. Her poems have appeared in such publications as *Prairie Schooner*, *The New York Times*, *Atlanta Review*, and *Ikebana International*. They have won several national awards and have been included in the anthology *Under a Gull's Wing: Poems from the Jersey Shore*. She collaborated on *Past and Present: Women in New Jersey's History*.

Victoria Redel is the author of four books, most recently a novel, *Loverboy*, and a collection of poems, *Swoon*. She teaches at Sarah Lawrence College and in the low-residency program at Vermont College.

Lisa Rhodes lives on Staten Island, New York, with Dave, Bonnie, and Lou. Her first collection of poems, *Strange Gravity*, is forthcoming from Bright Hill Press in 2004.

Martha Rhodes is the author of *Mother Quiet* (forthcoming from Zoo Press in 2004), *Perfect Disappearance* (2000 Green Rose Prize from New Issues Press), and *At the Gate* (Provincetown Arts 1995). She is the director of Four Way Books and teaches at the MFA Program for Writers at Warren Wilson College.

Nancy Richardson, born in Youngstown, Ohio, is an educator who lives and works in Vermont. She is enrolled in the MFA writing program at Vermont College and in her spare time is director of special education for eight school districts.

Susan Roney-O'Brien holds degrees from the University of Massachusetts, Anna Maria College, and Warren Wilson College. A middle school teacher, she is an editor of *Worcester Review*. Her chapbook, *Farmwife*, won the William and Kingman Page Poetry Award. She was named the 2002 Poet of the Year by the New England Association of Teachers of English.

Patricia Rose teaches English at Sewickley Academy in Pennsylvania. She has studied poetry at the University of Iowa and Trinity College in Cambridge, England. Her work has appeared in *Taproot* and *Cathedral Poets*.

Michael Ryan has published three books of poems, an autobiography, *Secret Life*, and a collection of essays about poetry and writing, *A Difficult Grace*. Two new books are scheduled for spring 2004: a memoir, *Baby B* (Graywolf Press); and a collection of poetry, *New and Selected Poems* (Houghton Mifflin). He is professor of English and creative writing at the University of California–Irvine.

Nicholas Samaras recently edited the book *To the Country of that Spirit: Selected Poems & Essays of Alexandros Gialas* (a.k.a. G. Verites) and wrote the introduction to the collection, published in Greece (1998). Having received degrees from the University of Denver (PhD, 1994) and Columbia University (MFA, 1985), Dr. Samaras has taught at the University of Denver (1989–1993) and at Columbia University and has been the recipient of numerous writing awards, such as the National Endowment for the Arts poetry fellowship (1997-98). Dr. Samaras currently teaches at Eckerd College in the Tampa Bay area of Florida.

Lois Sargent holds degrees in psychology and community counseling and is presently employed as a flight attendant (AA) based in Boston.

Nina Schafer has been a member of The Frost Place Poetry Festival for twelve years (1992-2003). She won a Philadelphia citywide poetry competition culminating in a reading at The Painted Bride in the spring of 2002. Numerous readings include the Philadelphia Free Library and Robins, the oldest independent bookstore in Philadelphia.

Jim Schley is an editor, teacher, and theater artist who has been part of The Frost Place resident faculty in 1997 and 2000. He and his family live in Vermont in a solar-powered home they built themselves, from the ground up.

Charles Simic was born in Belgrade, Yugoslavia, and emigrated to the United States in 1954. He received the Pulitzer Prize in 1990 and has been the recipient of many awards and honors, including a PEN International Award for translation, the Edgar Allan Poe Award, and the Harriet Monroe Award, as well as fellowships from Guggenheim, MacArthur, Ingram Merril, and Fulbright Foundations. He teaches in the English Department at the University of New Hampshire.

Jane Simon writes poetry and essays, and she had a small volume of poetry published years ago by Croton Review Press. "Glass Rose" describes the shock she felt at seeing a favorite violinist of her childhood dead on the autopsy table and how that experience helped her shift careers from forensic pathologist to psychiatrist.

George Singer lives in Santa Barbara, California, where he works as a faculty member at the University of California. He was a Zen Buddhist monk for several years and continues to make Zen training central to his day-to-day outlook. He attended The Frost Place Poetry Festival on four different occasions. His poems have appeared in several journals including *Prairie Schooner* and *Tar River Poetry*. He has completed a manuscript for a first book of poems and has begun the long hunt for a publisher. He is really grateful for the encouragement of the poets and The Frost Place and the kindness of its directors.

Tom Sleigh is the author of *The Dreamhouse* (University of Chicago Press, 1999), which was a finalist for the Los Angeles Times Book Prize; *The Chain* (1996); *Waking* (1990), which was a *New York Times* Notable Book of the Year for 1990-91; and *After One* (1983), which won the Houghton Mifflin New Poetry Prize. He has also published a translation of *Euripides' Herakles* (Oxford University Press, 2000). He is a professor of English and creative writing at Dartmouth College and lives in Cambridge, Massachusetts.

Bruce Smith teaches in the writing program at the University of Alabama. His previous collections of poetry are *The Common Wages*, *Silver, Information* (National Poetry Series Selection), and *Mercy Seat* (University of Chicago).

Elizabeth Anne Socolow taught poetry for the New Jersey State Council on the Arts, at Vassar and Barnard Colleges, and with The Writer's Voice and the Inside/Out Poetry Project in the Detroit area. More recently she returned to her Princeton home and has taught at high schools and Rutgers/Camden at Freehold. She won the Barnard Poetry Prize in 1987 and has published a book, *Laughing at Gravity: Conversations with Isaac Newton* (Beacon, 1988).

Margo Stever's first collection of poetry, *Frozen Spring*, was the winner of the 2001 Mid-List Press First Series Award for Poetry. Her chapbook, *Reading the Night Sky*, won the 1996 Riverstone Poetry Chapbook Competition. Her poems and reviews have appeared in *Webster Review*, *Ironwood*, and *New England Review*. She is the founder of The Hudson Valley Writers' Center.

Harriet Susskind was born in Brooklyn, graduated from Hunter College, and received an MA in English from Ohio State University. She was a professor in the English Department of Monroe Community College in Rochester, New York for twenty-eight years. Her poems have appeared in numerous journals, and twice she was awarded National Endowment for the Arts fellowships. When she passed away in 2002, she was married with three children and two grandchildren.

Jean Sinclair Symmes is a clinical psychologist and a playwright. Her mother said she started to write poetry when she picked up a pencil, but in the last ten years she has become persistent and slightly obsessed about poetry with the help of many good people at The Frost Place.

Jennifer Thomas lives in Quechee, Vermont, and works at University Press of New England. She first attended The Frost Place as a participant in 1981.

Parker Towle is a member of The Frost Place Board of Directors and Advisory Board. He is a former participant in The Frost Place Poetry Festival, lecturer at Frost Day, and for the past several years has served as an auditor faculty member at the Festival. He is also an assistant editor at *Worcester Review* and editor of their special issue on the poet and art curator Frank O'Hara. Parker Towle has published three chapbooks of poetry and edited an anthology of poetry. Currently he works as a clinical neurologist and faculty member at Dartmouth Medical School.

Jean Valentine was born in Chicago, earned her BA from Radcliffe College, and has lived most of her life in New York City. The author of eight other books of poetry, she has received a Guggenheim fellowship and awards from the National Endowment for the Arts, the Bunting Institute, the Rockefeller Foundation, the New York Council for the Arts, and the New York Foundation for the Arts, as well as the Maurice English Prize, the Teasdale Poetry Prize, and the Poetry Society of America's Shelley Memorial Prize in 2000. She teaches at Sarah Lawrence College, the Graduate Writing Program of New York University, Columbia University, and the 92nd Street Y.

Ellen Bryant Voigt is the author of six collections of poetry and *The Flexible Lyric*, a collection of craft essays. Her poems have appeared in *The New Yorker*, *Atlantic Monthly*, and *New Republic*. "Voices of 1918," a commissioned work based on her latest book, *Kyrie*, finalist for the National Book Critics Circle Award, was premiered by the Vermont Symphony Orchestra on its 2000 tour. She teaches in the low-residency MFA program for writers at Warren Wilson College.

Lynn Wagner was a participant in The Frost Place Poetry Festival in 1993 and 1995, a participant in the Seminar in 2000, and a visitor to New Hampshire most other years. She is currently a student in the MFA program at the University of Pittsburgh, where she won the Academy of American Poets prize in 2002 and served as the 2002-03 managing editor for the online journal *Nidus*. Her work has appeared in *Lullwater Review*, *Painted Bride Quarterly*, and *Two Rivers River*.

M. J. Wagner is alive and fairly well and sharing Time & Space in Bradford, Massachusetts, with two fiddling, flirting felines, a pair of prescient parakeets, numerous books, and a number of works in progress, the most recent being *Reflections: In The Wake of Traveling Light*, poems about a loved one's journey with cancer.

BJ Ward is the recipient of a 2003 Pushcart Prize for Poetry and a 2003 Distinguished Artist Poetry Fellowship from the New Jersey State Council on the Arts. His most recent book of poetry, *Gravedigger's Birthday*, was a finalist for the 2003 Paterson Poetry Prize. His work has been featured on National Public Radio's *The Writer's Almanac* and *Poetry Daily*, as well as in publications such as *TriQuarterly*, *Poetry*, *Painted Bride Quarterly*, *Puerto Del Sol*, and *Mid-American Review*. He lives in Washington, New Jersey.

David Watts is a physician and poet whose commentaries are heard regularly on National Public Radio's *All Things Considered*. Three books of his poetry have been published. He is the director of the Squaw Valley Community of Writers workshop on Writing the Medical Experience.

Ernest Wight is a retired teacher and jazz drummer. His work has appeared in *New England Review*, *Harvard Advocate*, *Interim*, and *Midwest Quarterly*. He lives with his wife in Randolph, Massachusetts.

Jack Wiler lives in New Jersey and has managed a blood distribution center, a senior citizen's lunch program, and sold weightlifting supplies. He works with the Geraldine Dodge Foundation in New Jersey as a visiting poet in the schools and as a group leader for the Foundation's "Clearing the Spring/Tending the Fountain" seminars for high school teachers. His book is *I Have No Clue* (Long Shot, 1996).

Irene K. Wilson, a native of New England, has published poems in *Calapooya Collage*, *Tucumcari Literary Review*, and *Redbook*. She lives with her husband in Lexington, Massachusetts.

Rosemary Gates Winslow is associate professor of English and director of writing at the Catholic University of America. Her poems have appeared in *Southern Review*, *Poet Lore*, and other magazines; and her critical and theoretical work has been published in numerous journals and books. She has received two Larry Neal Awards for Poetry. She lives in Washington, D.C.

Peter Wood is Professor Emeritus at the College of New Jersey, where he taught poetry and writing. He has attended The Frost Place Poetry Festival regularly from the beginning, acting as faculty to auditors in recent years.

Baron Wormser is the author of five books of poetry and the co-author of a text about teaching poetry. He codirects The Frost Place Seminar and The Frost Place Conference on Poetry and Teaching.

Afterthoughts and Thank Yous

Thank you, Robert Frost, for the gifts of your poems and your home. Both are incomparable!

Thank you, Donald Sheehan, for guiding us humanely through this process of making and sharing poems.

Thank you to all Frost Place poets for the gifts of your fine poems.

But your gifts include more than the poems . . .

Many many thanks to the scores of people who gave so generously of their time to bring *Breath I* and *II* to life:

To Sydney Lea for his kind heart and egalitarian editorship of *Breath II*. The task was monumental, his facility brilliant and graceful. From his essay at the opening of the book to his selection of the hundreds of poems, he captured the democratic essence of Donald Sheehan and The Frost Place.

To Baron Wormser—always available but never intrusive—for his constant and humble presence, for his insightful essay on William Matthews, and his intelligent input at every step of the way.

To Donald Hall for his brilliant foreword to *Breath I* and his intimate essay on Jane Kenyon in this volume.

And again to Donald Sheehan for his sage and perceptive introductions to the poets in *Breath I* and to Amy Clampitt in this volume.

To Jennifer Thomas and Keisha Luce, who worked so tirelessly as assistant editors.

To Frost Place poets Teresa Carson, Didi Goldenhar, David Keller, Howard Levy, and Molly Peacock who served as associate editors early on.

To Peter Cusack and Florenz Greenberg of CavanKerry and their assistant, Donna Rutkowski, for their herculean efforts to organize this second volume and bring it safely into the world.

Finally, we regret any errors or omissions. We hope, in keeping with Donald Sheehan's love for the human heart, we hurt no one's in the process.

Joan Cusack Handler
Publisher

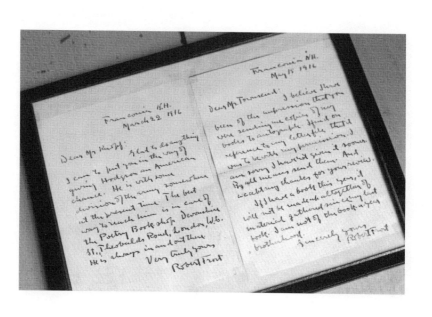